1975 RED SOX

American League Champions

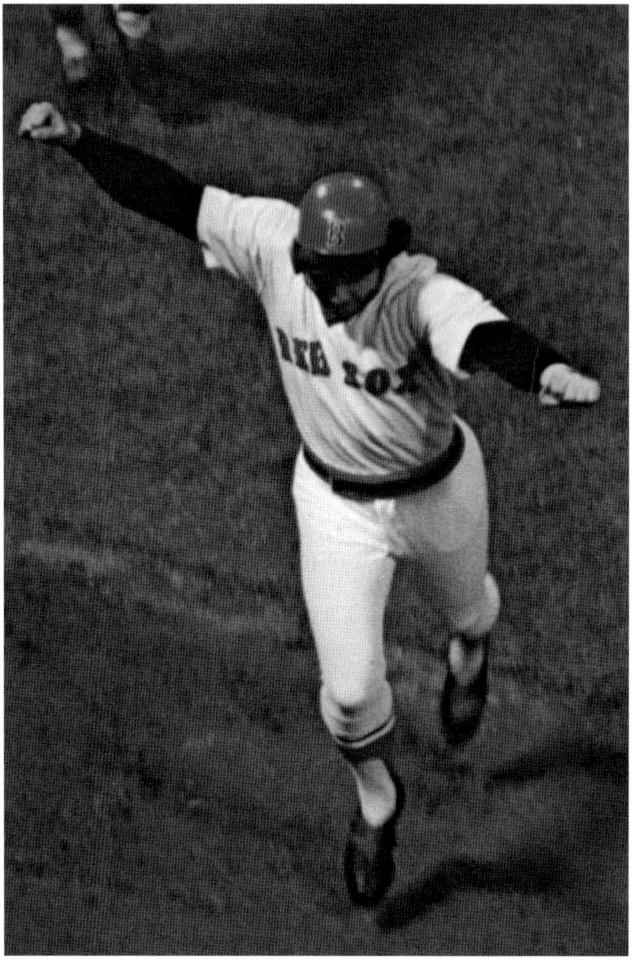

An exultant Bernie Carbo heads toward the Red Sox dugout following his eighth-inning, three-run homer that tied Game 6 of the World Series, setting up Carlton Fisk's iconic blast. Although Fisk's homer is recognized as one of the greatest home runs ever hit, a good number of the 35,205 people at Fenway Park that night will claim Carbo's blast was far more dramatic. In 2004, Carbo's home run became a part of the Red Sox Hall of Fame as one of the franchises' most memorable moments. In 1993, he founded the Diamond Club Ministry, which he still heads today. (Author's collection.)

FRONT COVER: Carlton Fisk is literally jumping for joy as he has just watched his 12th-inning smash of Game 6 of the 1975 World Series hit the foul pole. The home run made 7-6 winners of the Red Sox and extended the series to a winner-take-all seventh game. It also sent the Fenway Faithful throughout New England into delirium. Today, that foul pole is officially known as Fisk's Pole. (Author's collection.)

COVER BACKGROUND: Under Fisk's jumps of joy is Carlton Fisk rounding third base after the home run. Third base coach Don Zimmer is awaiting him with his hand extended. In pursuit are a few scattered members of the Fenway Faithful who bounded onto the field. Waiting at home plate are the 1975 Boston Red Sox. (Courtesy of Dick Raphael.)

BACK COVER: The rookie tandem of Fred Lynn and Jim Rice comprise the best rookie duo in the history of baseball. Together they powered the Red Sox offense in 1975, accounting for 32 percent of the team's home runs, 27 percent of the team's RBI, 25 percent of the team's runs scored, and 20 percent of the team's hits. They also tied for the team lead in stolen bases with 10 each, 30 percent of the team's stolen bases. (Author's collection.)

1975 RED SOX
AMERICAN LEAGUE CHAMPIONS

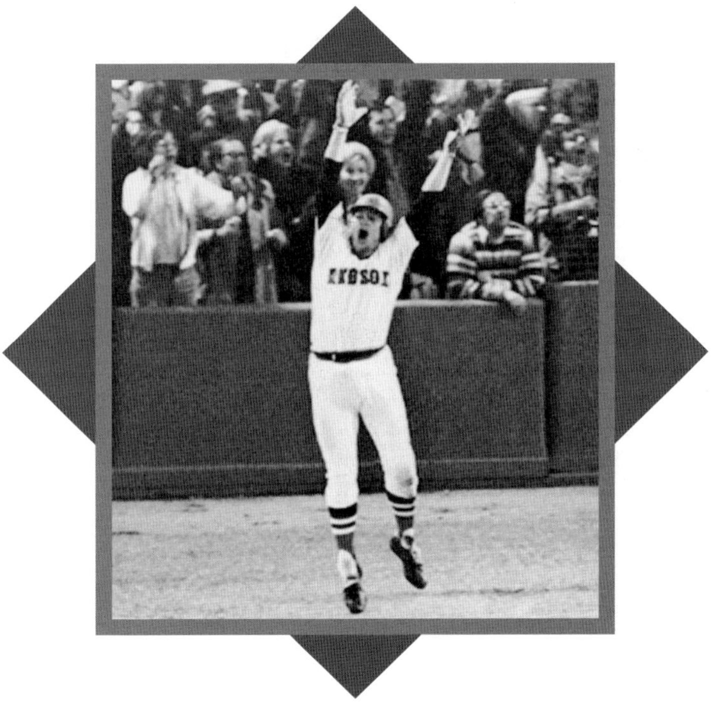

Raymond Sinibaldi
Foreword by Fred Lynn

ARCADIA PUBLISHING

For Jake, Addy, Brady, Reagan, and Quinn, who keep the hits coming, and for Zak, forever 26

ISBN 978-1-4671-2313-6

Published by Arcadia Publishing
Charleston, South Carolina

Printed in the United States of America

Library of Congress Control Number: 2014949903

For all general information, please contact Arcadia Publishing:
Telephone 843-853-2070
Fax 843-853-0044
E-mail sales@arcadiapublishing.com
For customer service and orders:
Toll-Free 1-888-313-2665

Visit us on the Internet at www.arcadiapublishing.com

CONTENTS

FOREWORD

My knowledge of the Red Sox was limited when they drafted me in 1973. Growing up in Southern California, I did not get to see them all that much. I knew a little about the 1967 team because they won the pennant and were on the NBC game of the week a few times, but that was about it.

My first taste of Fenway Park and Boston fans came in September 1974, and the following spring I went to Winter Haven, Florida, with my mind set on winning the center field position. I had a lot of confidence in my ability to play the game, but there was no way I, or anyone really, could have foreseen what was in store for the Red Sox and me in 1975.

When I think of that wonderful year, my first thoughts run to so many of the guys with whom I shared it. Luis Tiant battled like a warrior and would not leave the mound until the job was done. Carl "Yaz" Yastrzemski, the epitome of the word clutch, could still play a great outfield at 35, and Dwight "Dewey" Evens in right field had an arm that was simply like no other. The toughness and leadership of Carlton Fisk were evident both from behind the plate and in the clubhouse, and the hellfire brand of baseball played by Rick Burleson at short was embodied in his nickname, "Rooster." The slick, sure-handed veteran at third base, Rico Petrocelli, was so smooth he made it look easy, and the competitive energy of Bill Lee was fearsome. They called him the "Spaceman" because of his zany sayings and quirky off-field ways, but between the lines there was nobody who wanted to win more. And then there was Jimmy Rice, my fellow rookie, whose raw, naked power was a thing to behold. He could mishit balls that would leave the park. I will go to my grave convinced that were he not injured, we would have won that World Series!

I have often been asked what my first thoughts are when I think of the 1975 World Series, and the answer is simple—we lost. However, as the years have passed, I have come to appreciate what an honor and a privilege it was to have played in that World Series, which many credit with restoring the game of baseball to its rightful place in the pantheon of American sports. To have been a part of an event that has come to mean so much to baseball is something I will always cherish. And I did it in baseball's greatest park and in front of baseball's greatest fans. Thank you, Boston.

—Fred Lynn

ACKNOWLEDGMENTS

This project required the energy of many to come to fruition. At the top of the list are Fred and Natalie Lynn, who could not have been more gracious. Thank you, Bernie Carbo, for sharing your time and memories; Luis Tiant, who is as great a guy as he was a pitcher; and Rico Petrocelli and the depth of his graciousness. Sarah Coffin of the Red Sox was, as always, a force. Caitrin Cunningham and Ryan Easterling of Arcadia Publishing could not be more supportive and encouraging. Thanks to WBZ radio and Chart Productions' Jordan Rich, whose love of baseball and the Red Sox is a source of inspiration. A.J. Beecher, a kindred baseball spirit, thanks for your willingness to explore 1975 and taking care of the maps down the stretch. Thanks to Dave McCarthy of the Ted Williams Museum for bringing me together with so many. Coach Faulkner, Joe K., Jose, "Gut," Brendon, Callan, Richie, Mike, Steve, and Josh, I get to share a passion and love of this game with you every spring. My good friend, the walking encyclopedia known as Kerry Keene, has shown me grace, dignity, strength, and an unconquerable spirit in the face of life's cruelest adversity. And last, most, and as always, Lynda has taken me places in life I never thought I would go and shown me things I never dreamed possible.

All photographs are from the author's private collection, unless otherwise noted.

INTRODUCTION

Red Sox first baseman Cecil Cooper took the throw from Denny Doyle at second base, and the Boston Red Sox erupted on the field at Oakland's Alameda County Stadium. It was October 7, 1975, and they were on their way to the World Series for the eighth time in their history and first time since 1967.

Led by Fred Lynn and Jim Rice, a pair of rookies the likes of which Major League Baseball had never seen, the Red Sox had dethroned the World Champion Oakland A's and prevented them from capturing their fourth straight World Championship.

There was a formidable supporting cast for the pair of rookies the Fenway Faithful lovingly called the "Gold Dust Twins." There were two carryovers from the 1967 Cardiac Kids, Carl Yastrzemski and Rico Petrocelli. One drank from the fountain of youth and carried them through the American League Championship Series, and the other hit .290 with runners in scoring position. There was Carlton Fisk, the 27-year-old catcher who was destined for the National Baseball Hall of Fame. There were Dwight Evans, a 23-year-old right fielder, and Rick Burleson, a 24-year-old shortstop, both emerging all-stars. There were kids named Cooper, Beníquez, and Blackwell who meshed with seasoned role players named Miller, Griffin, Heise, and Montgomery. There was the requisite monumental mid-season acquisition Denny Doyle, who would hit .310, and there was a final comeback and goodbye for one of Boston's all-time favorite sons, Tony Conigliaro. And then there was Bernie Carbo, a most efficient fourth outfielder for whom destiny was waiting.

Luis Tiant, a grizzled veteran whose injuries once had ripped him from the elite of the league, was the ace of the pitching staff. He endured injuries, trades, and releases and clawed his way back to stardom through the minor leagues of two franchises to once again emerge as one of the game's best. The rest of the rotation included a wise man (Rick Wise), a Spaceman (Bill Lee), a city's namesake (Reggie Cleveland), and a 24-year-old phenom named Dick Pole who would be leveled by a line drive to the face after delivering a pitch in June. The bullpen was comprised of a patchwork of names: Drago, Willoughby, and the team's oldest player, Diego Segui. And as was true for all teams of that era, there was the swingman, the guy who bounced back and forth from the starting rotation to the bullpen. For this Red Sox team it was Rogelio Moret, a 25-year-old southpaw who went 14-3 in 36 appearances, 16 of them as a starter.

The Red Sox were heading back to the World Series and only eight years after their previous visit to the fall classic: a marked distinction from the two previous Red Sox squads to win the pennant. The 1946 team returned the Red Sox to the series after 28 years and the 1967 team after a 21-year World Series hiatus.

Baseball had undergone significant and dramatic changes in just eight years. The mound was lowered five inches after the pitching-dominated year of 1968, and baseball went to divisions within each league the following year. The first-ever player strike struck in 1972, and it was followed by the dissolution of the reserve clause, free agency, and the designated hitter.

And through that short span of only eight years, the Red Sox went through some wonderful highs, woeful lows, and bitter disappointments that a decade later would find the Fenway Faithful describing their beloved Red Sox and their history in curse-ridden terms.

And it all began in the midst of one of the franchise's shining moments.

It was the sixth inning of Game 7 of the 1967 World Series. With the Red Sox trailing, Jim Lonborg struck out Curt Flood to end the inning. Sensing the inevitability of the Red Sox's fate and Lonborg's departure from the game, the Fenway Faithful rose and cheered the American League's best pitcher. It was an acknowledgment of a man, a team, and a year that would echo down through the ages. St. Louis defeated Lonborg and the Red Sox 7-2 in that seventh game, behind the arm of series MVP and future Hall of Famer Bob Gibson and the bat and legs of future Hall of Famer Lou Brock. The powerful Cardinals lineup was too much for the 25-year-old soon-to-be Cy Young Award winner as he took to the hill on just two day's rest.

The 1967 Cardiac Kids had taken the Fenway Faithful on a magical journey, and they were young, the youngest Red Sox team since the days of Babe Ruth. Coupled with the fact that general manager Dick O'Connell had added veteran hurlers Ray Culp and Dick Ellsworth, this buoyed the hopes of the faithful for the 1968 campaign. As Christmas approached, all of New England looked forward to spring training, just two months away. However, on the ski slopes of Lake Tahoe on Christmas Eve, it all began to unravel when Cy Young Award–winner Jim Lonborg tore ligaments in his left knee while skiing, portending the Red Sox story of 1968. Right fielder Tony Conigliaro would miss the entire 1968 season as the result of a fastball to the face, which damaged his eye in August 1967. And by season's end, there was talk that the damage would claim his promising career.

Conig's replacement, Ken "Hawk" Harrelson, more than made up for the loss of Conigliaro's bat when he hit .275 with 35 home runs and a league-leading 109 RBI. However, the increased output began and ended there, as the remaining Red Sox regulars collectively hit 19 points lower, with 55 less homers and a whopping 215 less runs batted in than they had in 1967.

The Red Sox opened 1968 at Tiger Stadium, and they won 7-3. The day ended with the Red Sox in a five-team first-place tie. It was the first, last, and only time they occupied the top spot the entire season.

The face of baseball changed forever in 1969, and as Major League Baseball celebrated its 100th year in existence, its shortest era came to a close. Implementing its second expansion in a decade, two teams were added to each league, creating two six-team divisions. In the American League, the Kansas City Royals replaced the Athletics, who headed to Oakland. The Seattle Pilots would last but one year before moving to Milwaukee and becoming the Brewers. In the senior circuit, the San Diego Padres became California's fifth big-league franchise, and the Montreal Expos officially marked Major League Baseball as an international game. The era of two 10-team leagues had lasted only seven years, and now a five-game series between the winners of each league's eastern and western divisions would determine the combatants for the fall classic, adding the term post-season play to baseball's lexicon.

At Baltimore's Memorial Stadium, the Red Sox opened the 1969 campaign as Tony Conigliaro returned and led them to an extra-inning win. They battled the Orioles for the top spot into early June, but by July they were 10 out and gone. Despite Baltimore's 109 wins and a sweep of the Twins in the first American League Division Series, it was the Amazin' Mets who made history, winning the series in five games and in only their eighth year of existence. In 1969, the Red Sox drafted a California southpaw named Bill Lee, and a hardnosed New England catcher named Carlton Fisk made his debut.

Under new manager Eddie Kasko, the 1970 Red Sox once again spent exactly one day in first place, following an opening day win in Yankee Stadium. Despite four players with 20-plus homers, three players with 100-plus RBI, and the best offensive season of Tony Conigliaro's career, the Red Sox finished a distant third as the Orioles ran away with the East, winning 108 games and again sweeping the Twins in the American League Championship Series. There would be no October upsets this time; Brooks Robinson put on the finest defensive display in World Series history, and they dispatched the Reds in five games.

In September, the 1975 swingman arrived when a 20-year-old lefty, Rogelio Moret, made his major-league debut. And during the World Series, the Red Sox made their second unpopular trade in as many years: sending homegrown Tony Conigliaro to the California Angels.

The 1971 season brought hope to the Fenway Faithful, and the Red Sox were the best team in the American League East until early June. However, it would be the Orioles who would prevail as they cracked the 100-win mark for the third year in a row.

The Red Sox, however, spent 37 days in first place—their longest stretch atop the heap since August and September 1948. By year's end, they added two mammoth pieces to the 1975 puzzle: within 22 days they signed Luis Tiant and drafted an 18-year-old kid out of T.L. Hanna High School in Anderson, South Carolina, Jim Rice.

On April 1, 1972, the first-ever strike in the history of professional sports took place when the players walked out of spring training camps. Their primary issue was their pension fund. It lasted 13 days, and the 86 games lost would prove devastating to the Red Sox.

The 1972 version of Boston's Old Town Team epitomized and embodied Fenway Faithful frustration. In first place on September 7, they dropped two of the season's last three games to the Tigers in Detroit, and the Tigers prevailed by only a half game. Why? The strike! Detroit played one more game than the Red Sox.

The American League added the designated hitter in 1973, and into August the Red Sox were within a game of first place. However, the summer belonged to the Orioles, and the fall belonged to the Oakland A's, as they won their second World Series in a row.

Off the diamond, the 1975 vision came more into focus as they drafted Fred Lynn of the University of Southern California. Before the end of the year, the Red Sox had acquired Dick Drago and, in two separate deals with St. Louis, Rick Wise, Reggie Cleveland, Diego Segui, and Bernie Carbo.

The 1974 season was one of excitement, hope, joy, and ultimately frustration for the Red Sox and their beloved Fenway Faithful. They spent 101 days in first place, and following Tiant's 20th win of the year on August 23, they were 7.5 games up with only 38 games to go. The faithful were chafing in anticipation of Boston's first post-season appearance under the new playoff format. Then came 11 losses in the next 13 games, including eight in a row, five shutouts, and three runs or less scored in every game but one. They finished in third, seven games out. An astounding 14-game turn around in only 38 games! It was the single greatest collapse in their entire history.

Yet lined within the darkest of the August and September clouds was a glimmer of golden light named Rice and Lynn. The Gold Dust Twins had arrived, and the final pieces were now in place for the celebration of the Red Sox's diamond jubilee.

1

The Bridge between Two Pennants

There were 41,429 Detroit partisans present in Tiger Stadium when the Red Sox kicked off the 1968 campaign. Behind two home runs by Carl Yastrzemski, three RBI from Rico Petrocelli, two hits and an RBI from Reggie Smith, and a complete game win from newly acquired lefty Dick Ellsworth, they beat the Tigers 7-3. Seven regulars hammered 10 hits, giving the appearance they were they were picking up right where they had left off in 1967. Alas, it was not to be. The 1968 Boston Red Sox spent exactly one day in first place, finishing in fourth place, 17 games out of first.

Although the championship promise of 1967 never really came to fruition, the fact remains that the Boston Red Sox were now a winning franchise. They put together a string of eight consecutive winning seasons, something they had not done since they ran off 10 straight winning campaigns from 1909 through 1918. The onset of divisional play saw them become contenders, coming close but never quite capturing the brass ring. In fact, the ways they found to not win began weaving a fabric of folklore that would become the stuff of which the Curse of the Bambino was made.

Although they were winning, they never finished closer than 17 games from 1968 through 1971. By the arrival of the 1970s, Dick Williams was gone, off to Oakland, and many big names followed him out of town: Conigliaro, Lonborg, Scott, and Smith. Cecil Cooper and Bill Lee arrived in 1971, and in 1972, a local kid catcher by the name of Fisk captured the Rookie of the Year Award. Joining him was Luis Tiant, an aged pitcher who went from reclamation project to superstar. Dwight Evans, a 20-year-old September call-up in 1972, would never again play in the minor leagues. In a span of six weeks in the fall of 1973, the Red Sox acquired Rick Wise, Bernie Carbo, Reggie Cleveland, and Diego Segui from the Cardinals and Dick Drago from the Royals—all of whom played key roles in the 1975 pennant chase. And in May 1974, Rick Burleson played his first game at shortstop, a position he would occupy for the next seven seasons. By September, Rice and Lynn arrived to stay. The pieces to the puzzle were on the table, and manager Darrell Johnson was charged with putting the puzzle together.

The year of the Red Sox diamond jubilee began on April 8 at Fenway; batting third, fourth, and fifth for the Red Sox were Carl Yastrzemski, Tony Conigliaro, and Rico Petrocelli, the only three remaining players from the 1967 Impossible Dream team.

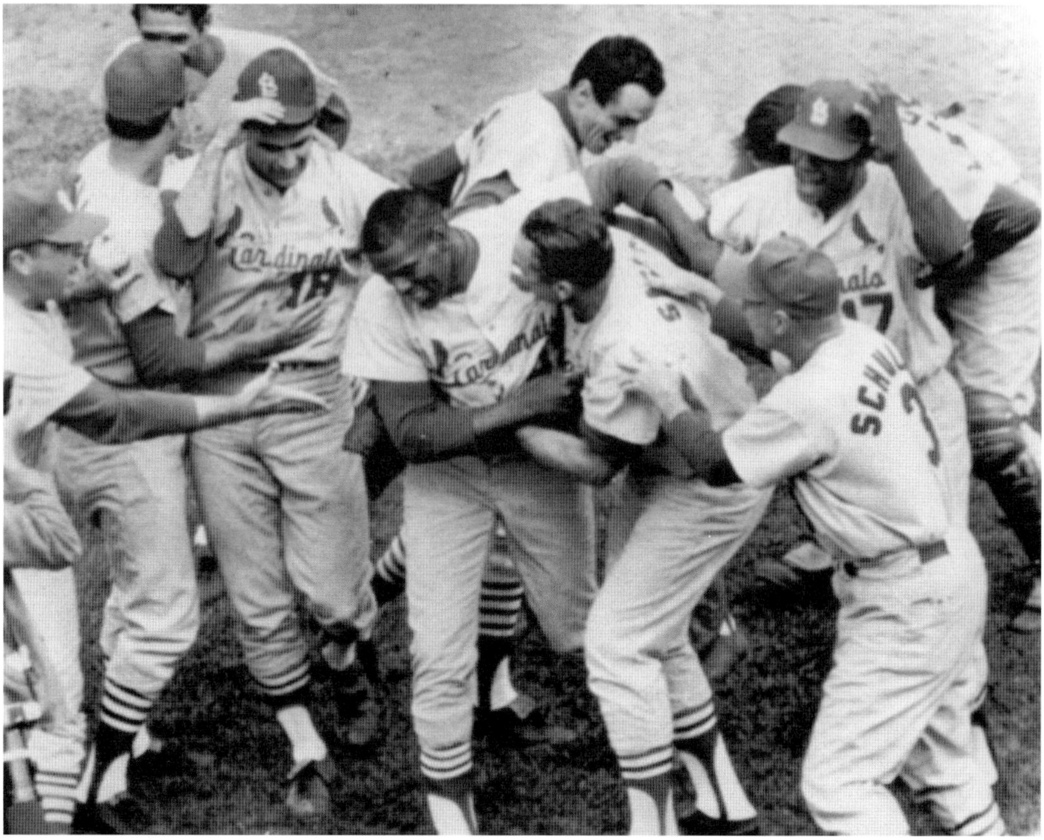

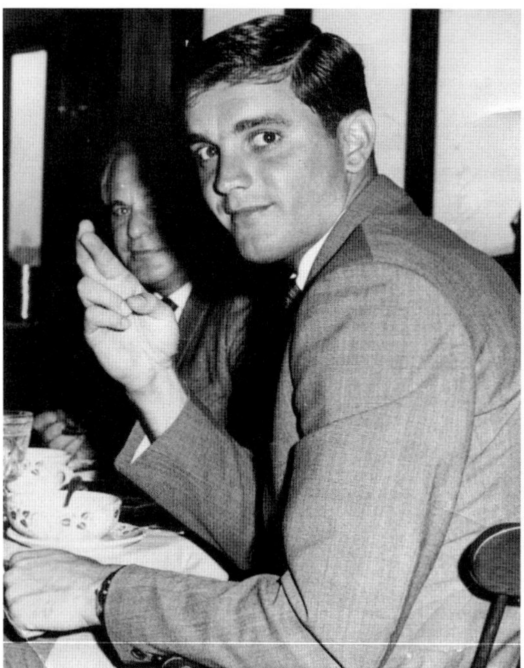

St. Louis Cardinal pitcher Bob Gibson (center) is mobbed by his teammates leaving the field at Fenway Park following his 7-2, three-hit victory over the Red Sox in Game 7 of the 1967 World Series. Although defeated in the World Series, the future of the Red Sox was indeed bright, as their starting lineup averaged 23 years of age.

Through the promise of the future however, ominous clouds were gathering. Star right fielder Tony Conigliaro would sit out the 1968 season as a result of the beaning he took on August 18, 1967. Here, he indicates his hopes for the 1968 season, but they did not come to fruition.

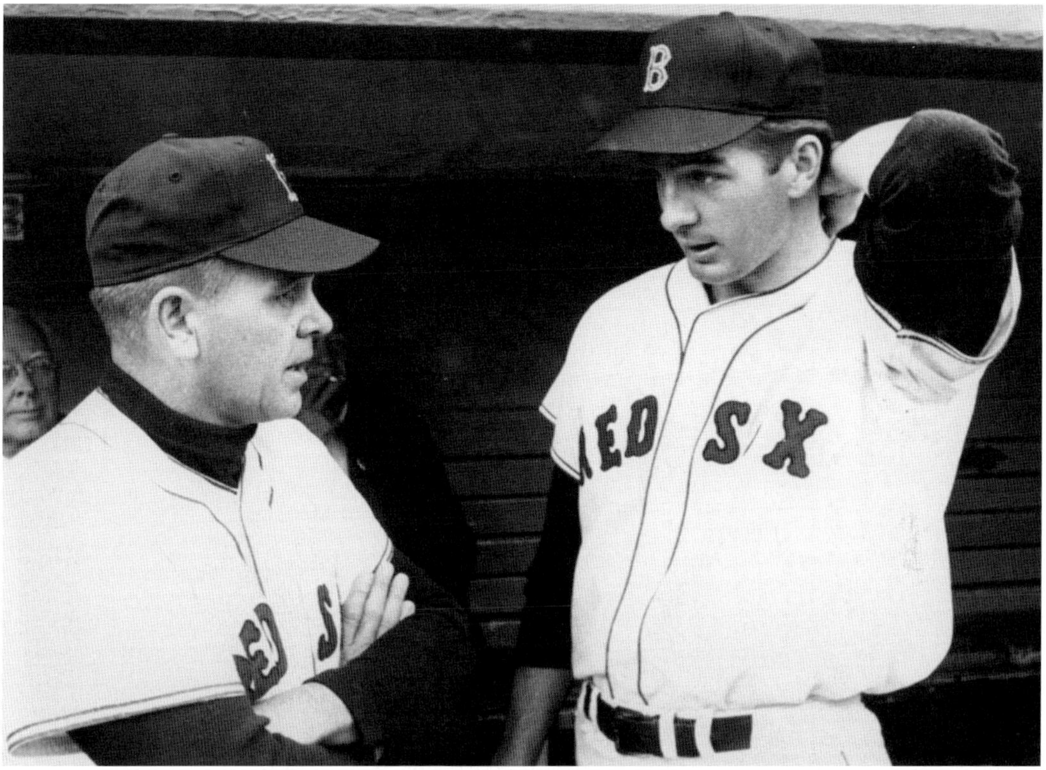

Within weeks, the clouds grew darker when Jim Lonborg (right), seen here with manager Dick Williams during the 1967 World Series, severely tore two ligaments in his left knee in a Christmas skiing mishap at Lake Tahoe. Though he would pitch in 1968, it took years to regain any semblance of his 1967 form. He went 6-10 with a 4.29 ERA in 1968. Williams was fired in June 1969.

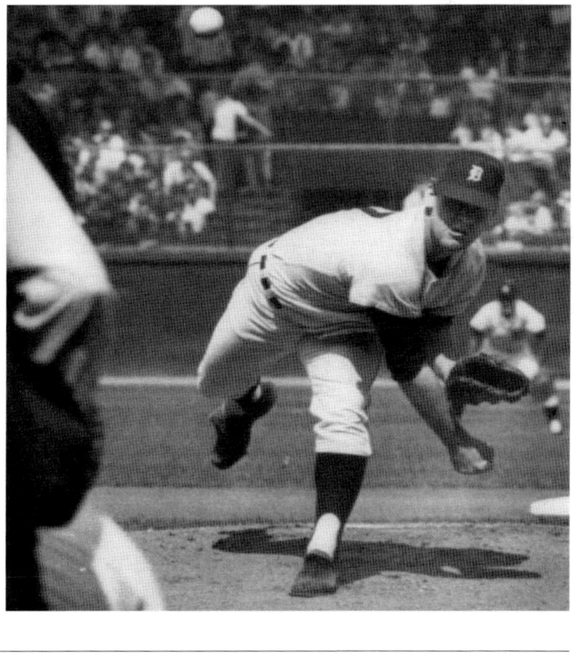

In 1968, Tigers pitcher Denny McLain made history, winning 31 games with an ERA of 1.96. He hurled 336 innings, completing 28 of his 41 starts, and became the first American League pitcher to win both the Cy Young and MVP Awards. The following year, he became the first American League pitcher to win back-to-back Cy Young Awards. He is baseball's last 30-game winner.

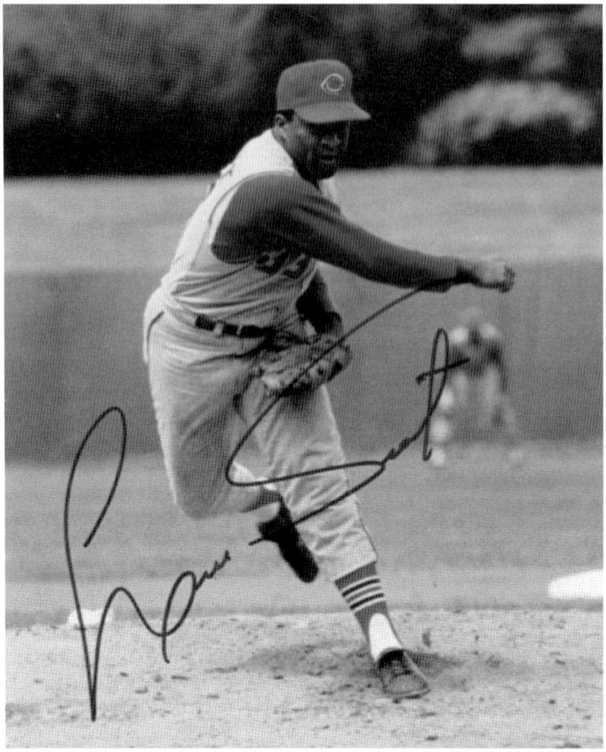

Were it not for McLain, Cleveland's Luis Tiant surely would have captured the American League Cy Young Award. He went 21-9, leading the league with a 1.60 ERA and nine shutouts, finishing fifth in the league MVP voting. He was four years away from wearing a Red Sox uniform.

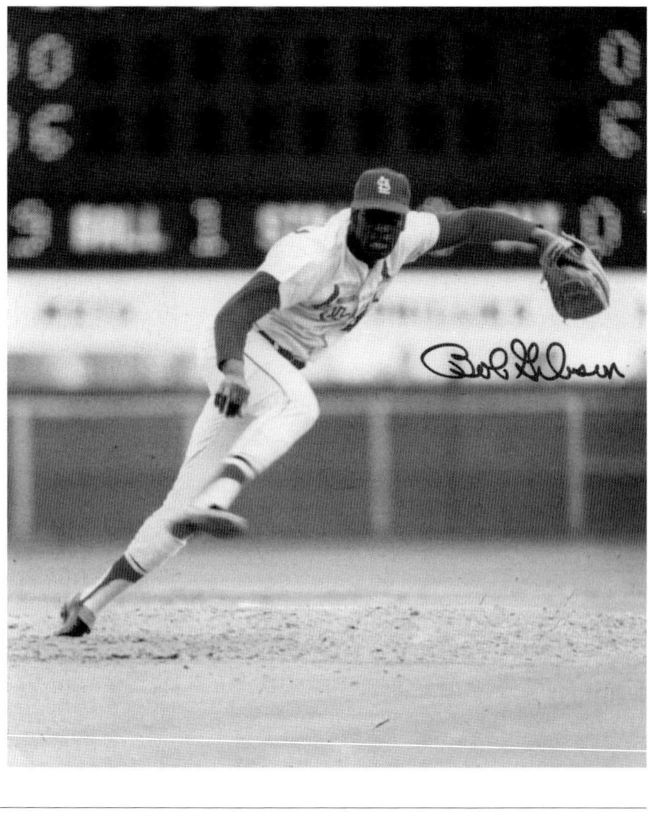

The year of the pitcher was capped off by Bob Gibson's 1968 campaign. Going 22-9, his ERA was a microscopic 1.12, the lowest since Red Sox hurler Dutch Leonard's 0.96 in 1914. His 13 shutouts were the most since 1916, and he led the league in strikeouts. Both he and McLain captured MVP and Cy Young Awards in their respective leagues, the only time this has occurred in the same season in both leagues.

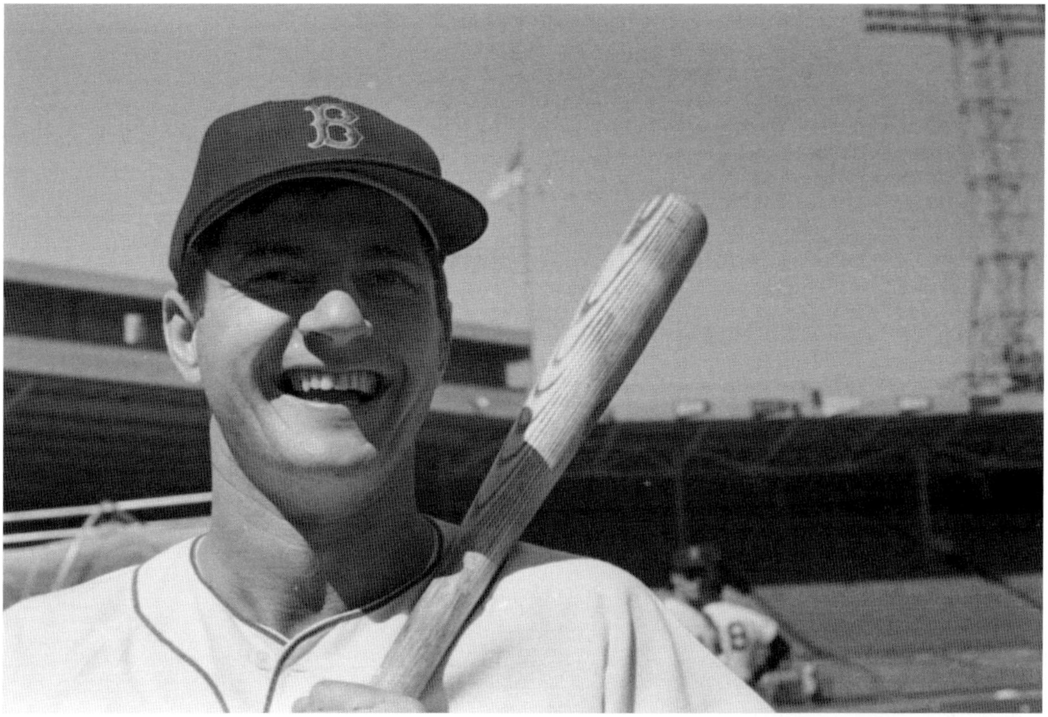

Perhaps the truest measure of the year of the pitcher is that in 1968, only six players in all of baseball hit over .300. Carl Yastrzemski won his second batting title in a row, albeit with a .301 average. He was the only American Leaguer to hit .300. The year of the pitcher prompted the most radical rule change in seven decades, as the pitcher's mound was lowered from 15 to 10 inches in 1969.

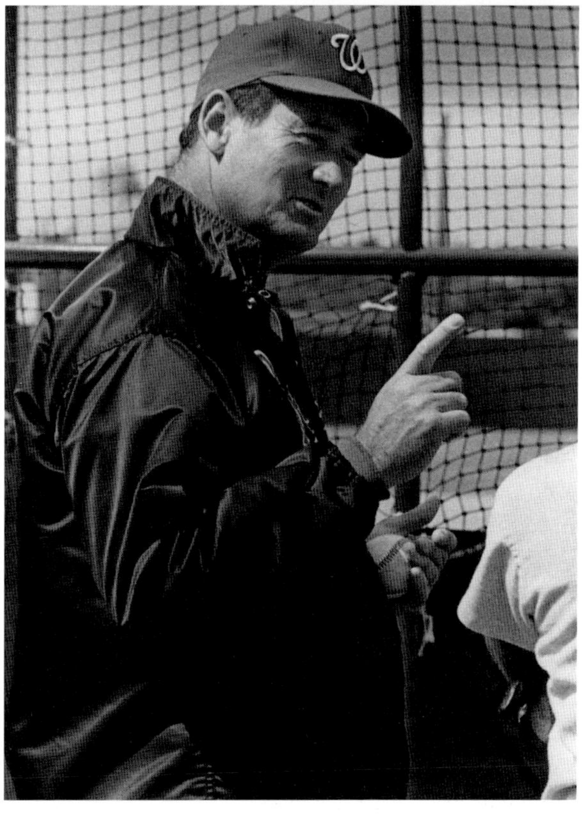

The baseball world was abuzz in 1969 with the return to the diamond of Red Sox all-time great Ted Williams. The "Splendid Splinter" took the helm of the Washington Senators, created in 1961 to replace the old Senators who had moved to Minnesota. He piloted them to their best record ever in 1969 (86-76). He stayed with them through their first year in Texas before retiring to do more fishing.

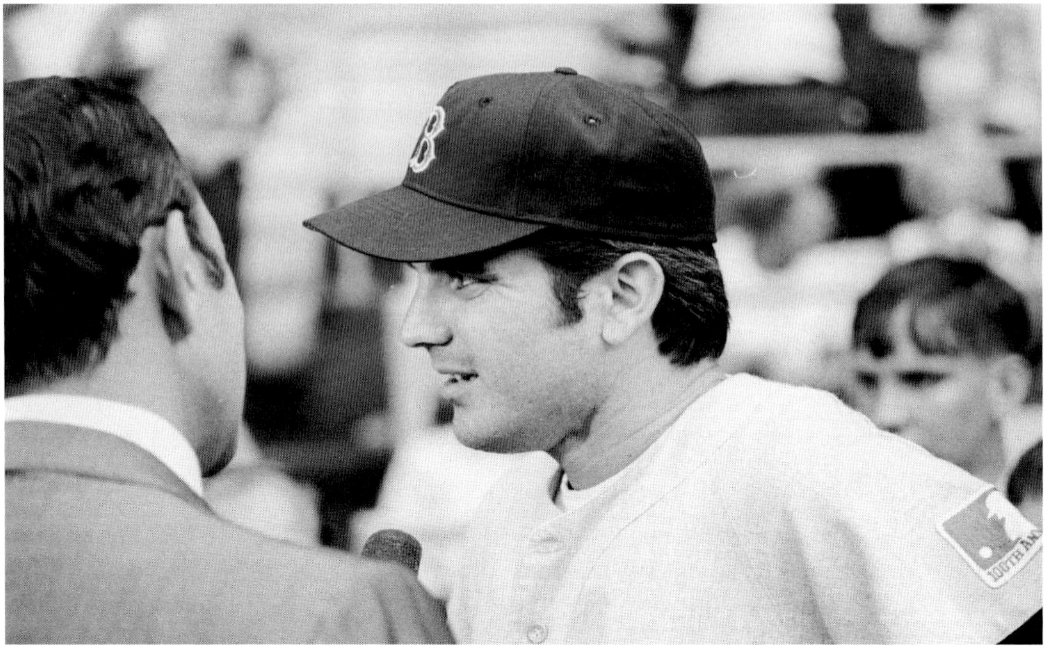

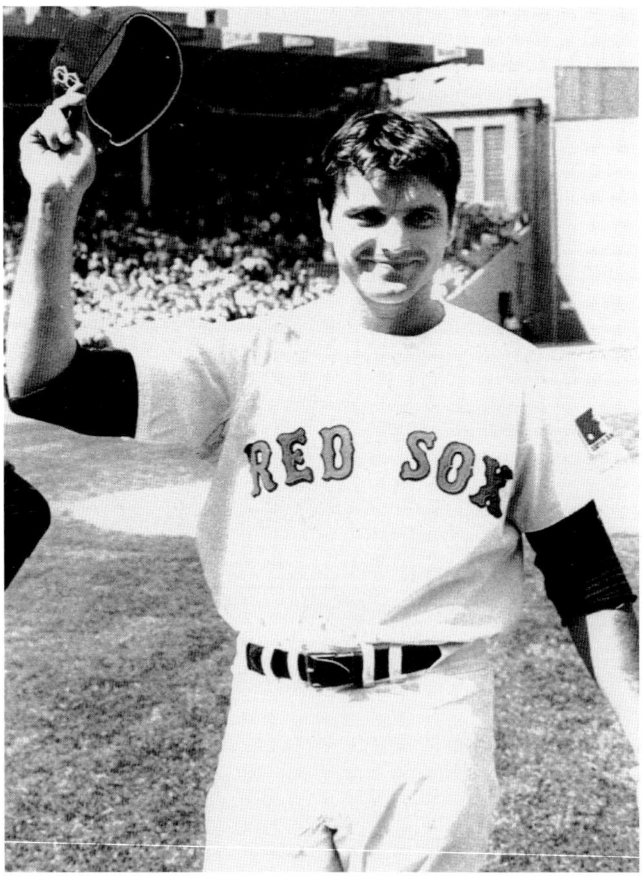

The Red Sox opening of the 1969 season was befitting a Hollywood script. Tony Conigliaro, who had sat out the entire 1968 season with what was thought to be permanent eye damage, returned like a thunderbolt! Seen here (above) in Baltimore on opening day, he came to bat in the top of the 10th in a 2-2 game. He proceeded to hit a two-run homer. Frank Robinson homered in the bottom half of the frame to retie it. Conigliaro eventually scored the winning run in the 12th. Six days later at Fenway Park, (left) the faithful welcomed him back. The author, a 16-year-old junior in high school, played hooky and watched from the last row of the right field bleachers as Conig singled, driving in what proved to be the game-winning run in the fourth inning.

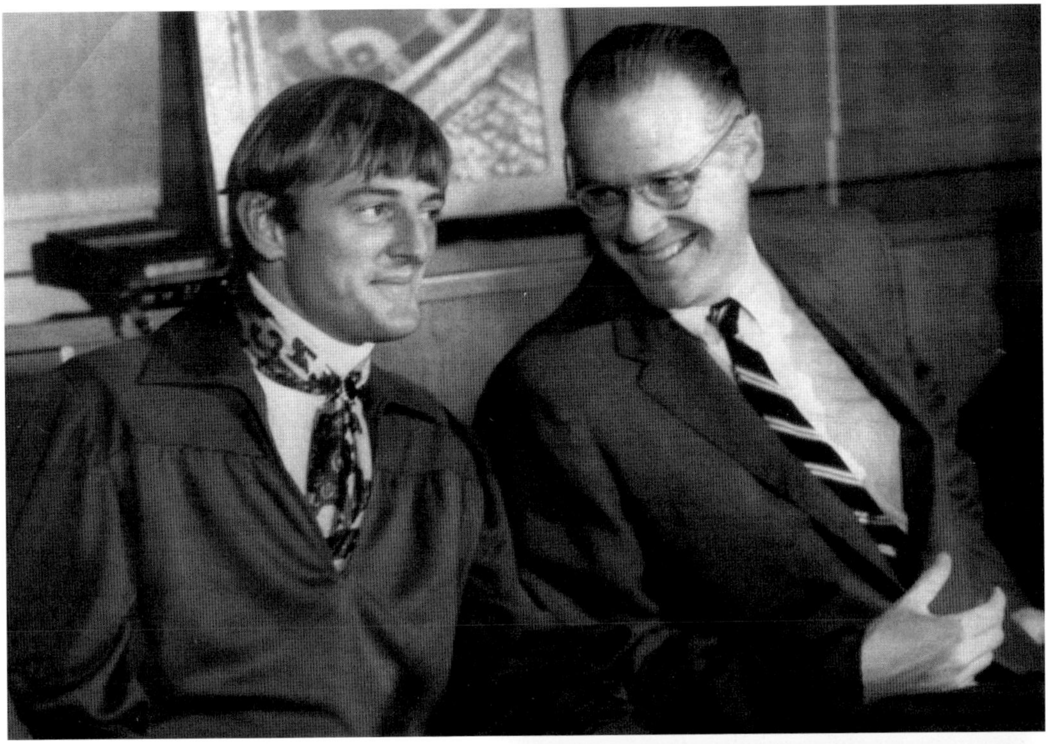

Days later, the Sox season took a surreal turn. On Friday, April 17, the Indians came to town. The Red Sox shelled Luis Tiant with five homers, and leading the attack was Ken Harrelson (two homers and three RBI). The "Hawk" had become a megastar in Boston with his pronounced beak, Nehru jackets, and playboy lifestyle. Not to mention he had hit 35 homers and led the league in 1968 in runs batted in. The following day, the Red Sox shocked the Hawk and the baseball world when they announced he had been traded to the Indians in a blockbuster, six-player deal. The Hawk balked, and on Sunday, the author was in the crowd, which was in a constant buzz about the trade. Nearly 30,000 were in attendance, and they reached frenzied proportions when the rumor spread that Hawk was in the stands. After a meeting with Commissioner Bowie Kuhn (above) and a significant bump in salary, Harrelson reported to the Indians.

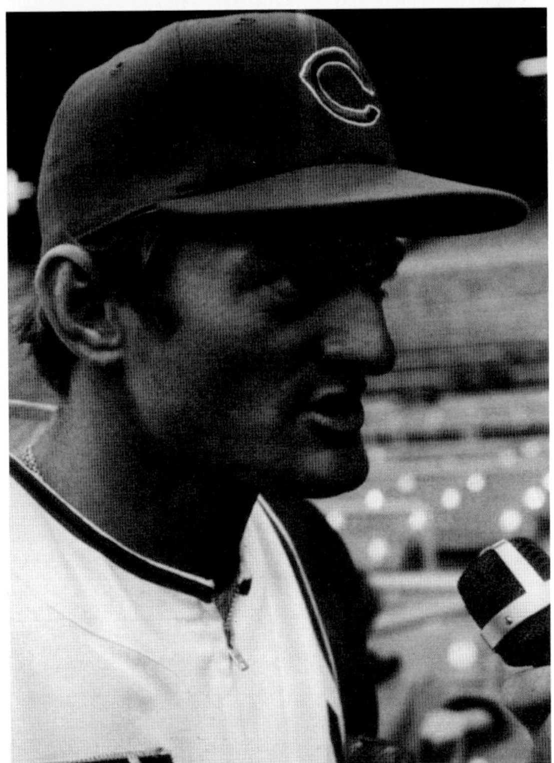

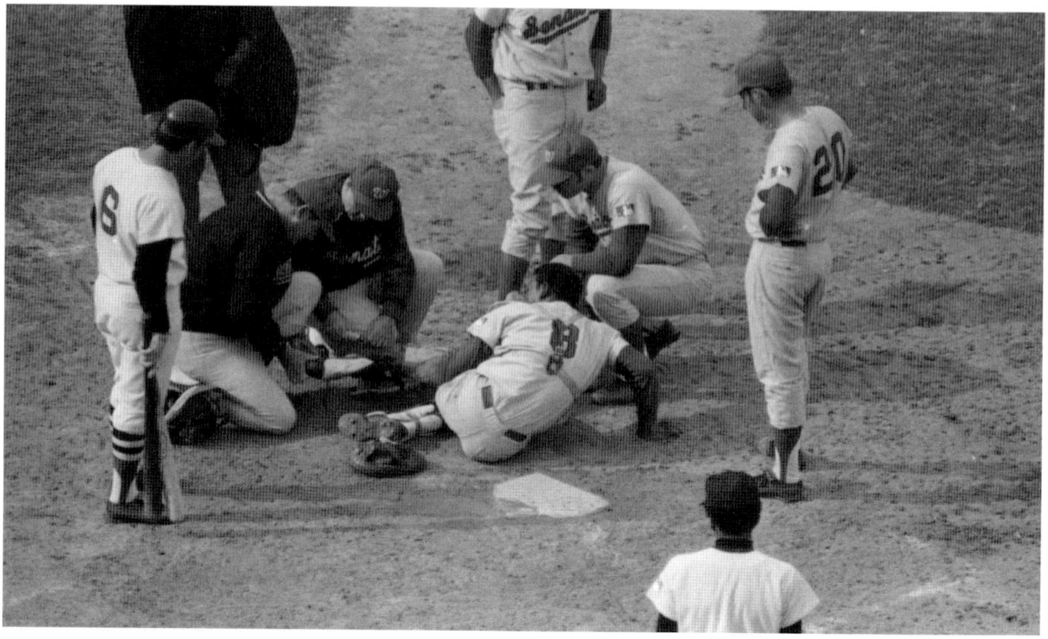

On April 23, the principals of the Harrelson trade were in uniform and ready to go. However, the drama of a few days earlier faded as an entire new chapter was unfolding with Ted Williams making his return to Fenway Park in a Washington Senators uniform. He is seen here (third from left) tending to catcher Paul Casanova (8), felled by a Rico Petrocelli (6) foul ball, while two teammates and pitcher Joe Coleman (20) look on. Casanova stayed in the game. Below, Tony Conigliaro deposits a Joe Coleman pitch into the left field screen in the second inning, giving the Red Sox a 1-0 lead. Paul Casanova is catching, and the umpire is Art Franz. Washington won 9-3. (Both, courtesy of Lynda Fitzgerald.)

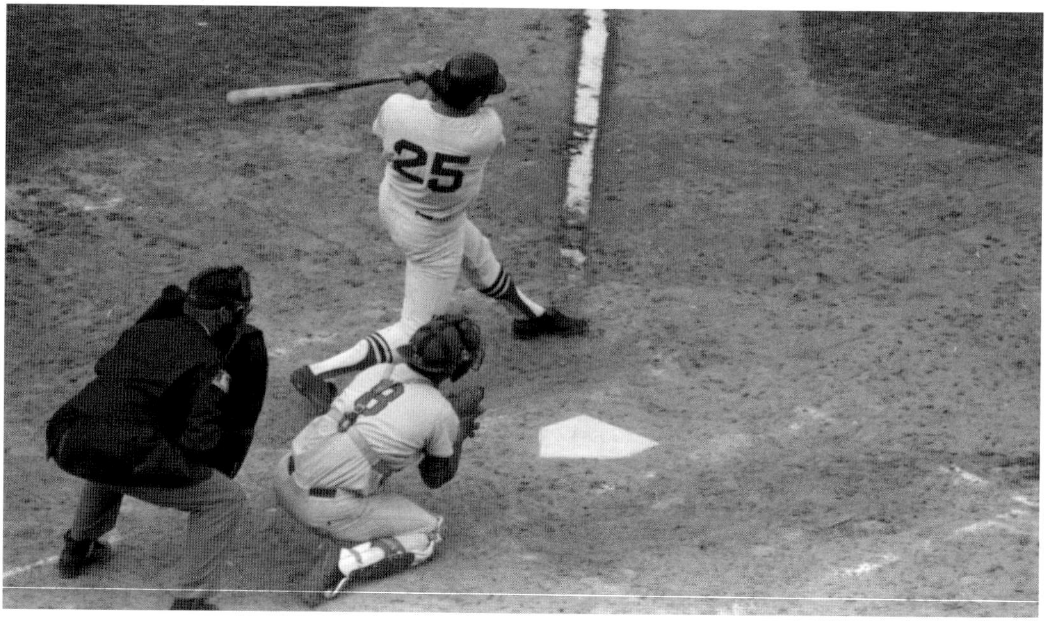

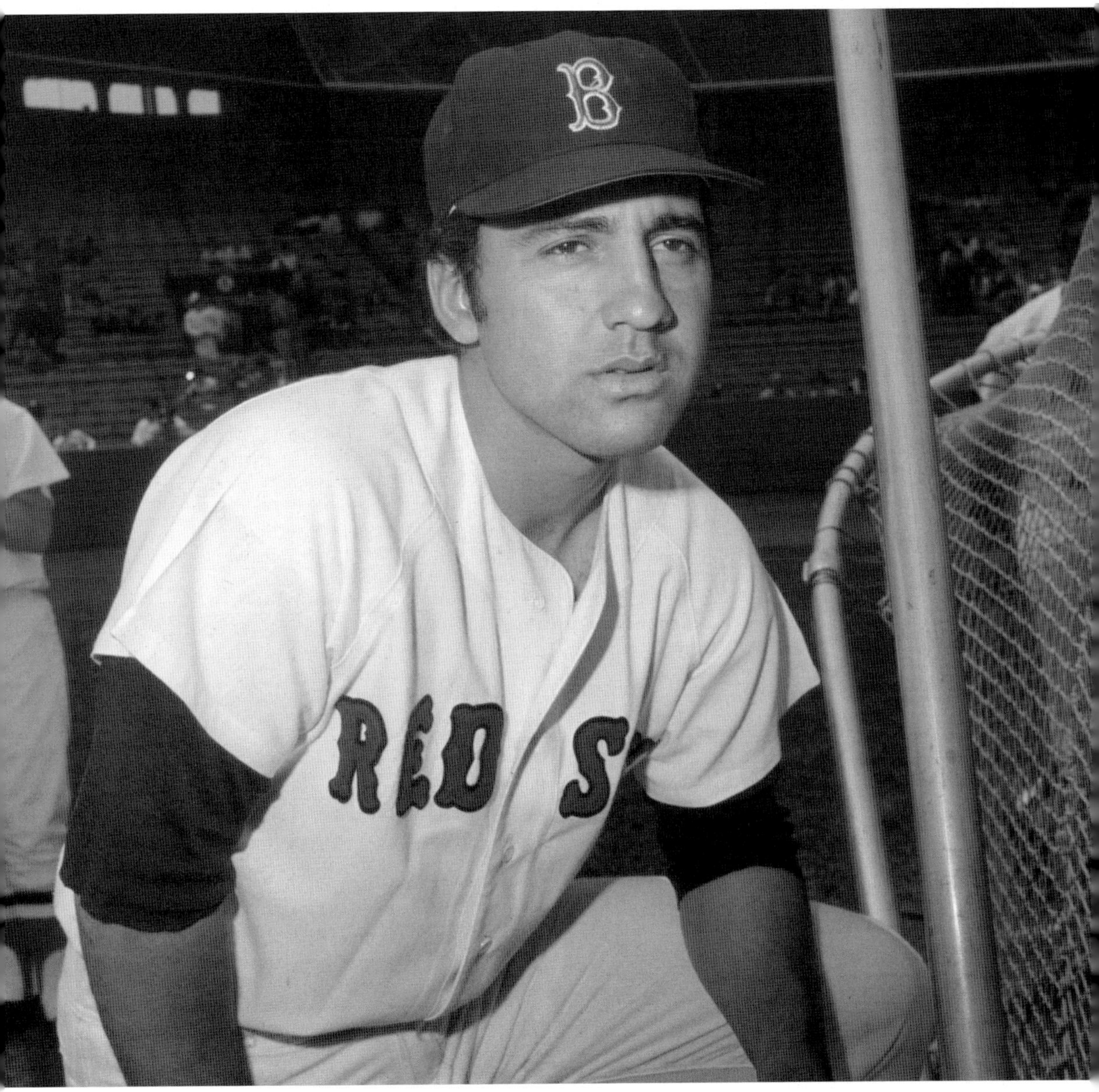

In 1969, Rico Petrocelli became the first American League shortstop to hit 40 home runs in a season. He hit .297, knocked in 97 runs, and was the starting shortstop on the 1969 all-star team. Just how productive Petrocelli was in 1969 is borne out by the Sabermetric statistic called wins above replacement (WAR). It calculates the number of wins a player generated above what that of a replacement player would have done. The measuring stick goes like this: a WAR of eight or above is an MVP-type season, while five or more would be an all-star year. The highest WAR by any position player was 14 by Babe Ruth in 1923, followed by Carl Yastrzemski's 12.5 in 1967. Petrocelli's WAR in 1969 was 10. The only other Red Sox position players to attain a WAR of 10 or more are Ted Williams and Yastrzemski. In 1969, Petrocelli had one of the most productive seasons in Red Sox history.

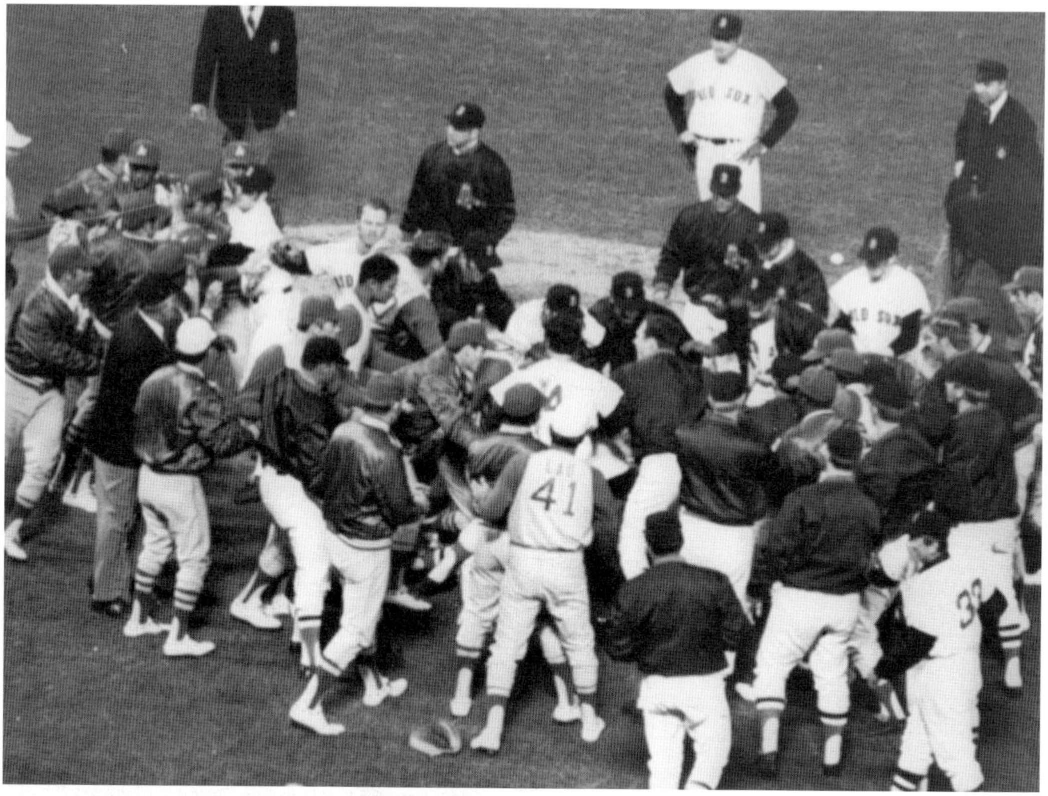

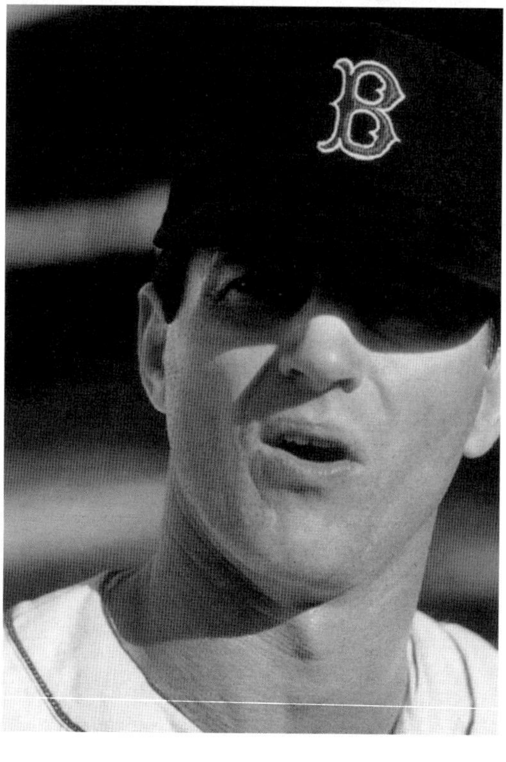

The Red Sox were in the hunt for only a month in 1970. In this photograph, benches cleared twice, this last time after Red Sox pitcher Sonny Siebert plunked Reggie Jackson. Order was restored, and Jackson went back at Siebert. The Red Sox won the game 5-3, and on May 5, they were only 1.5 games out. They then dropped 14 of their next 20 and were gone.

In 1970, Carl Yastrzemski became the first Red Sox player to have back-to-back 40 home run seasons—he hit .329 with 40 homers and had 102 RBI. His .329 mark was the highest of his career, but he lost his fourth American League batting title when Angel's outfielder Alex Johnson took himself out after the fourth inning of his final game when he surpassed Yaz for the crown.

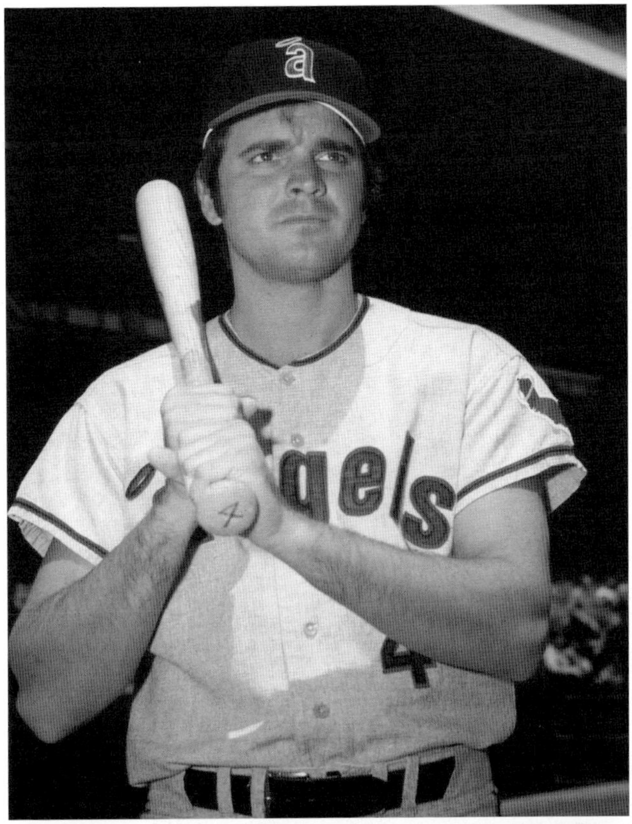

Tony Conigliaro had his most productive year in 1970, hitting .266 with 36 home runs and a team-leading 116 RBI. However, in the midst of the World Series, the baseball world was shocked when he was traded to the California Angels. Conig and two others brought Doug Griffin and Ken and Jarvis Tatum. Doug Griffin (2), seen here tagging out "Cookie" Rojas in a game at Fenway on May 16, 1975, opened the 1975 season as the Red Sox second baseman. Conig would write his final chapter as a player in a Red Sox uniform in the spring and early summer of 1975.

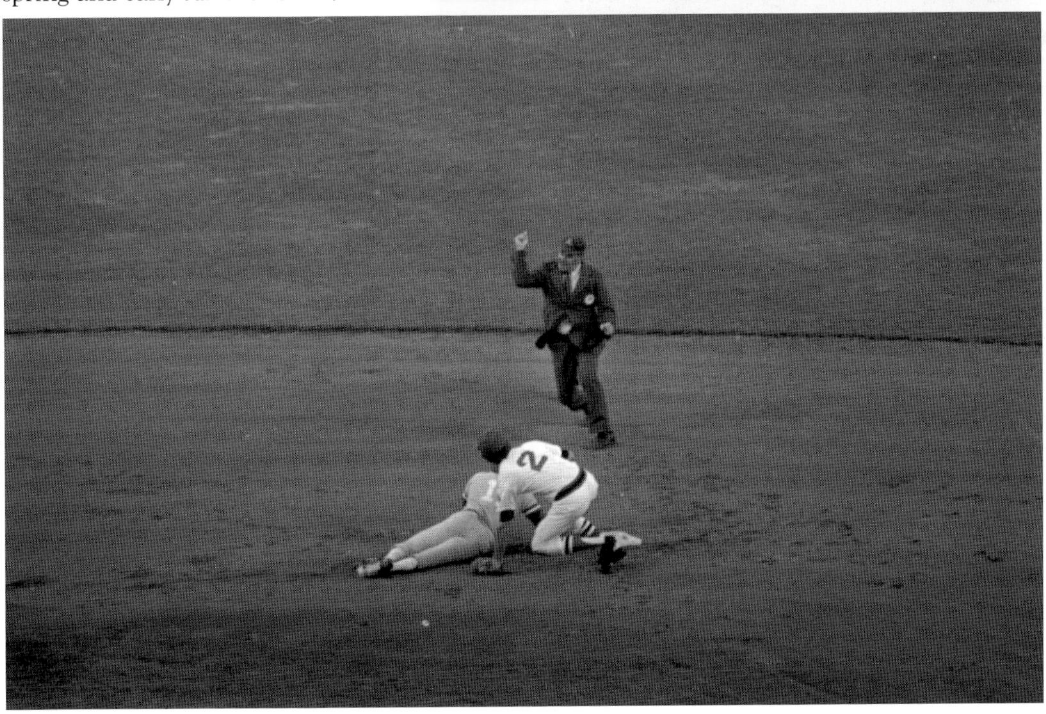

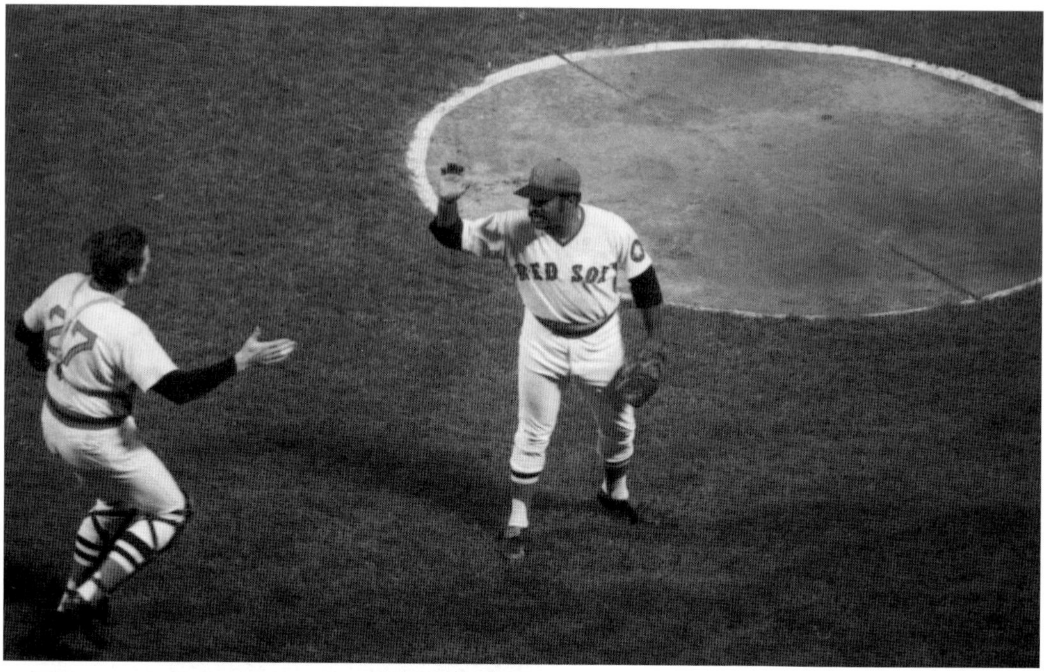

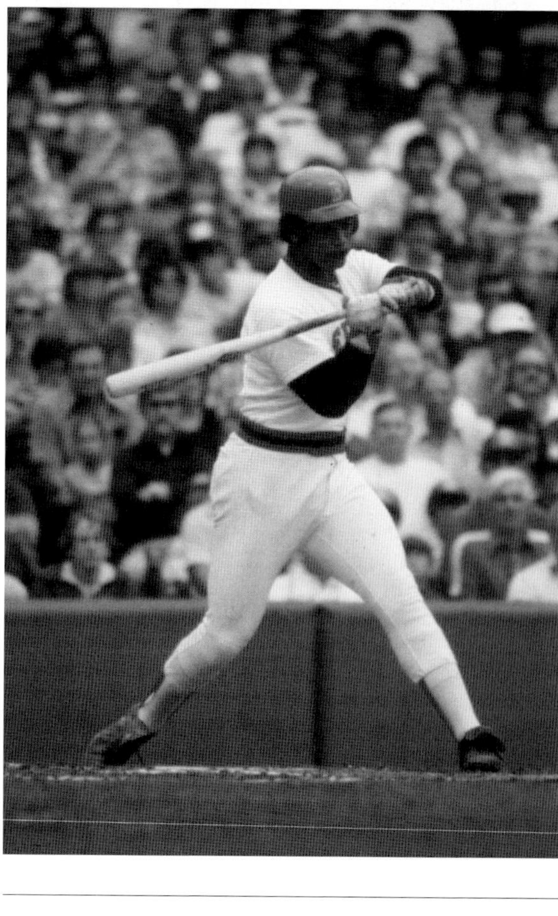

The year 1971 saw the Red Sox mired in the middle of the pack, finishing third in the American League East for the third straight year—a full 18 games out. However, within three weeks they acquired two significant pieces of what would become the 1975 pennant puzzle. Luis Tiant (seen here with Carlton Fisk, left, following a 1975 win) signed with the Red Sox on May 17 and reported to AAA Louisville, and on June 8, the team made Jim Ed Rice of T.L. Hanna High School in Anderson, South Carolina, their first pick in the amateur draft. Within one year, Tiant would be the ace of their staff, and Rice would become the AA Player of the Year at Bristol in 1973 and the AAA Player of the Year at Pawtucket in 1974 before his legendary rookie season in 1975.

The Red Sox acquired Luis Aparicio (right) in 1971. Ever the team player, all-star shortstop Rico Petrocelli (left) moved to third base to make way for him. The tandem would anchor the left side of the Red Sox infield through the 1973 season. Aparicio became the first Venezuelan native inducted into Cooperstown in 1984.

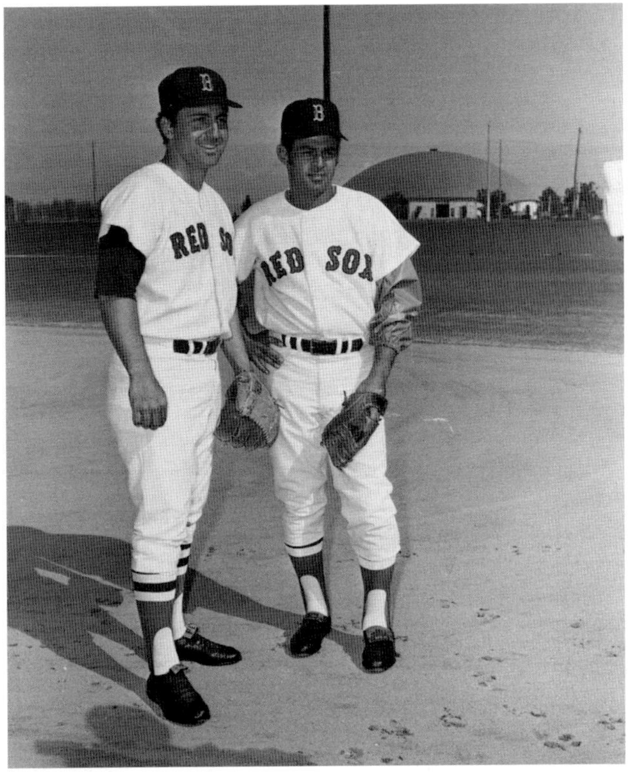

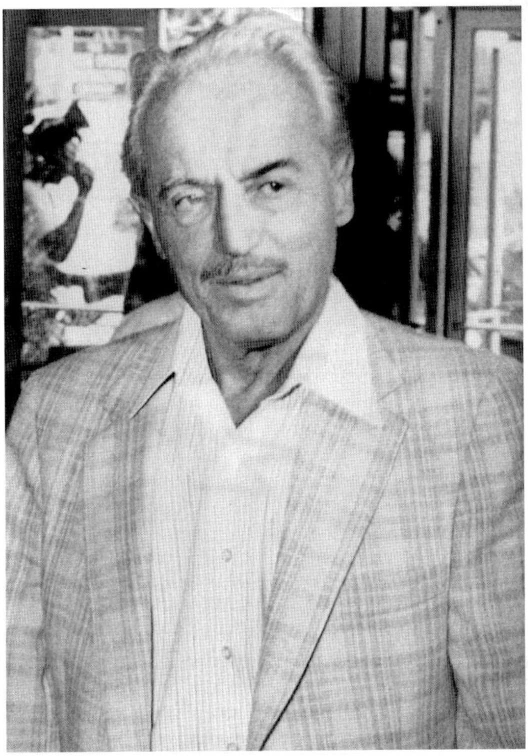

Under the leadership of Players Association director Marvin Miller, the first strike in baseball history took place from April 1 to April 13, 1972, causing the loss of 86 games. The primary issue was the players' pension plan. The result was a $500,000 increase to their pension fund and the right to salary arbitration. The owners lost $5 million and the players $1 million during the stoppage. The uneven schedule cost the Red Sox dearly by year's end.

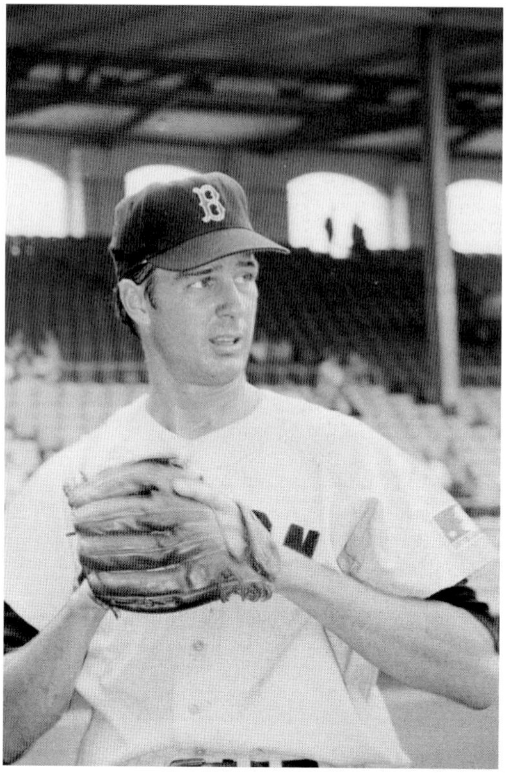

The 1971 World Series brought yet another Red Sox blockbuster trade. This was a nine-player deal in which the Red Sox sent 1967 heroes Jim Lonborg (left) and George Scott (below) along with southpaw Ken Brett, outfielders Joe Lahoud and Billy Conigliaro, and backup catcher Don Pavletik to the Milwaukee Brewers. In exchange, they received pitchers Lew Krausse and Marty Pattin and outfielder and speedster Tommy Harper. Lonborg had just begun to regain his 1967 form and would spend a year with the Brewers before being dealt to the Phillies where he became an 18-game winner. Scott would regain his form as well, hitting .285 with 36 homers and 109 RBI in 1975. He would return to the Red Sox in 1977, but Krausse, Pattin, and Harper were not around by 1975.

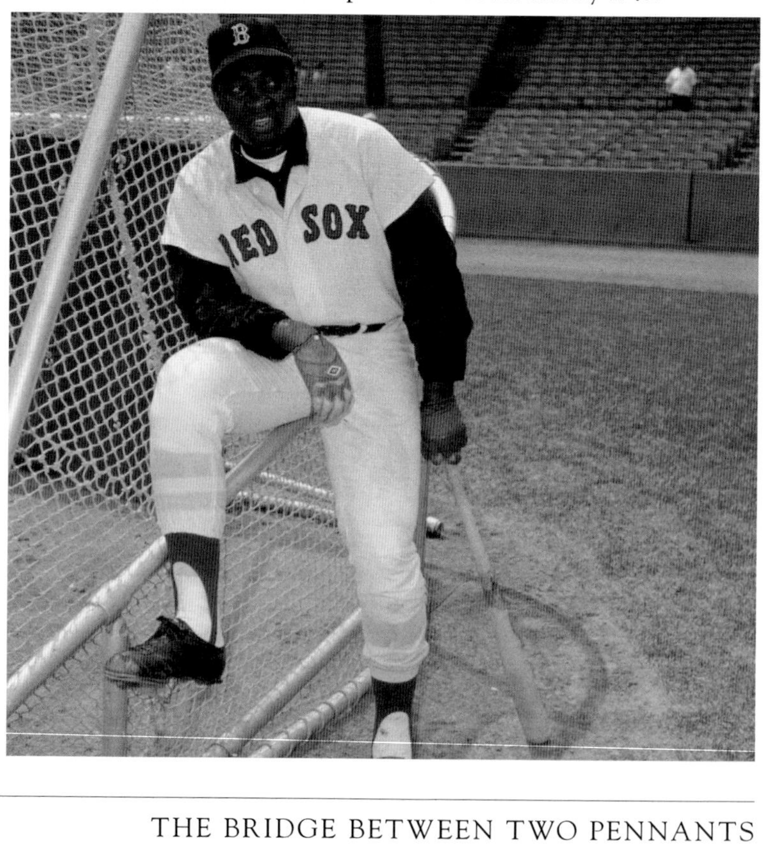

Carlton Fisk arrived on the scene to stay in 1972. Born in Bellows Falls, Vermont, and raised in Charlestown, New Hampshire, Fisk was the Red Sox's first-round draft pick (fourth overall) in 1967. He made his debut in 1969, played two games, and returned for 14 games in September 1971. Although he was turned upside on this play (below) at Yankee Stadium in July 1972, it was he who turned the American League on its head—hitting .293 with 22 homers, 61 RBI, and a league-leading nine triples. That year, Fisk won the first unanimous vote for American League Rookie of the Year. Despite his tender age of 24, he emerged as a clubhouse leader as well.

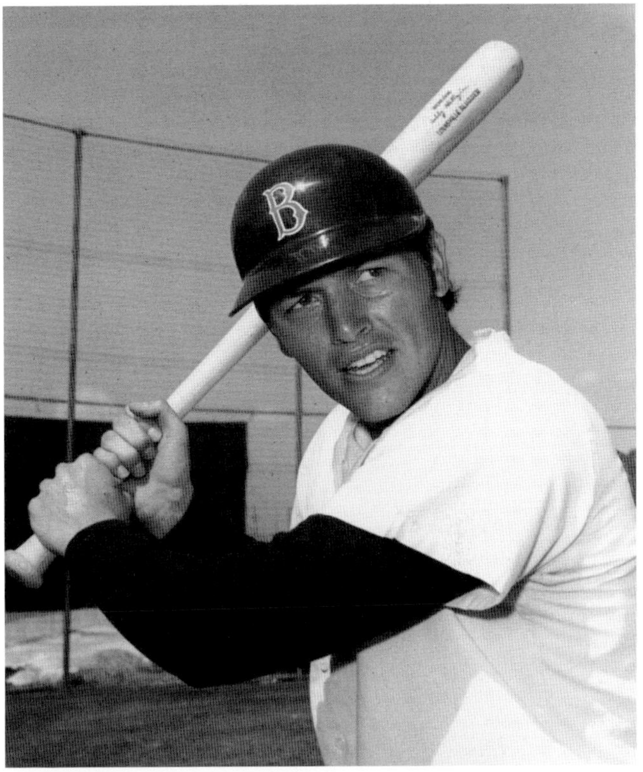

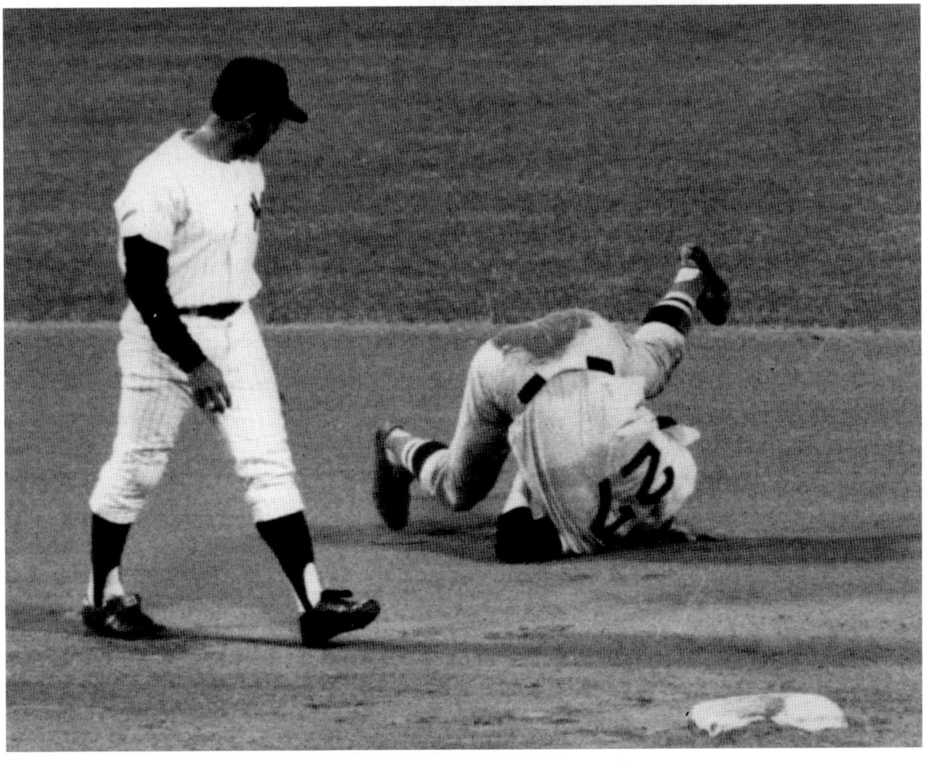

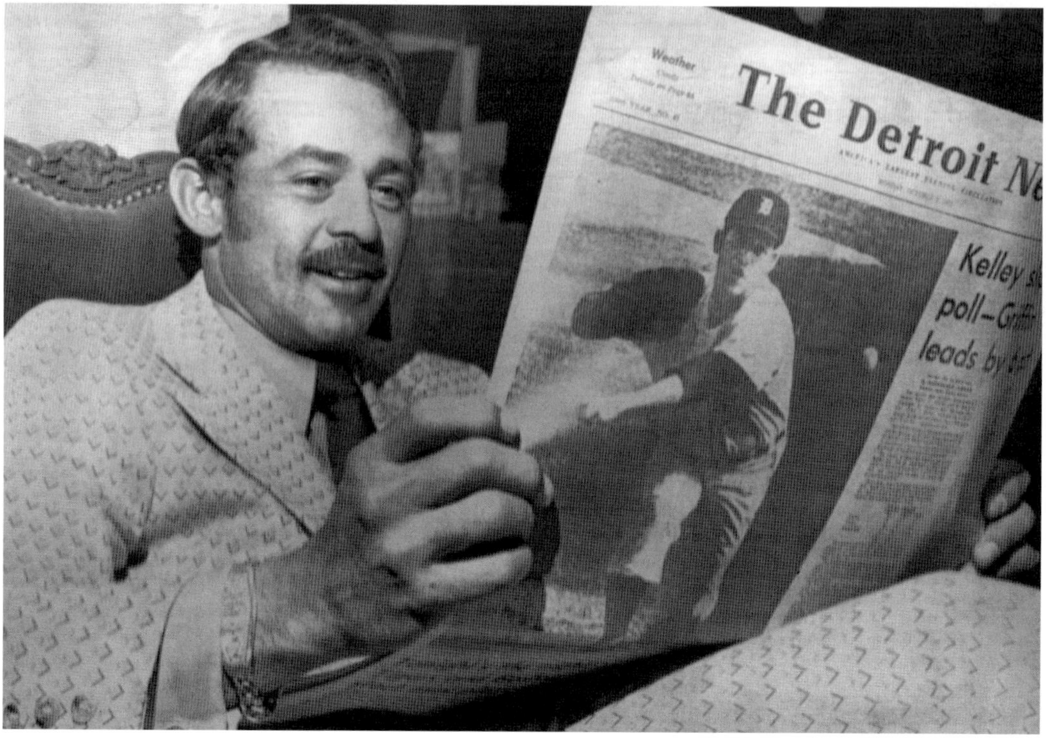

The race for first came down to a three-game series in the Tigers' lair. The first game of the series had John Curtis facing Tiger ace Mickey Lolich. Red Sox shortstop Luis Aparicio is pictured above reading the *Detroit News* with Lolich on the front page. The Red Sox lost 4-1, with their only run coming on a Yastrzemski double scoring Tommy Harper. Aparicio slipped rounding third, causing Yaz to be thrown out at third. Instead of the Red Sox ahead 2-1, one out, and Yaz on third, it was 1-1, two outs, and a runner on third. The following day, the Tigers beat Luis Tiant 3-1, clinching the American League East and setting off a fan celebration on the Tiger Stadium field (below). Boston won the last game good enough for a second-place finish, half a game back. They were struck down by the strike at the season's outset.

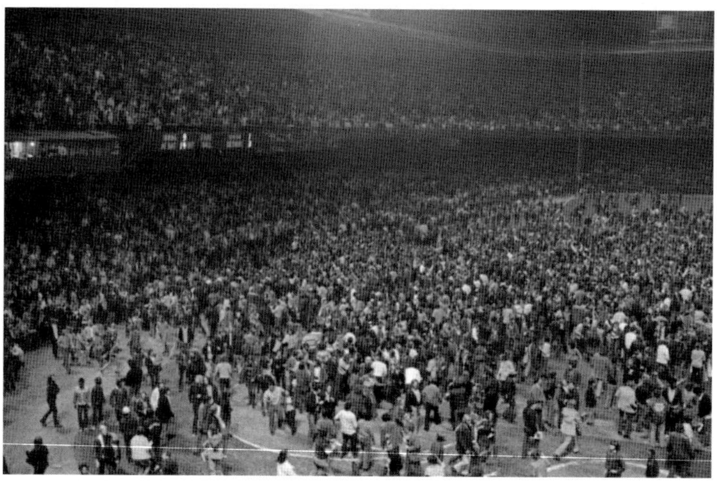

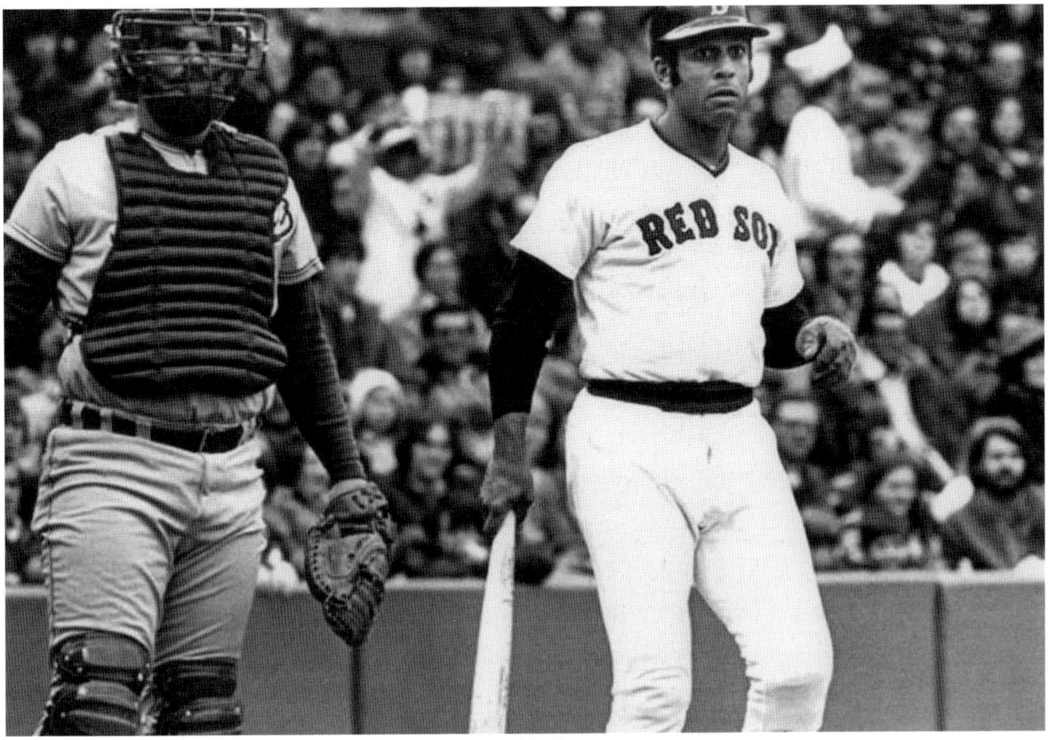

The 1973 campaign ushered in the designated hitter, prompting the Red Sox to sign Orlando Cepada, who had been released by the Oakland A's. The "Baby Bull," or "Cha Cha" as he was also known, turned out to be a great choice as the Red Sox inaugural designated hitter. He hit .289 with 20 homers and 86 RBI, among the team leaders in all categories.

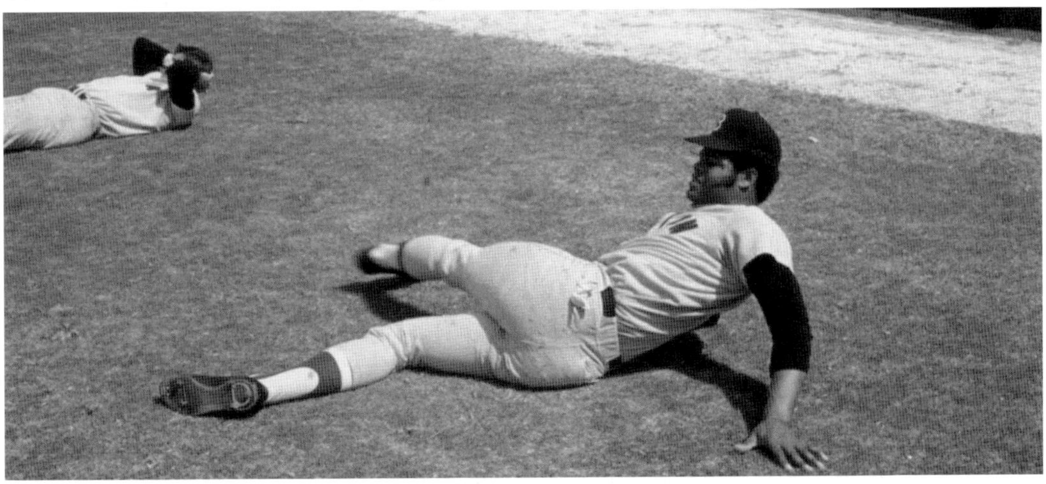

In October 1973, the Red Sox traded their star center fielder, Reggie Smith, to the St. Louis Cardinals. In eight years with the Red Sox, the switch-hitting Smith cracked 20 or more homers five times. His best year came in 1970 when he hit .283 with 30 homers and 96 RBI. The Red Sox acquired two key pieces to the 1975 puzzle in this deal: pitcher Rick Wise and outfielder Bernie Carbo.

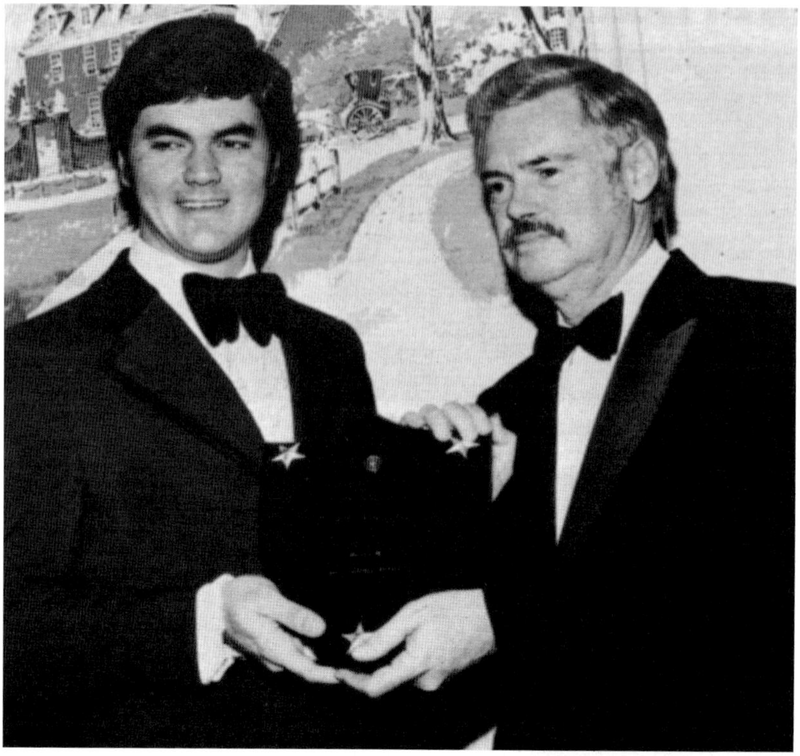

Another piece of the 1975 puzzle, Dwight Evans (left), receives the Red Sox 1973 Rookie of the Year Award from the Boston Baseball Writers (BBWA). Boston BBWA president Charles Scoggins of the *Lowell Sun* presented Evans with his hardware.

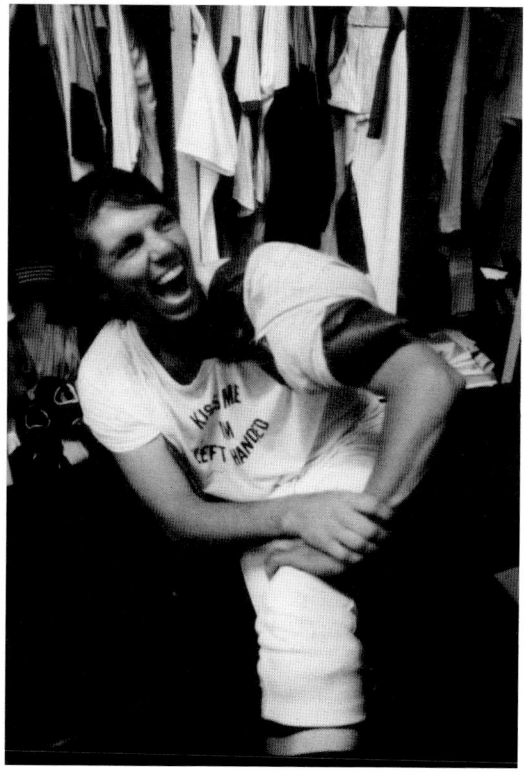

In 1973, Bill Lee won 17 games for the Red Sox, becoming their winningest left-handed pitcher since Mel Parnell in the late 1950s. He would, in fact, win 17 games in three successive seasons with the Red Sox, culminating in their pennant-winning 1975 season.

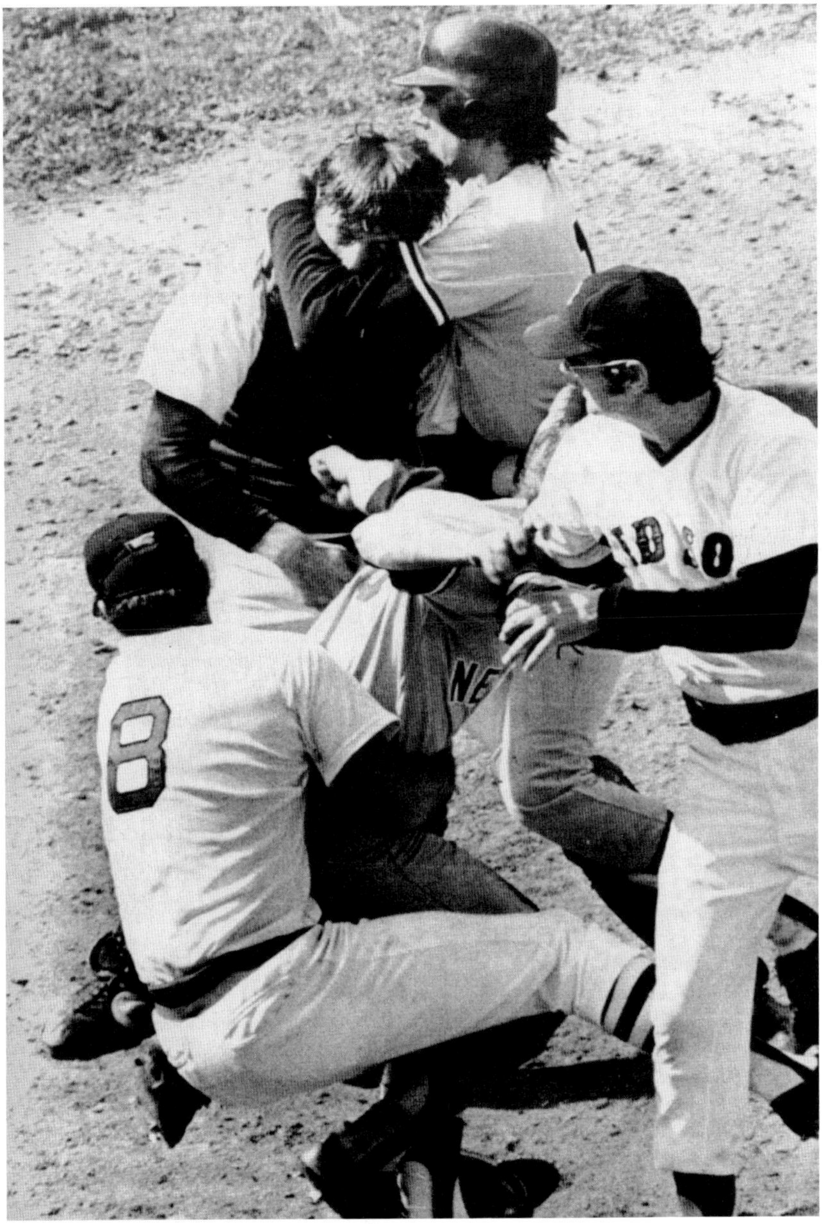

The 1973 season ratcheted up the Red Sox–Yankee rivalry. Dormant since the late 1940s, it was renewed in the personalities of their catchers, Thurman Munson (1970 Rookie of the Year) and Carlton Fisk (1972 Rookie of the Year). The hardnose style and leadership of both redefined the rivalry, which bristled in the late 1970s. It was August 1, 1973, one out, top of the ninth of a 2-2 game. Batter Gene Michael (with a choke hold on Fisk) missed a bunt on an attempted suicide squeeze. Munson barreled into Fisk, who hung on to the ball, and a donnybrook ensued. Yaz (8) has Munson around the waist as pitcher John Curtis arrives to lend a hand. Both catchers were ejected, and the Red Sox won the game with a run in the ninth. The tone for the rest of the decade was set.

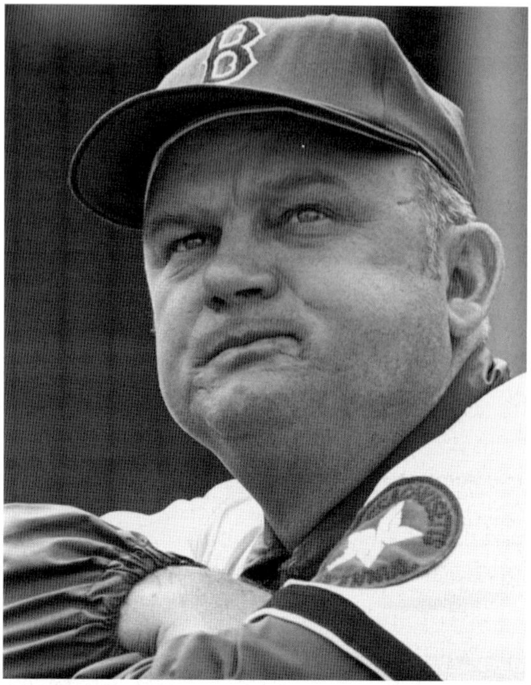

Don Zimmer arrived in 1974 as Darrell Johnson's third-base coach. He would occupy that capacity in 1975 as well, and halfway through the 1976 season, he would become the Red Sox's manager, holding that post through the 1980 season. The Red Sox were 411-304 under manager Don Zimmer for a .575 winning percentage.

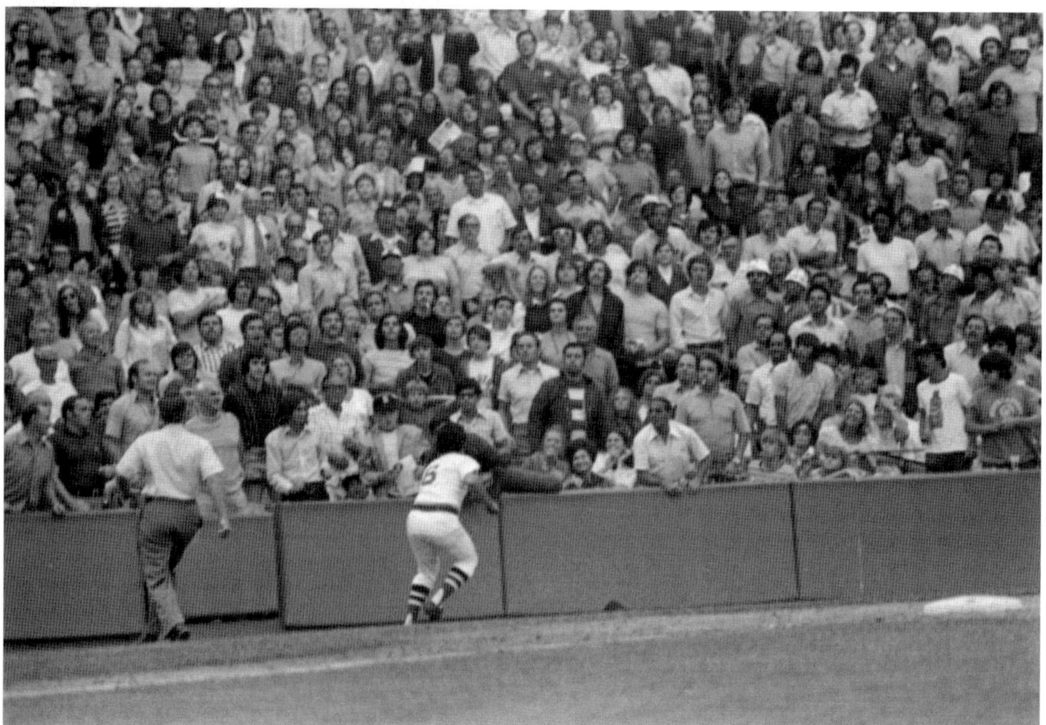

On April 21, 1974, the Red Sox captured their first walk-off win of the year. It came in the 10th inning, after Rico Petrocelli (6) doubled to tie the game in the ninth. Pertocelli is pictured here giving chase to a foul popup by Indians catcher Dave Duncan in the fifth inning.

On June 11, 1974, old friend Dick Williams (right) returned to Fenway in the capacity of analyst for NBC's Monday night Game of the Week. Williams had resigned as manager of the Oakland A's following their 1973 World Series win, as he had simply had enough of owner Charlie Finley. Three weeks from this game, a 10-9 Red Sox win, Williams joined the Angels.

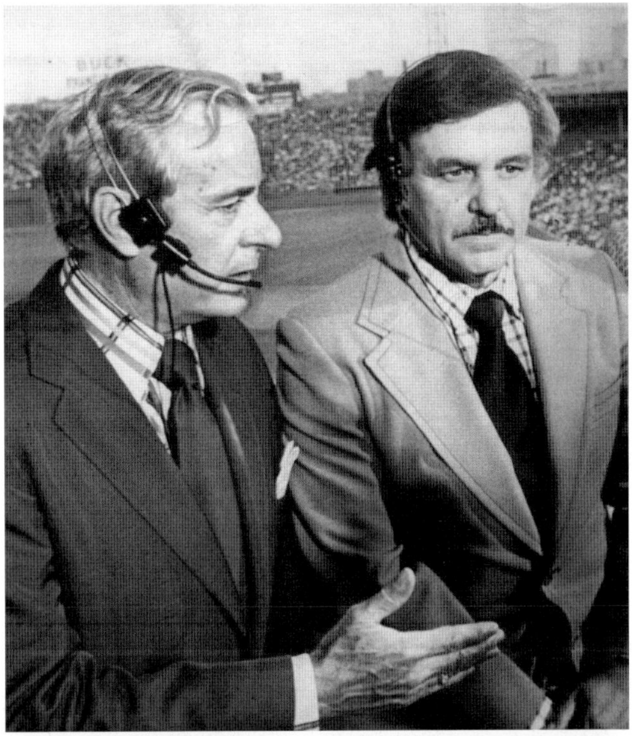

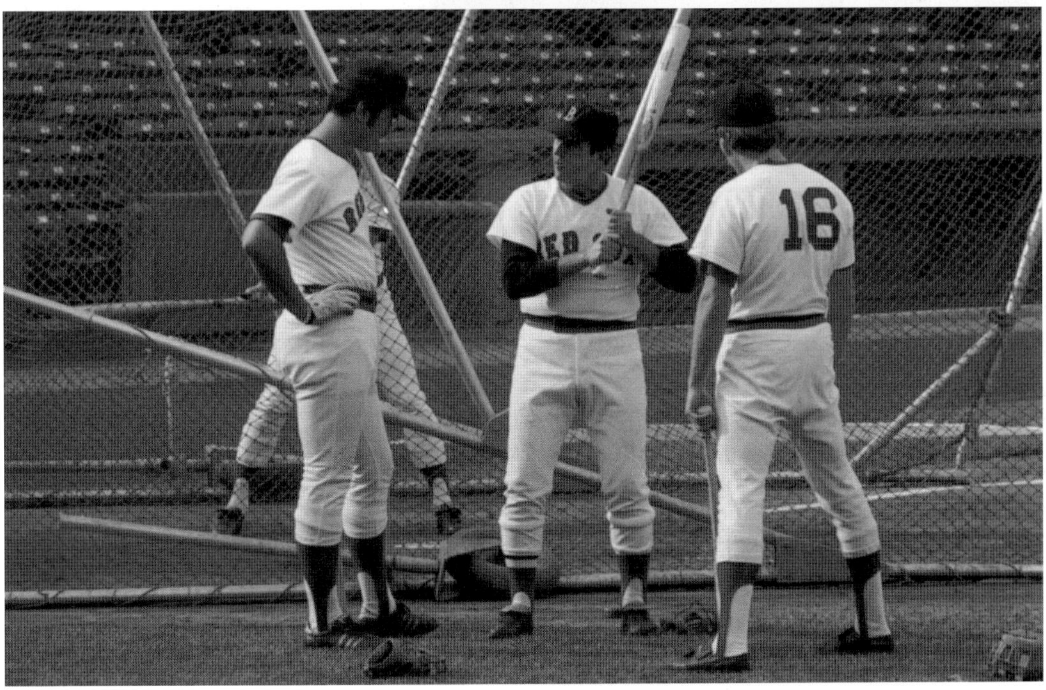

The Red Sox beat Milwaukee 9-0 on the June 24, putting the team in first place by 4.5 games. Before the game, Dwight Evans (left) and Rick Miller (right) discuss the finer points of hitting with coach Johnny Pesky.

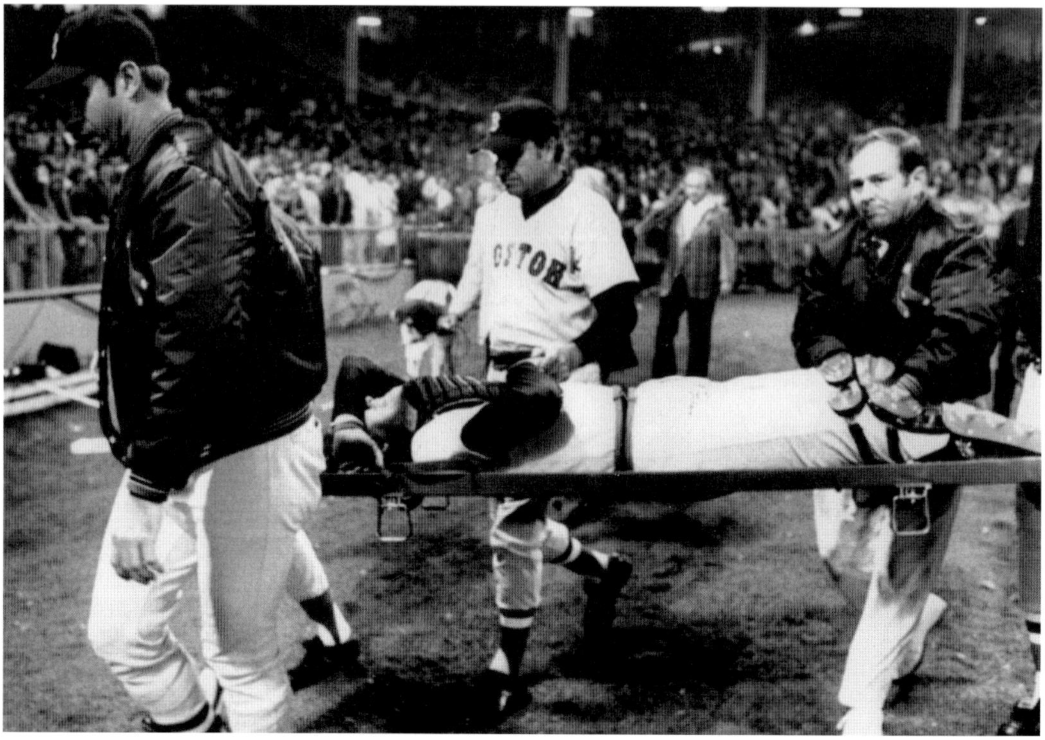

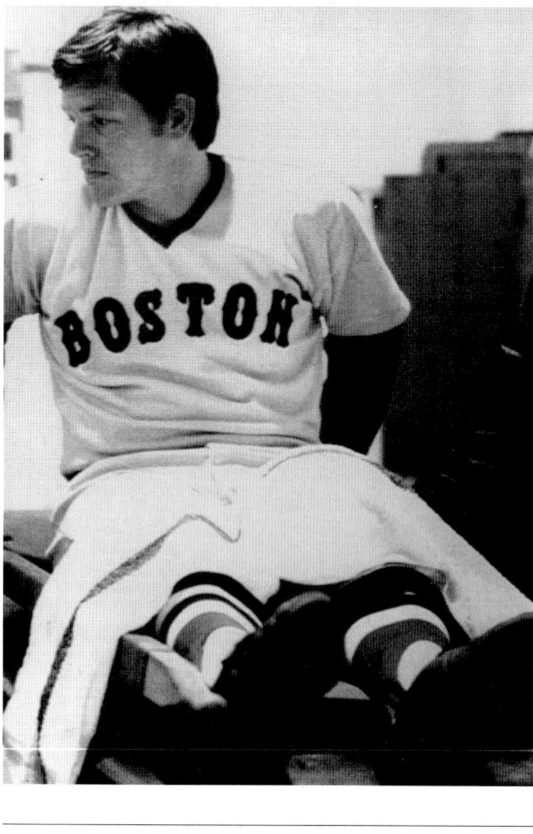

In Cleveland Stadium, the career of a Red Sox catcher nearly came to an end. It was June 28, 1974, and the score was 1-1 in the bottom of the ninth. With one out, Indians left fielder Leron Lee walked, and George Hendrick doubled to left field. Lee came all around to score from first base, sliding into Fisk's left knee, ending the game and the season for Fisk. He was carried off the field (above) and is pictured here waiting to be transported to the hospital (left). Suffering major ligament damage to his knee, some thought his career was over. He recovered, but during spring training in 1975 he broke his wrist, which sidelined him until June that same year. It was a blessing in disguise, as it gave his wounded knee three more months to heal.

Jim Rice (left), seen here with Carl Yastrzemski in 1975, made his major-league debut on August 18, 1974, against the White Sox. In his second at-bat, he recorded his first RBI, a sacrifice fly scoring Yastrzemski. Both men ended up in the National Baseball Hall of Fame—Yaz in 1983 and Rice in 2010.

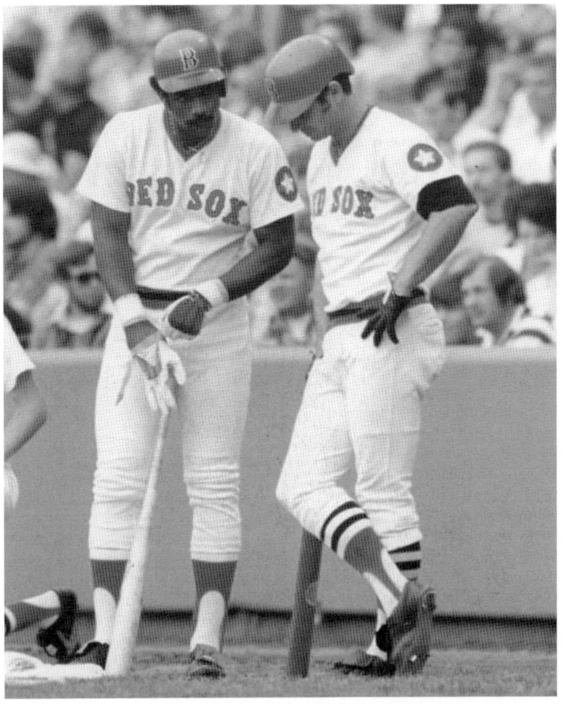

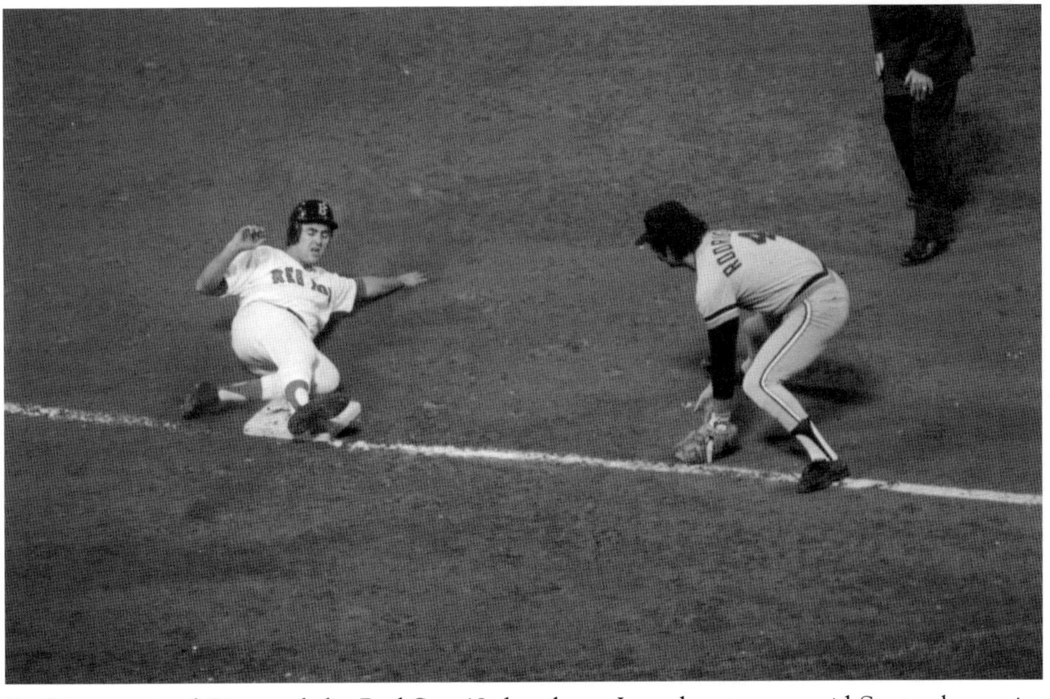

Fred Lynn joined Rice and the Red Sox 18 days later. In a three-game, mid-September series against the Tigers, in the midst of the Red Sox collapse, Lynn gave the Fenway Faithful a prelude of what was to come in 1975. He is pictured here sliding into third for the first triple of his career, in an 8-5 win on September 18. He went 4-5 with three RBI that night.

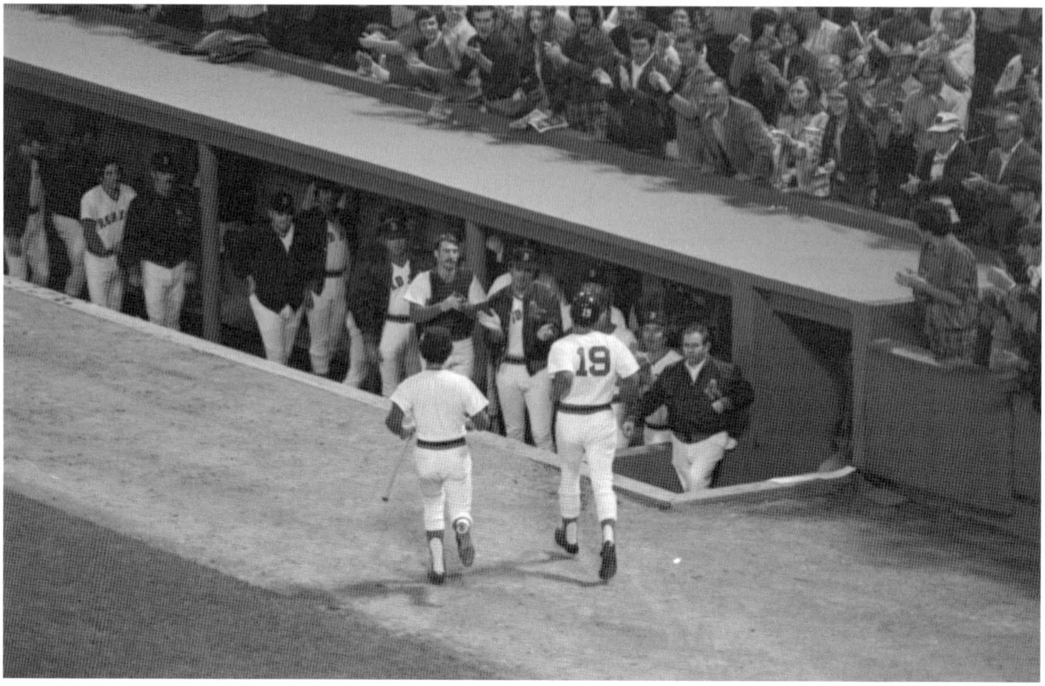

The following night, Fred Lynn hit his first Fenway Park home run—a solo shot in the second inning off Tiger pitcher Vern Ruhle. He is seen here being welcomed in the Red Sox dugout following the blast. It was the only Red Sox run in a 3-1 loss. He would hit 70 more home runs at Fenway, accounting for 71 of his 306 career home runs.

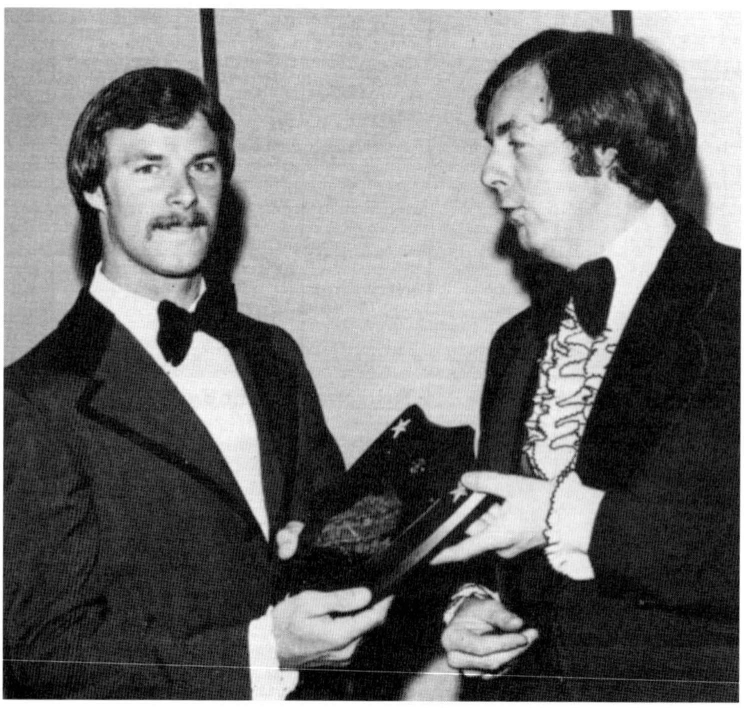

He made three errors in his major-league debut, but by year's end, shortstop Rick Burleson had finished fourth in the voting for American League Rookie of the Year. He became a four-time all-star and a fixture at shortstop for the remainder of the decade. Here, he accepts the BBWA Red Sox Rookie of the Year Award from Peter Gammons in January 1975.

2

THE RED SOX DIAMOND JUBILEE

The Red Sox and the Fenway Faithful were reeling following the team's collapse in the 1974 season. On August 23, Luis Tiant won his 20th game of the season, a 3-0 shutout of the Oakland A's. It was his sixth whitewash of the year, the Red Sox's fifth win in a row, and most importantly, it put the Red Sox in first place by seven games, their largest lead of the season. The following night they lost to Oakland's Catfish Hunter 4-1, sending them into a tailspin the likes of which the Fenway Faithful had never seen. In the next 13 games, the Red Sox won only two of them. They were shut out six times, including three in a row in Baltimore, and scored a grand total of 23 runs in those 13 games. In a span of 12 days, their seven-game lead evaporated, and they fell out of first place. Not quite flatlined, they rallied to win two in a row and regain a share of the lead, but death came quietly when they dropped five of their following six games and sank to third place, four games out. From the apex of their season on August 23 until September 20, the Red Sox had gone from seven games up to four games back. In that span of 26 games, they won but seven and from that same apex to season's end, they were an abysmal 14-24, surpassed in futility by only the lowly Kansas City Royals.

However, there were glimmering stars on the horizon, one named Rice and the other named Lynn, and there were the stalwarts Yaz, Petrocelli, and Tiant. There was a question behind the plate: could another budding star named Fisk come back from major knee surgery? And as always there were questions about the pitching past the fabulous El Tiante.

They were sluggish in spring training and out of the gate but played .640 baseball in May as things began to click. Rice and Lynn emerged, and Fisk returned in June. And through it all was the consistent veteran leadership of Yastrzemski, Petrocelli, and Tiant. New England reveled that summer, which melted into a fall that would rejuvenate the game of baseball in the hearts and minds of America.

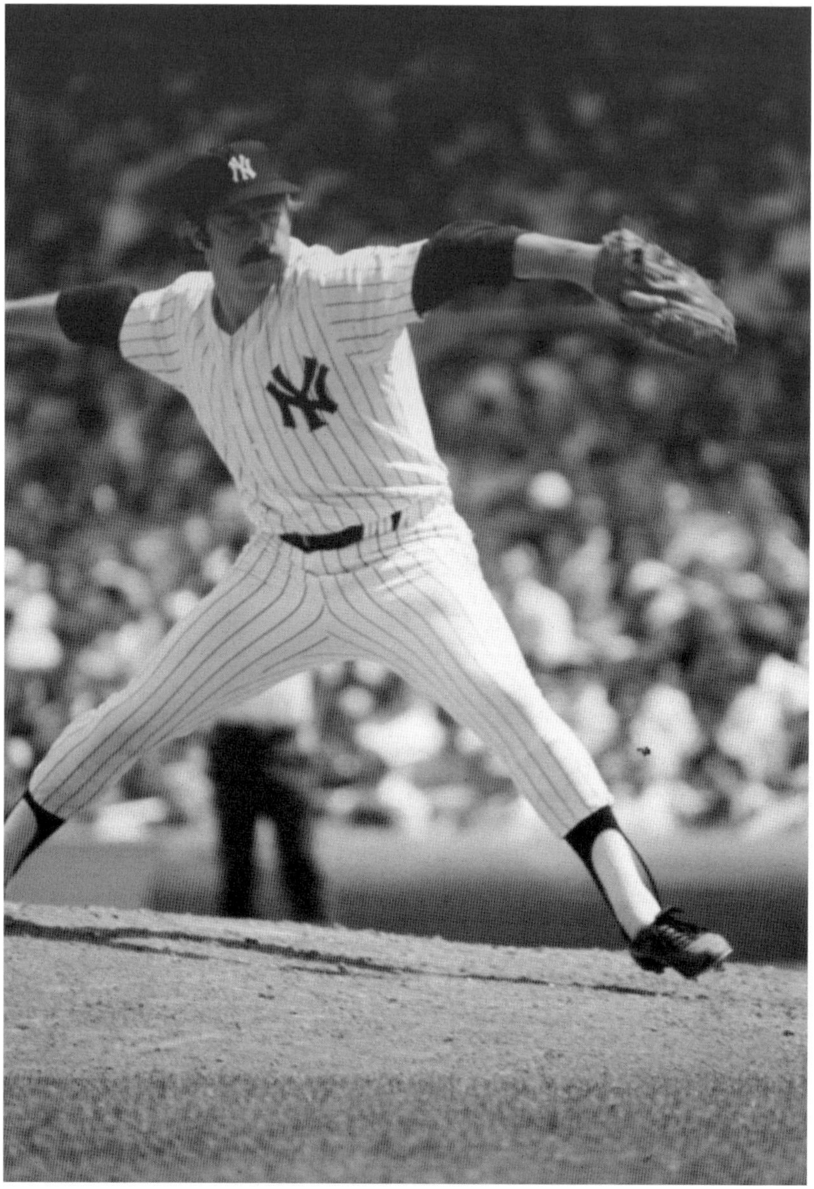

The Oakland A's James Augustus "Catfish" Hunter, pitcher extraordinaire, became baseball's first true free agent in December 1974. Oakland's cantankerous owner Charlie Finley committed an inexplicable blunder by not depositing checks into Hunter's insurance annuity fund per the terms of his contract. An arbitrator ruled in favor of Hunter, and Major League Baseball's first bidding war was on. Hunter's decision came down to the Red Sox or Yankees. With Tom Yawkey willing to pay $4 million to procure his skills, Catfish chose the Yankees. The sum broke down as follows: $100,000 per year for five years, $53,000 annual annuities for 10 years, 15 years at $100,000 per year deferred until 1994, $25,000 college endowments for his children, $200,000 in attorney's fees, and a brand-new Buick every year for five years. The major league's yearly average salary was $41,000—the genie was out of the bottle.

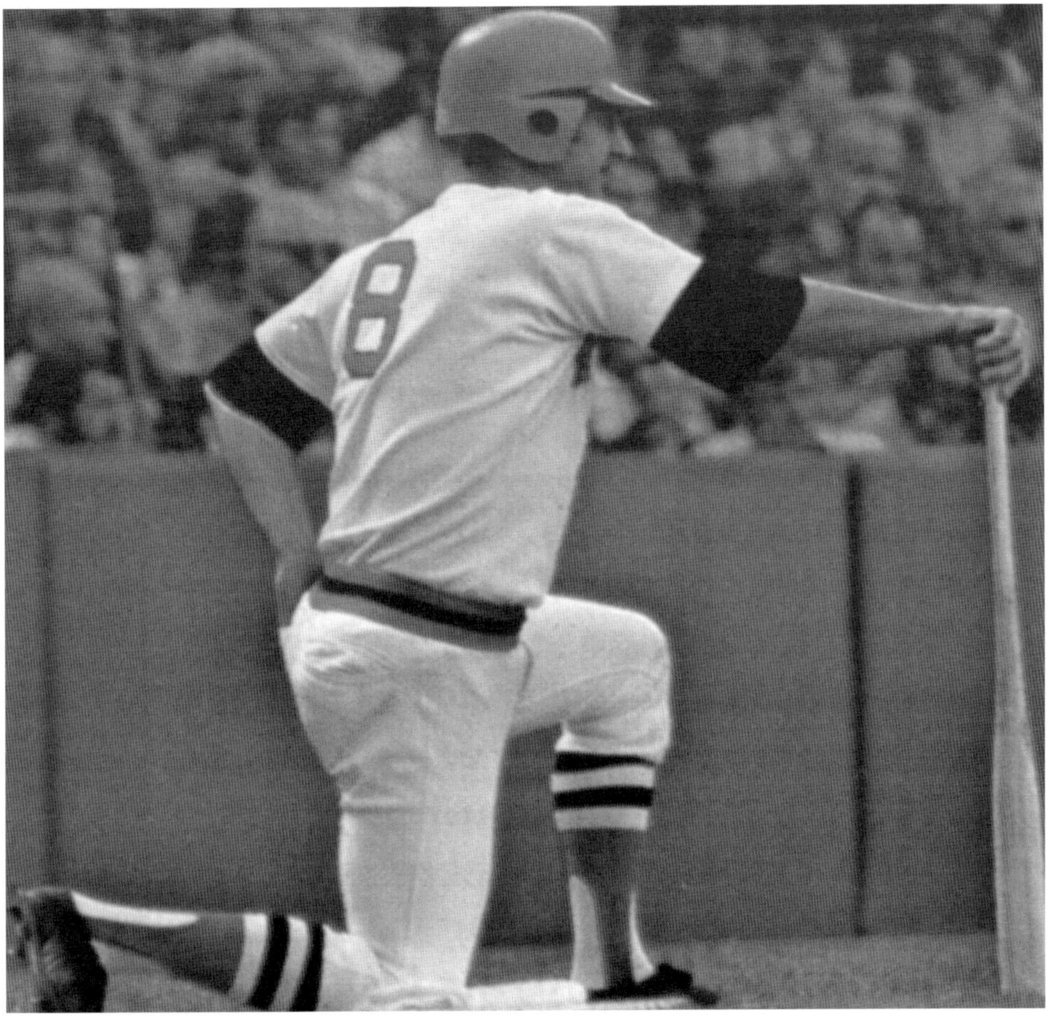

Carl Yastrzemski was entering his 15th season in the spring of 1975. An 11-time all-star and three-time batting champ, he had become the first Red Sox player to enjoy back-to-back 40 home run seasons. However, a love-hate relationship had established between Yaz and the Fenway Faithful, as his remarkably historic 1967 season could not be reproduced. It was in 1975 that he rose to iconic status when he battled a shoulder injury throughout the summer to lead his team through the playoffs and into the World Series. It began at the end of a poor spring, when he challenged them, "If we play in the season, the way we played this spring . . . we'll finish in last place . . . we have to execute and hustle . . . we're not going to overpower anyone . . . we've got to start and finish as a unit."

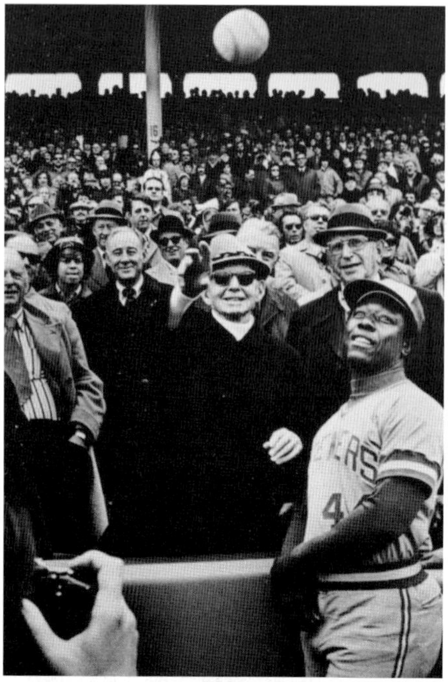

The Red Sox opened up at Fenway on April 8, 1975, a chilly day. It was indeed a special day, as newly crowned home run king Hank Aaron made his American League debut as the designated hitter of the Milwaukee Brewers. Here, Aaron joins Red Sox Hall of Famer George "Duffy" Lewis as he throws out the first pitch. Lewis was the left fielder on the Red Sox 1918 World Championship team.

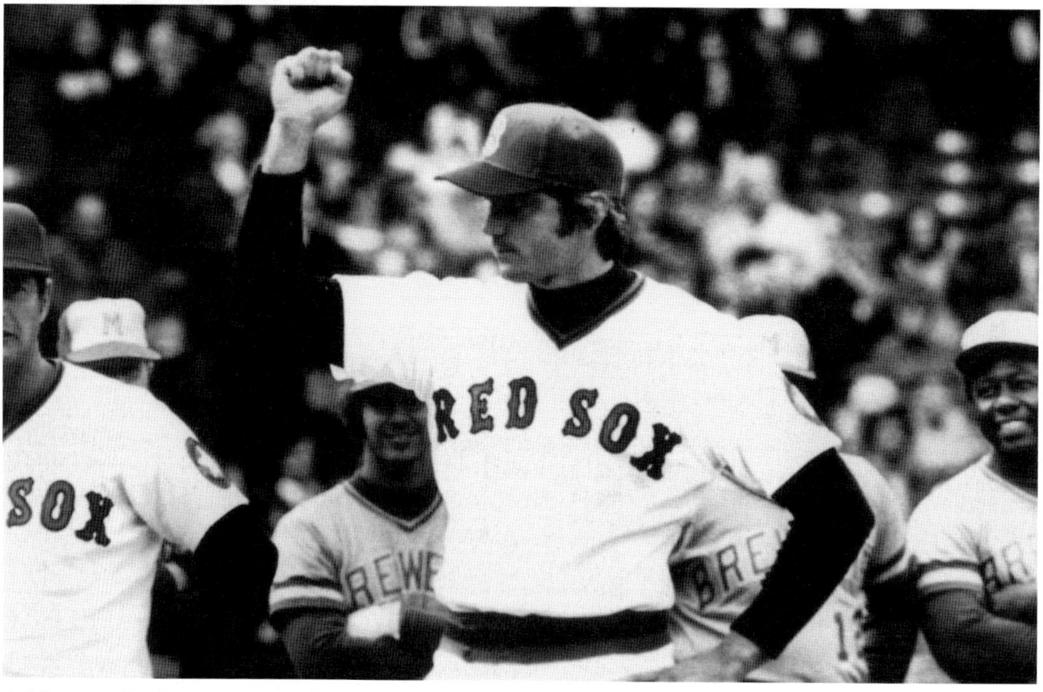

Adding to the festivities was the return of Tony Conigliaro, acknowledging the crowd, as a smiling Hank Aaron looks on (right). After three years absent from the game, he fought back to make the Red Sox squad as the designated hitter. After singling in his first at-bat, he and Yaz executed a double steal with Yaz scoring the game's first run, stealing home. The Red Sox won 5-2, and 1975 was under way.

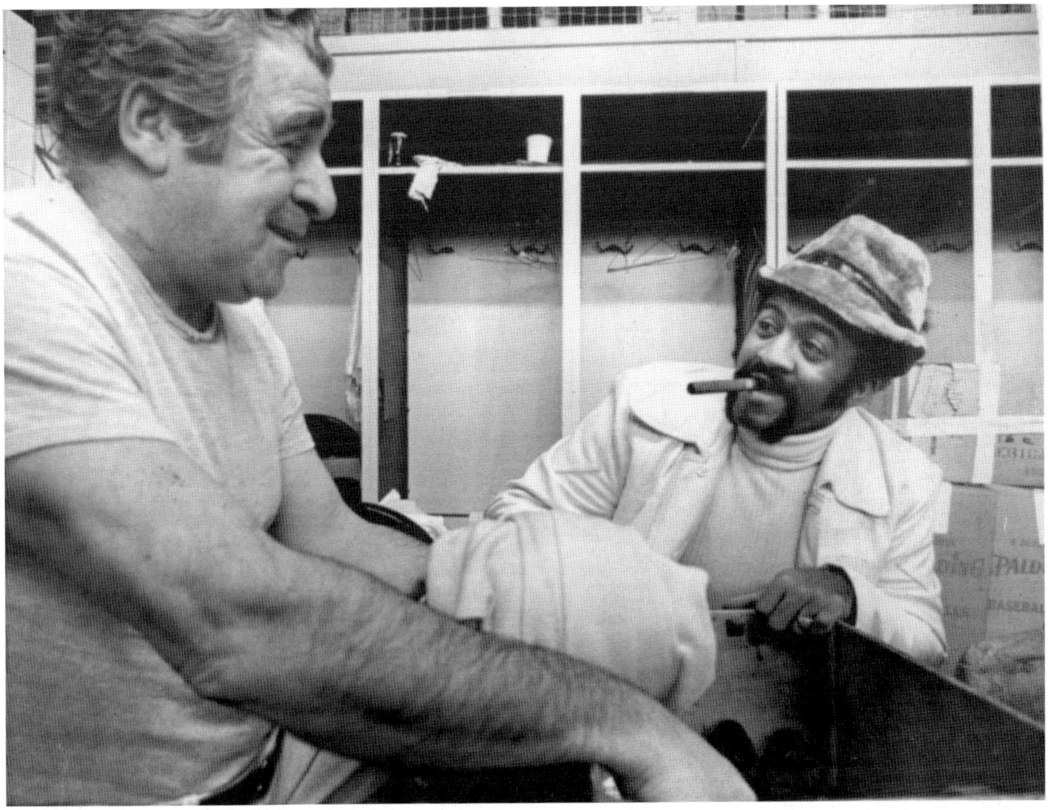

Luis Tiant arrived in Winter Haven, Florida, for 1975 spring training, ready to do his part to rectify the debacle of 1974. Since joining the Red Sox rotation in 1972, El Tiante was 57-32 with back-to-back 20-plus-win seasons in 1973 and 1974. One of the premier pitchers in all of baseball, Tiant (right) shares a light moment with equipment manager Vince Orlando in the Winter Haven clubhouse.

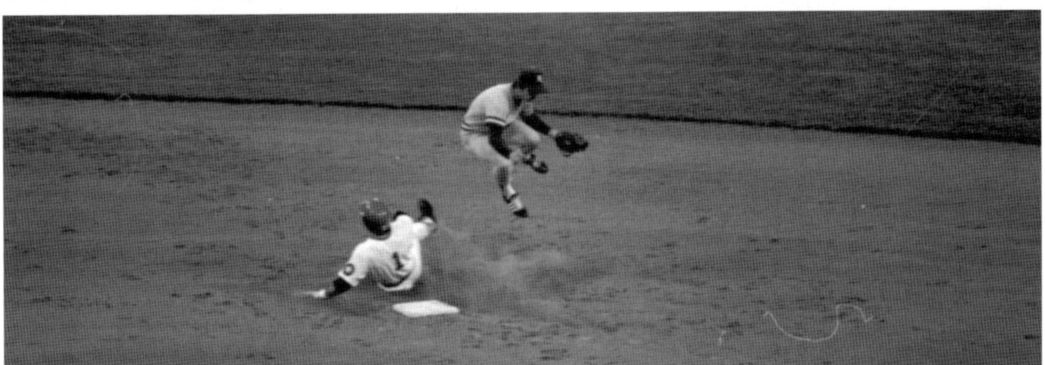

On May 15, the Kansas City Royals came to town, matching up 26-year-old Steve Busby against Luis Tiant. The game was scoreless until the sixth, and Busby threw a four-hit shutout as the Royals won 3-0. It was the Red Sox's third straight loss. Bernie Carbo (1) is forced at second in the first inning—one of three Red Sox to even touch second base. The flying Royals shortstop is Freddie Patek.

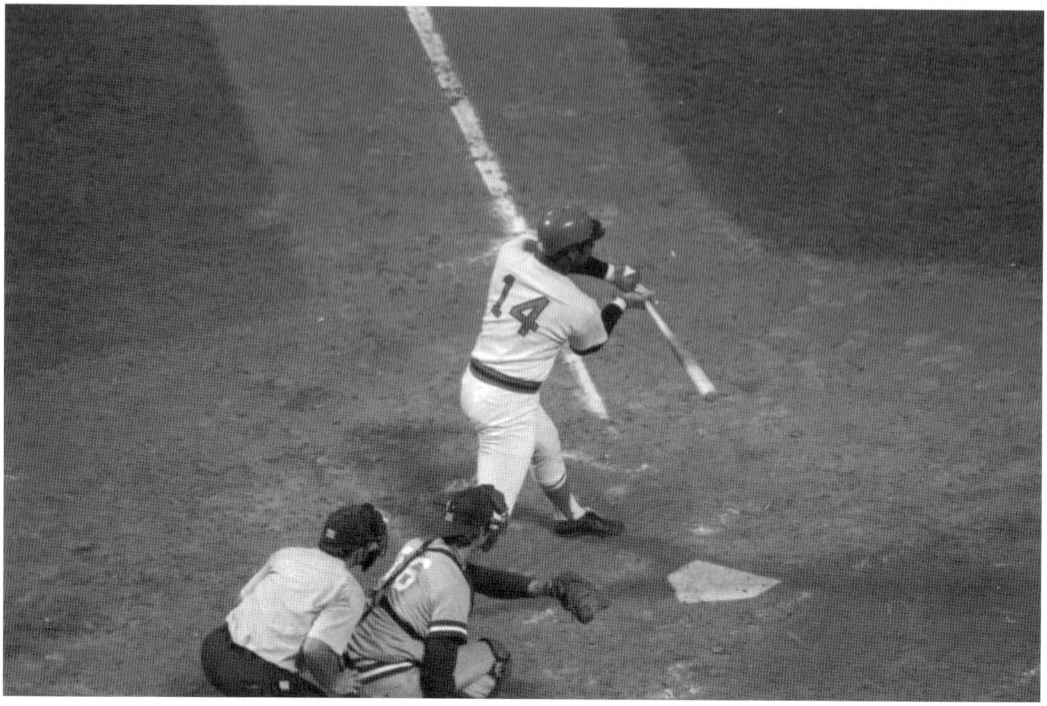

May 15 proved a particularly difficult night for Jim Rice (14) as well. He came into the game mired in a 1-16 slump in his previous five games. His woes continued as he went 0-4, and Busby struck him out four times.

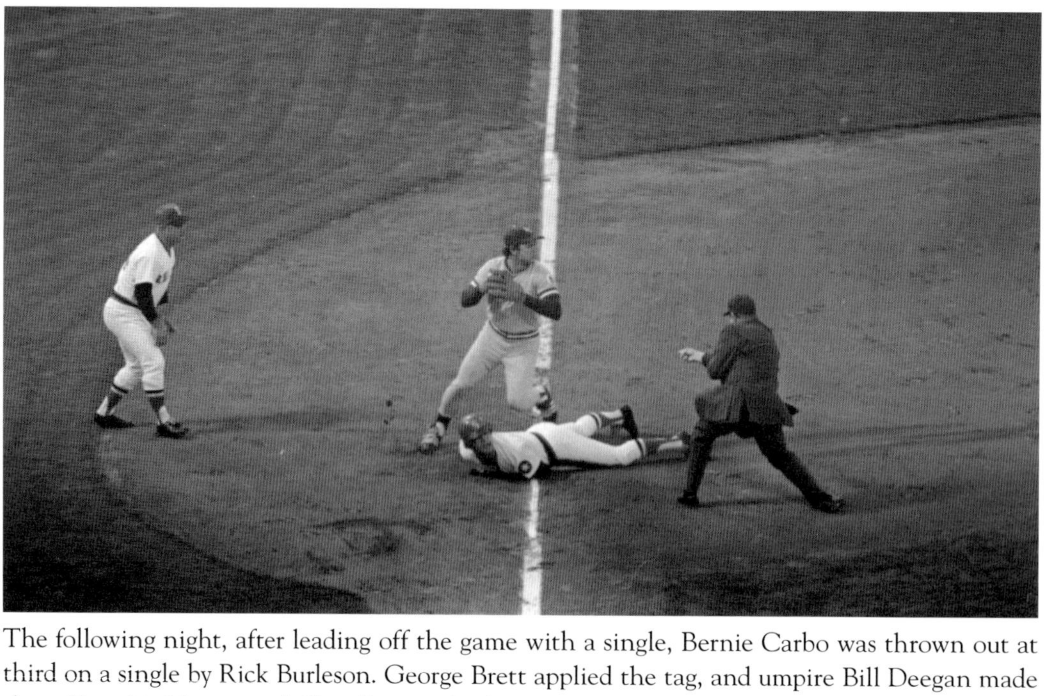

The following night, after leading off the game with a single, Bernie Carbo was thrown out at third on a single by Rick Burleson. George Brett applied the tag, and umpire Bill Deegan made the call as third-base coach Don Zimmer looks on.

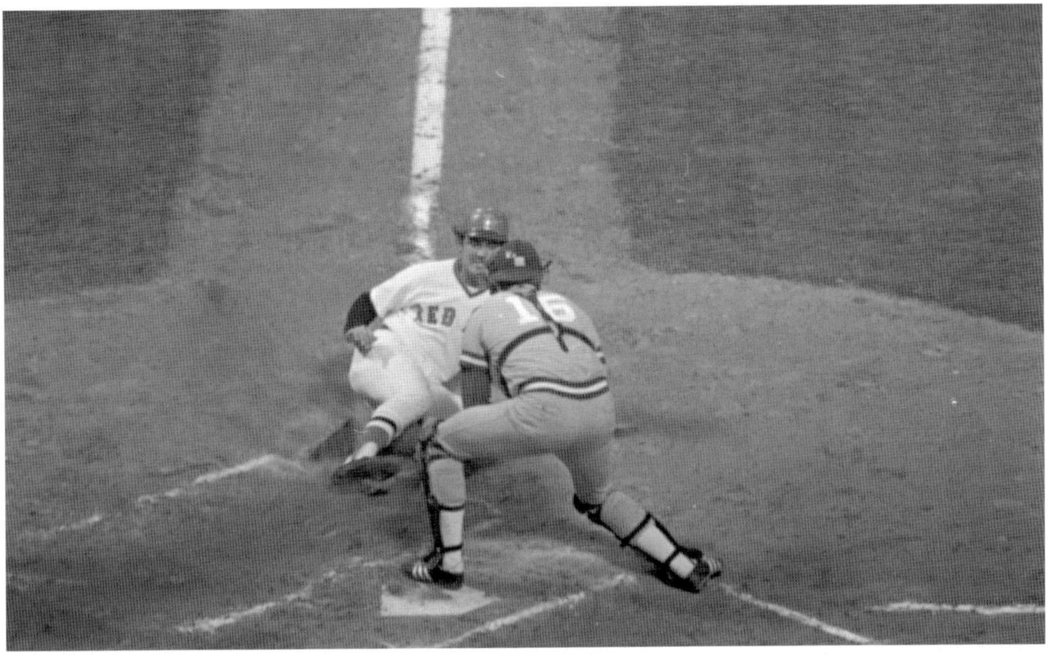

In the Red Sox second inning, Dwight Evans (sliding) reached on a fielder's choice and attempted to score on a double by Bob Montgomery. The throw came from center fielder Amos Otis to Freddie Patek at short and then to catcher Fran Healy, seen here tagging Evans out.

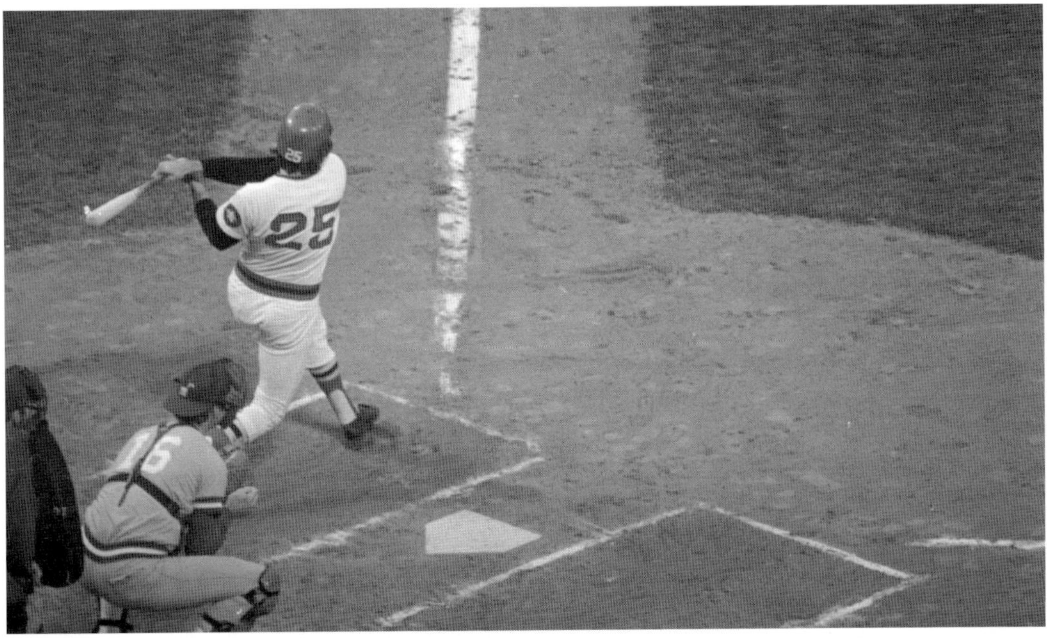

The Royals had a 5-1 lead in the bottom of the sixth when Tony Conigliaro (25) brought Rick Burleson home with a sacrifice fly to right field. Conig had been struggling, going into the game hitting .121 with a home run and three RBI. He had only four hits in the 11 games he played as designated hitter.

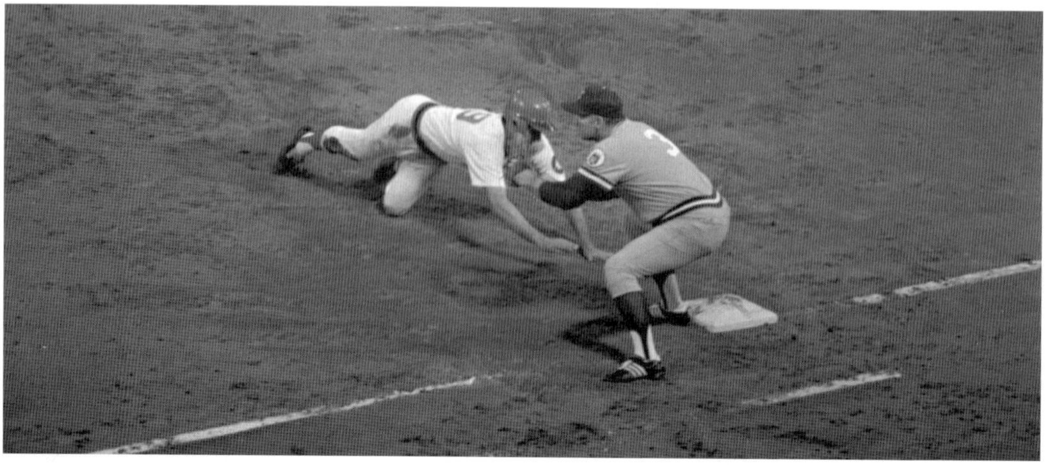

The Red Sox had an opportunity in the ninth when Fred Lynn reached on an error and Rico Petrocelli walked, bringing the tying run to the plate with one out. Here, Lynn dives safely back to first on a throw over from pitcher Dennis Leonard. The Royals prevailed 5-2, the Red Sox's fourth loss in a row. The Red Sox were now four games out of first, the farthest behind they would be all year.

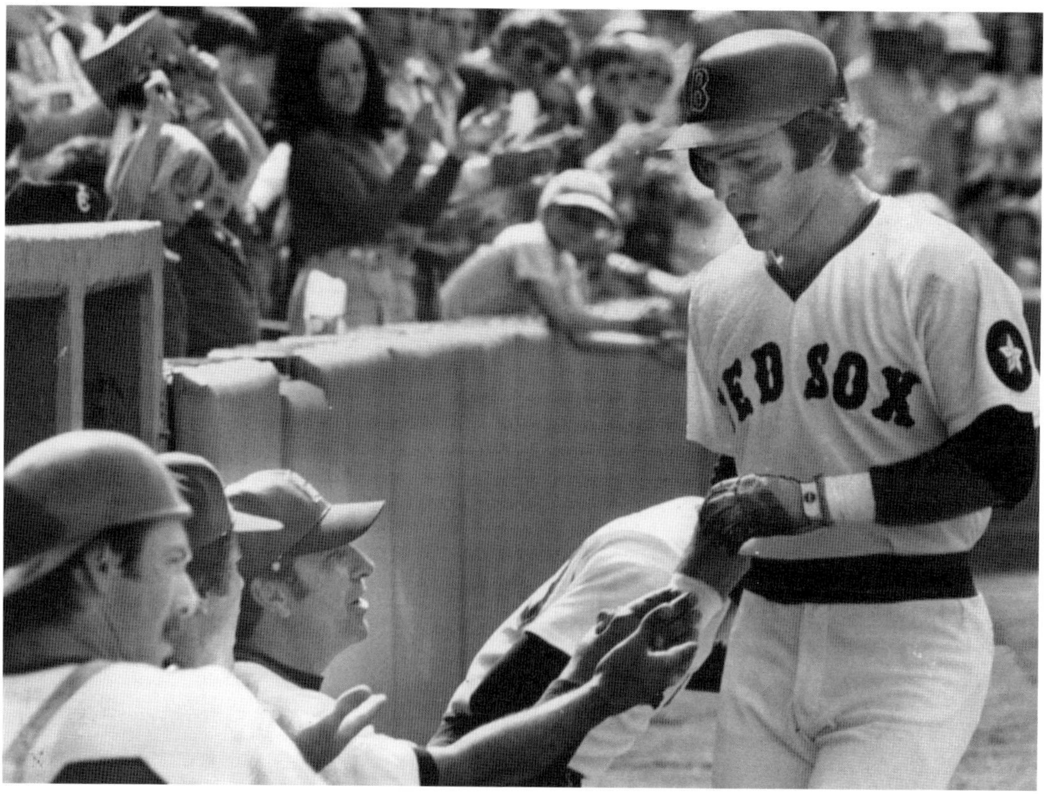

It was all Bernie Carbo on May 18, as he provided all the offense with two home runs and four RBI in a 4-2 win against the Royals. Here, he is welcomed back to the dugout by manager Darrell Johnson following his second homer in the fifth. The win halted a five-game losing streak.

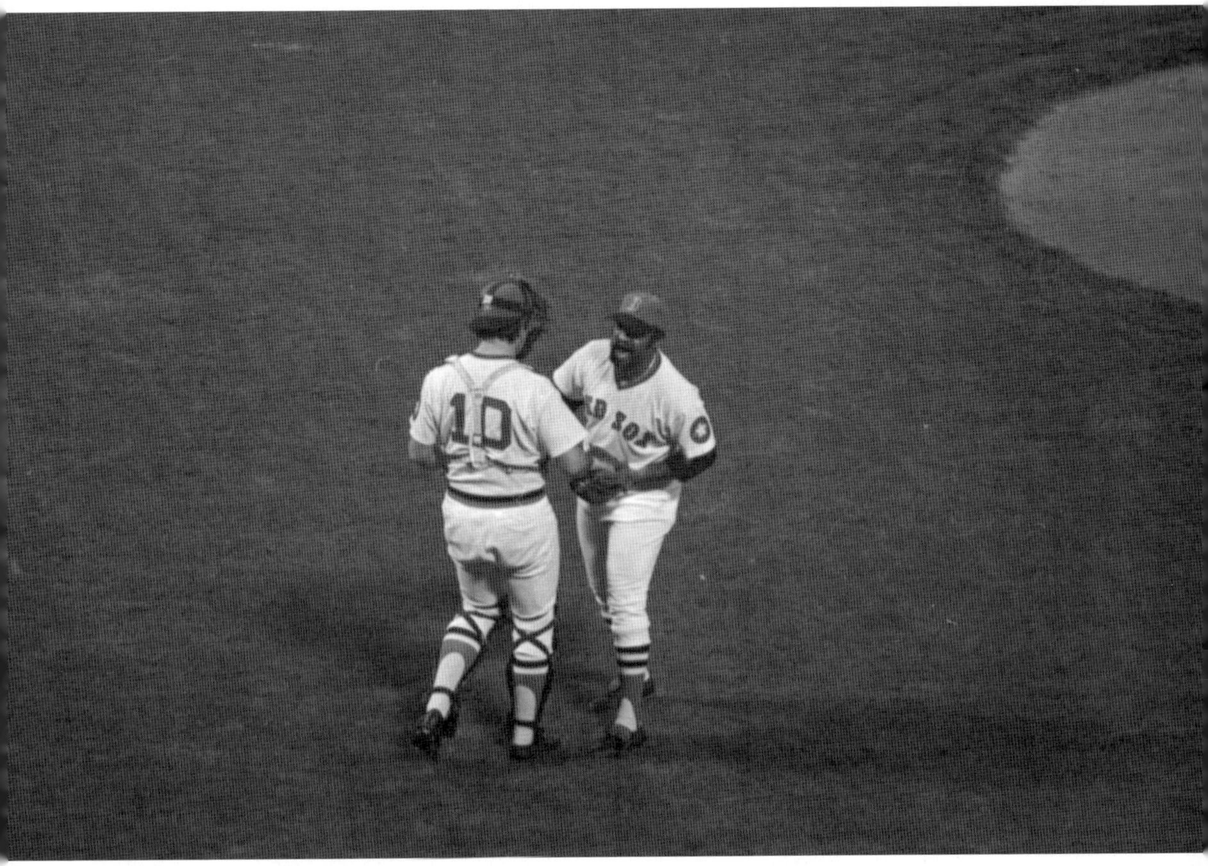

On Monday, May 19, the Sox beat the defending champion Oakland A's 10-5. Jim Rice and Rick Burleson led the offense, each going 2-4, with Rice knocking in three and Burleson a pair. Luis Tiant, seen here shaking hands with catcher Bob Montgomery at game's end, pitched a complete game, upping his record to 4-5 that year.

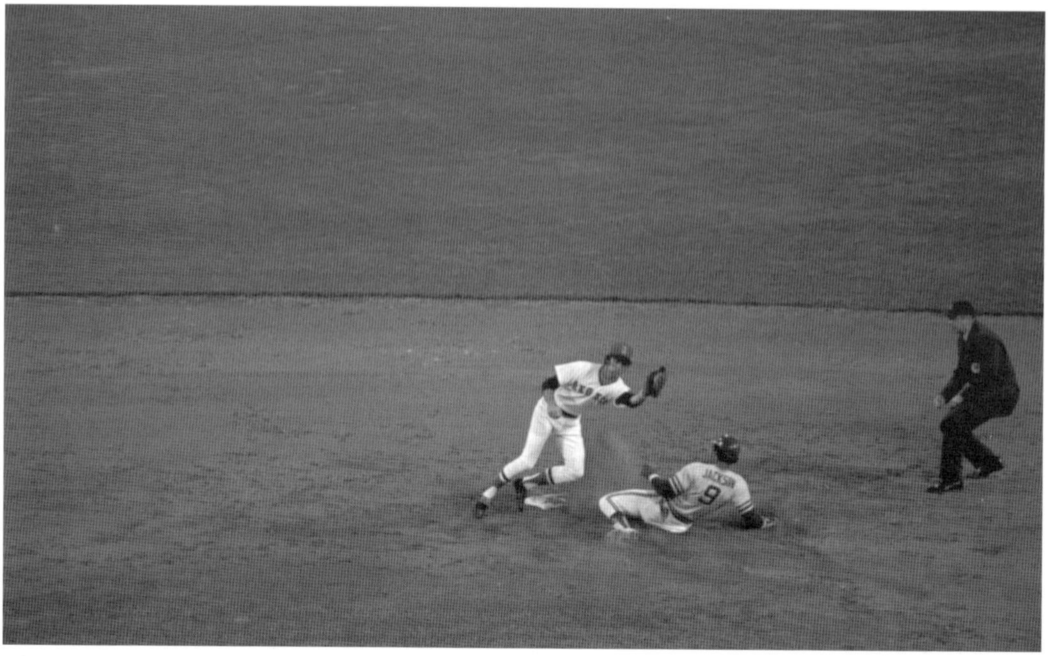

The next night pitted Oakland southpaw Ken Holtzman against Reggie Cleveland. In the second inning, Reggie Jackson (9) reached on a fielder's choice and with two outs, stole second. The following hitter, Joe Rudi, doubled, scoring Jackson and giving the A's a 2-1 lead.

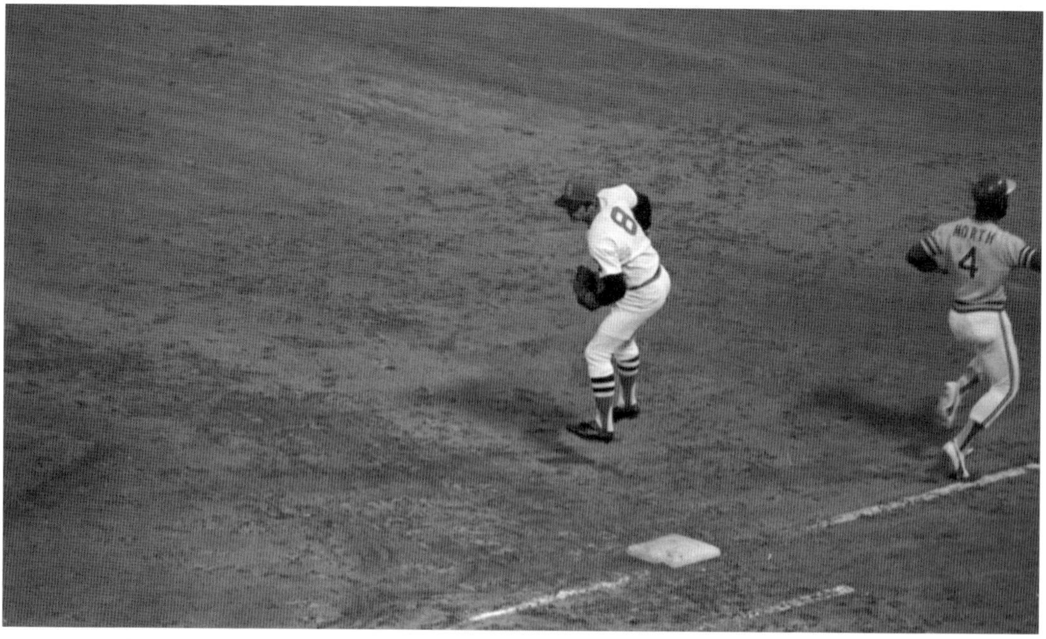

Bill North (4) had led the inning with an infield single. North was safe, as first baseman Carl Yastrzemski made a great play to keep the ball from scooting by him. North was forced by Jackson, and it was Yastrzemski who provided the difference in the game with a grand slam home run in the seventh, ushering in a 7-3 win—the Red Sox's fourth win in a row.

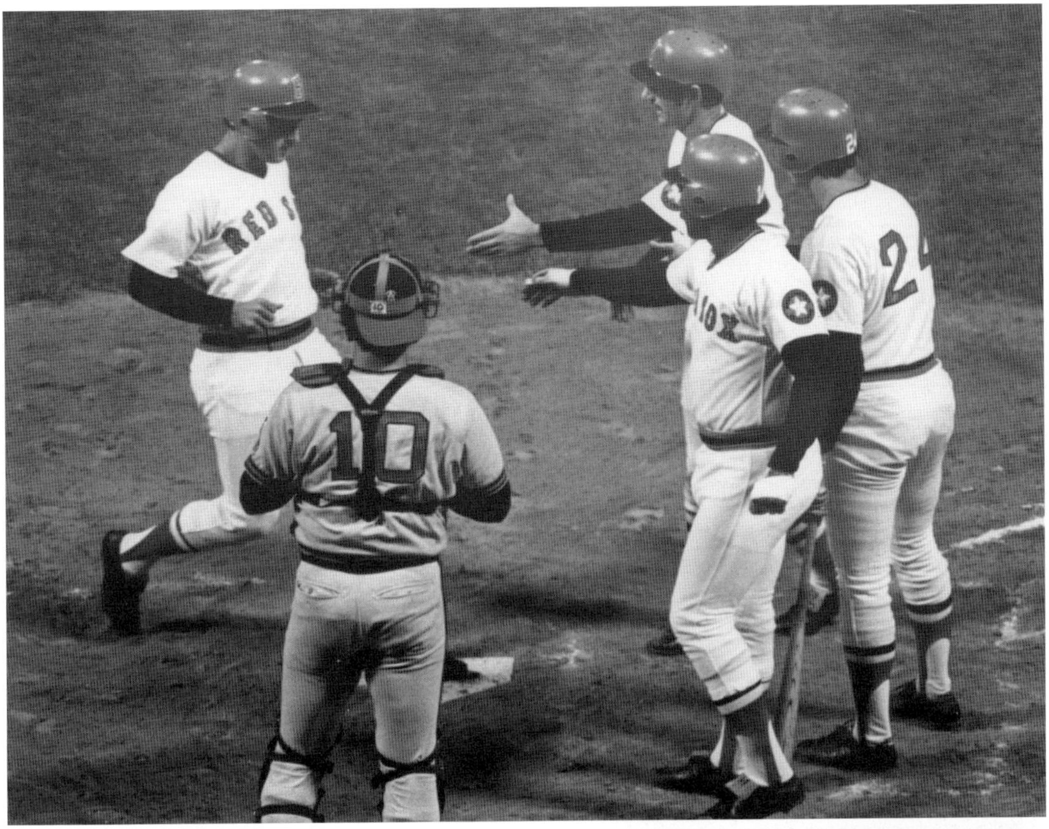

Fred Lynn is welcomed home by team members Carl Yastrzemski (left), Dwight Evans (24), and Jim Rice (right) after a three-run homer in third inning of a May 22 game against the Angels. Angels catcher Tom Egan looks on. Lynn went 3-4 in his 11th multi-hit game of the season and his third in a row, but the Sox lost 7-3. Lynn came out of the game hitting .337.

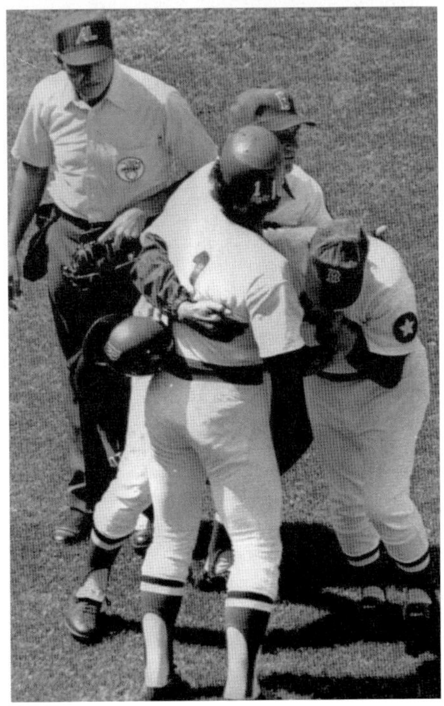

On May 25, the Sox again battled the Angels. With two outs in the second inning, Bernie Carbo (1) was called out on strikes. Infuriated, Carbo's protest led to his ejection by umpire Lou DiMuro. He is restrained by manager Darrell Johnson (left) and Johnny Pesky (right). Four innings later, both Carl Yastrzemski and Johnson were tossed for the same reason, protesting a third strike call. Yaz covered the plate with dirt and bounced his helmet on his way out.

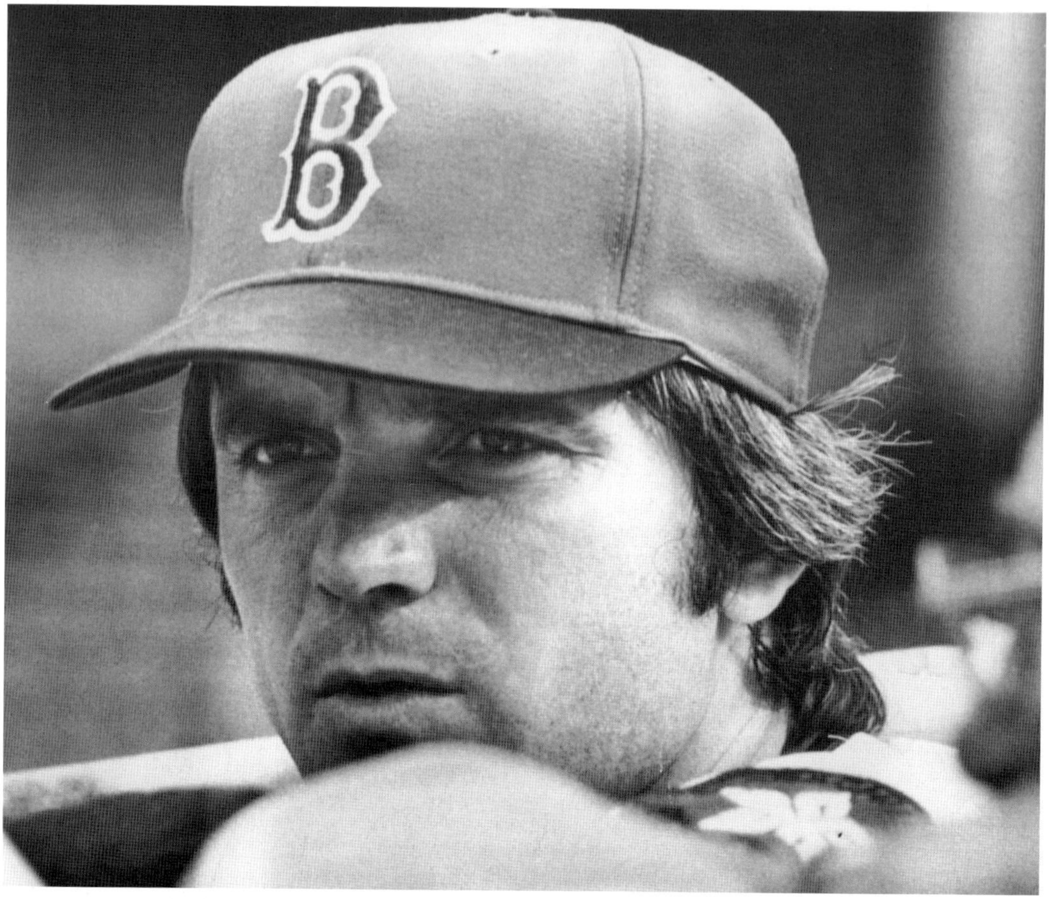

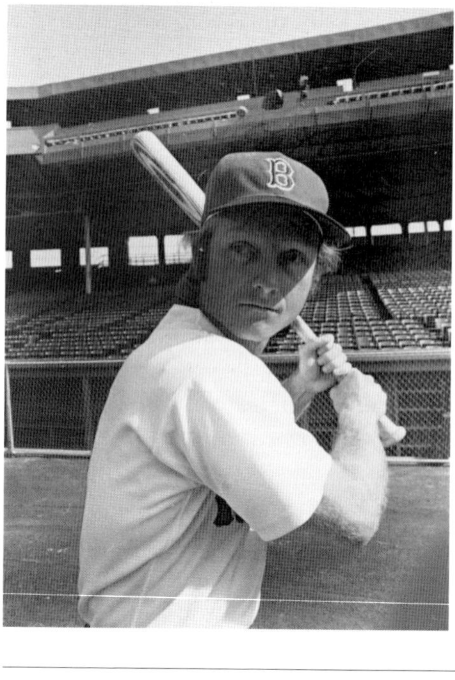

Tony Conigliaro leans on the batting cage prior to the May 20 game with Oakland. Conig went 2-4 with an RBI single in the second inning and a solo homer in the fourth. It was his last home run. Four years away from the game was too much to overcome. He was optioned to AAA Pawtucket and played in 37 games before retiring for the final time.

On June 14, the Red Sox acquired second baseman Denny Doyle from the California Angels. Doyle was at second for 89 of the remaining 107 games, hitting .310 with four homers and 36 RBI while playing a solid second base. He added eight hits in the World Series and was the only player to get a base hit in every World Series game.

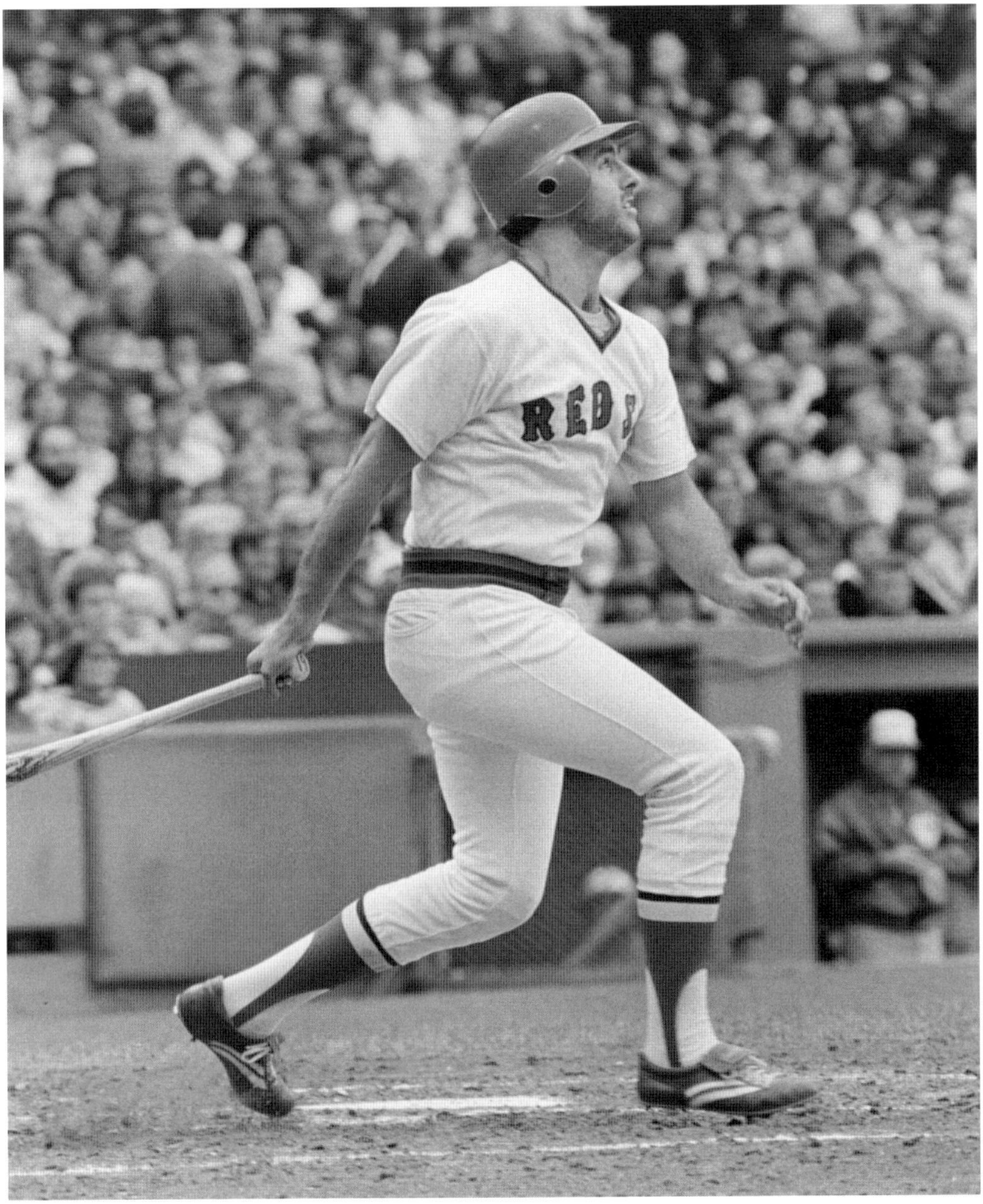

Three days after acquiring Doyle, the Red Sox found themselves in Tiger Stadium. That night, Fred Lynn's 20-game hitting streak was snapped. Having trouble sleeping, he got up in the middle of the night and was walking the streets of Detroit. Four decades later, he told the author it was "a real sign I was a rookie," as he walked in what could best be described as an unsafe area. The following night, Lynn had Dwight Evans pitch him some extra batting practice. The results were astonishing. In his first at-bat in the first inning, he hit a two-run homer; in the second inning he hit a two-run homer; and in the third inning he hit a two-run triple, missing a home run by about a foot. In the ninth inning he hit a three-run homer. On that night, he went 5-5, scored four runs, and tied an American League record with 10 RBI. The Red Sox won 15-1.

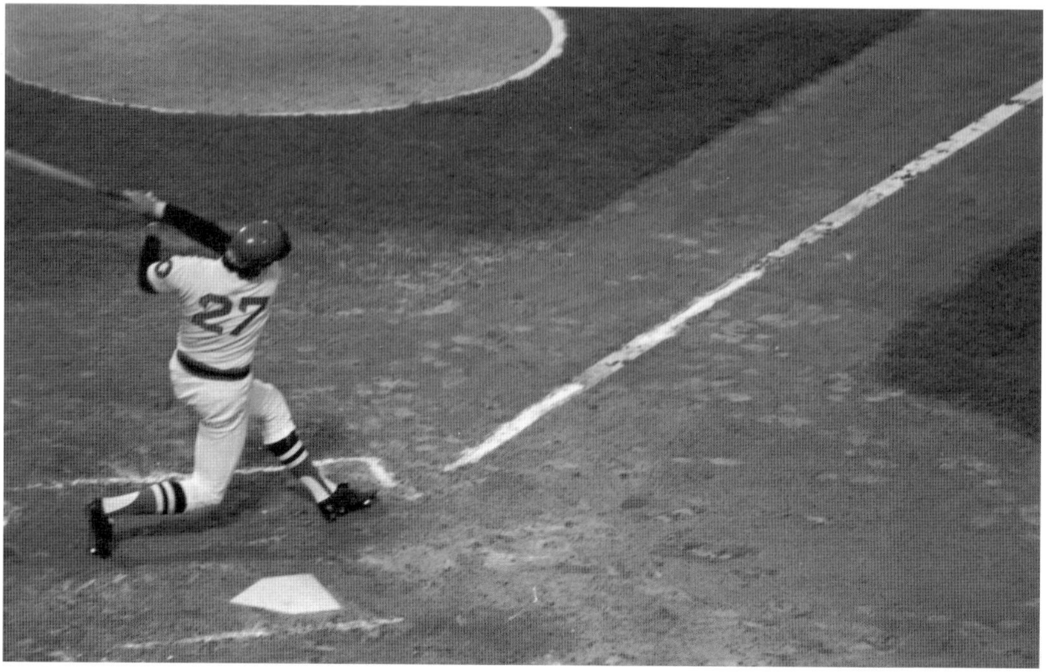

On June 26, the Yankees came into Fenway Park with a 1.5-game lead. In the second inning, Carlton Fisk (27) singled in Fred Lynn to put the Red Sox ahead 1-0; Lynn is pictured below sliding behind Yankee catcher Thurman Munson. It was Fisk's first RBI of the season, as he had just joined the team on June 23 after recovering from a broken wrist in spring training. It had been one day short of a year that he was carried off the field in Cleveland Stadium with a shattered knee, leaving many to wonder if his career was indeed over.

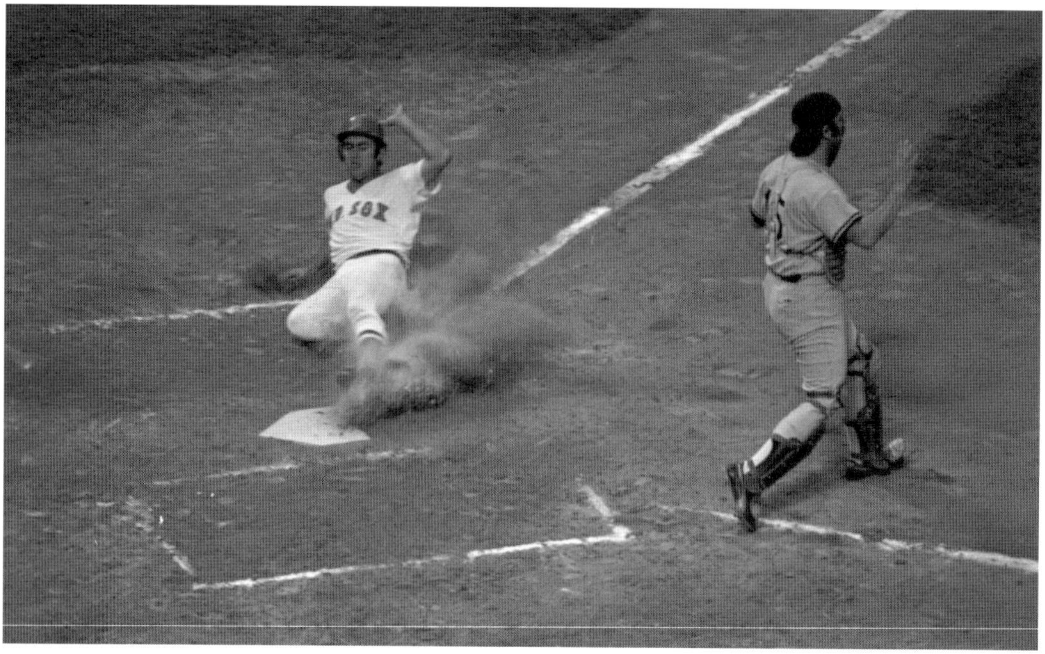

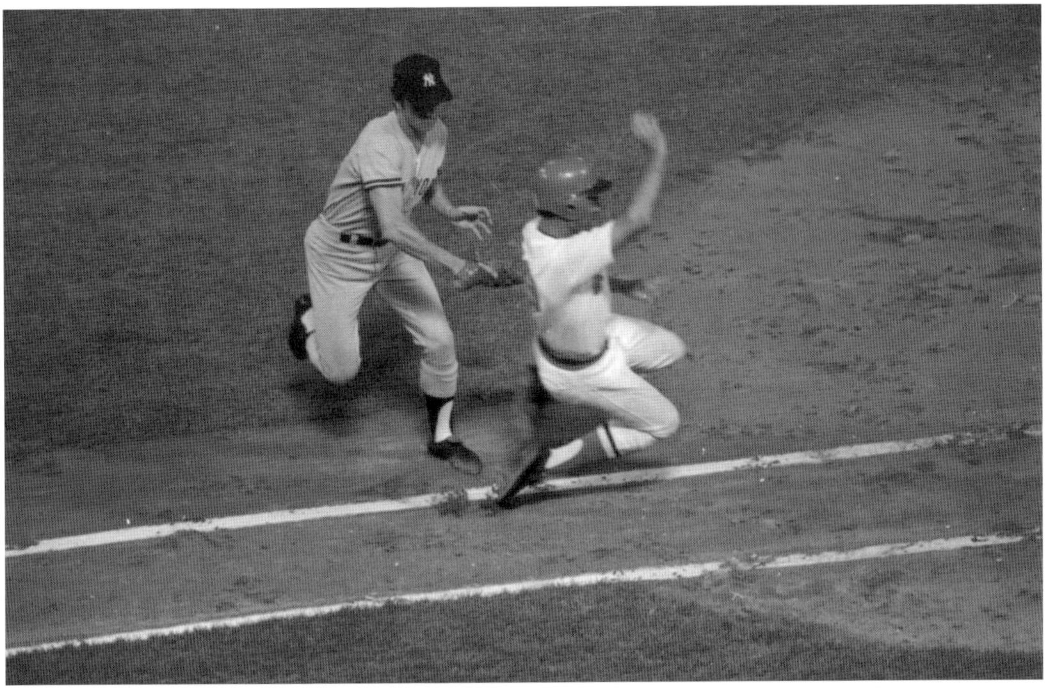

Fred Lynn is tagged out by Yankee pitcher Larry Gura, leading off the fourth inning. Gura made a nice play to record the unassisted out, fielding Lynn's chopper down the first-base line.

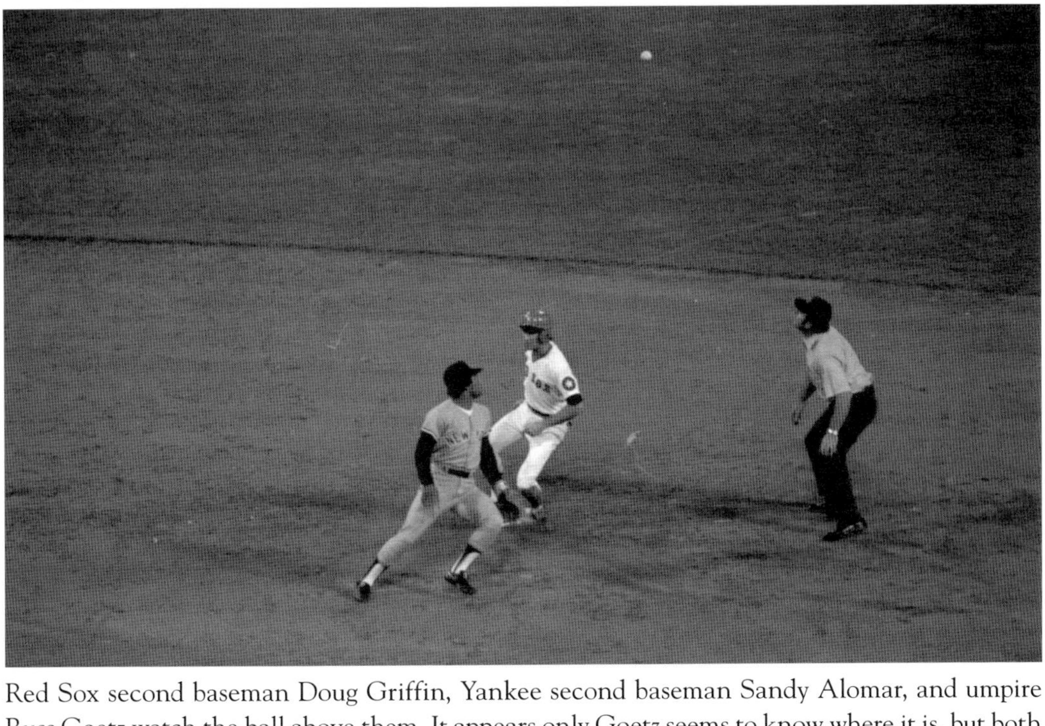

Red Sox second baseman Doug Griffin, Yankee second baseman Sandy Alomar, and umpire Russ Goetz watch the ball above them. It appears only Goetz seems to know where it is, but both Alomar and Griffin found the ball. Griffin wisely stayed at second on the play.

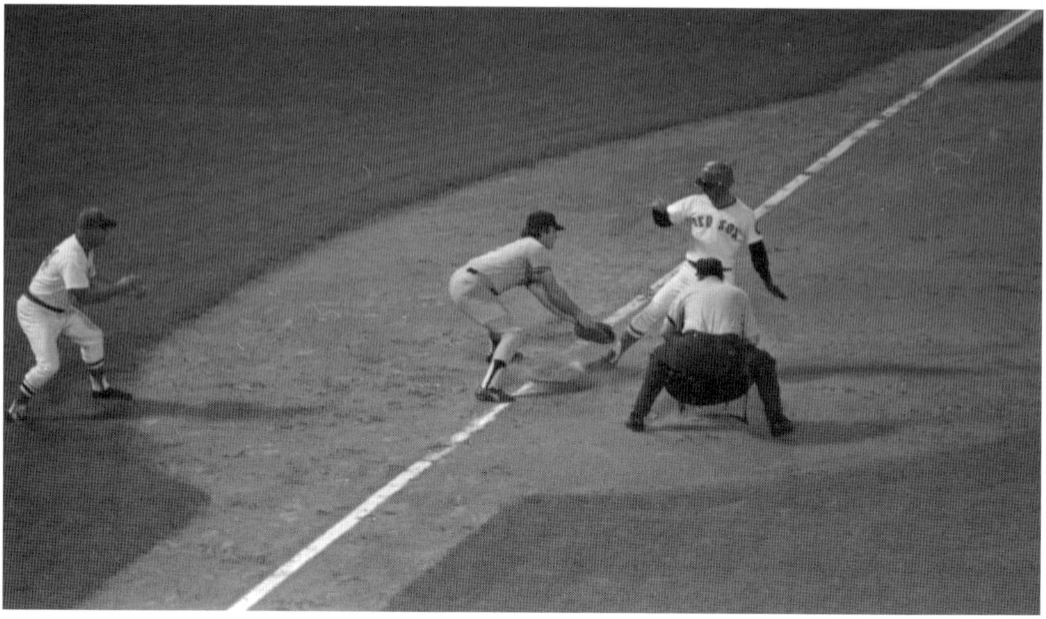

Red Sox shortstop Rick Burleson slides safely into third base on a Carl Yastrzemski double. The "Rooster" had led off the inning with a single. Third baseman Graig Nettles applies the tag too late while home plate umpire George Maloney moves into position to make the call. Red Sox third-base coach Don Zimmer is helping Maloney along.

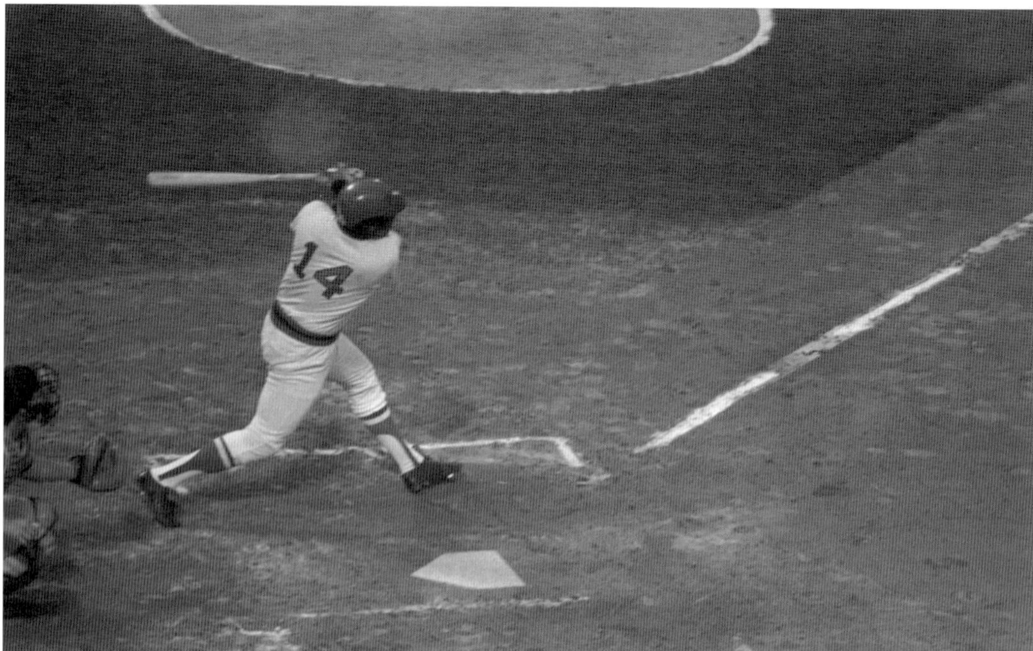

Jim Rice launches a fly ball to right field, which was caught by Yankee right fielder Fred Whitfield. It was, however, deep enough to score Rick Burleson, giving the Red Sox a 6-0 lead.

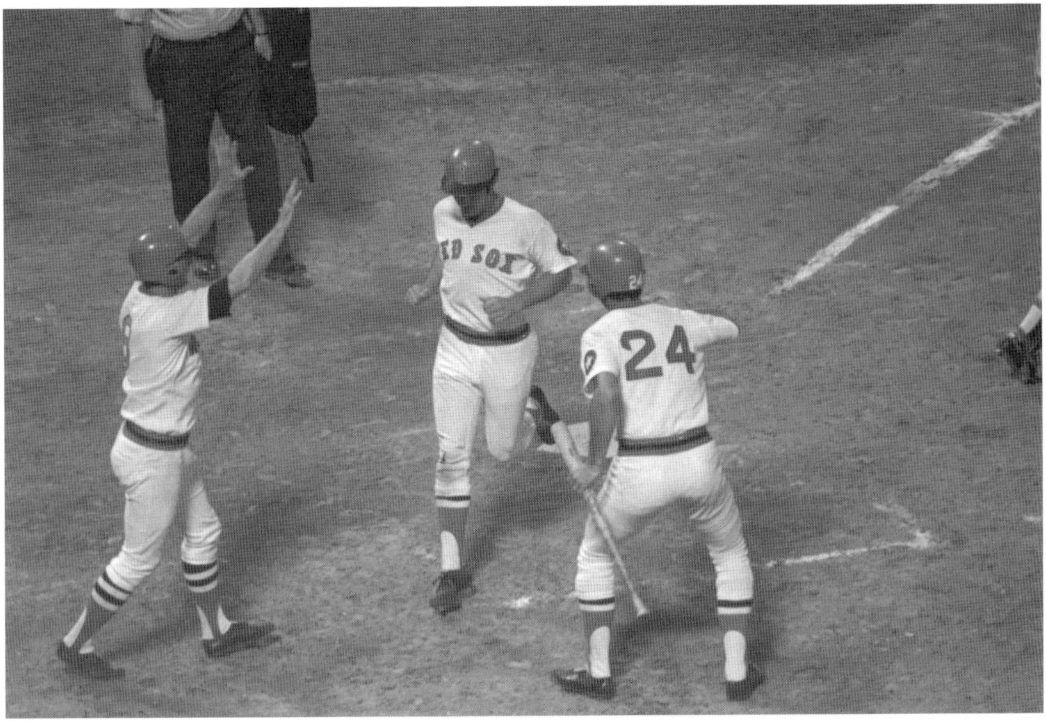

Carl Yastrzemski (hands up) tells Fred Lynn there is no need to slide, as Dwight Evans (24) cheers him on. Lynn and Yaz both scored on Rico Petrocelli's fifth-inning double, giving the Red Sox an 8-0 lead. The Red Sox won the contest 9-1, giving them sole possession of first place in the American League East.

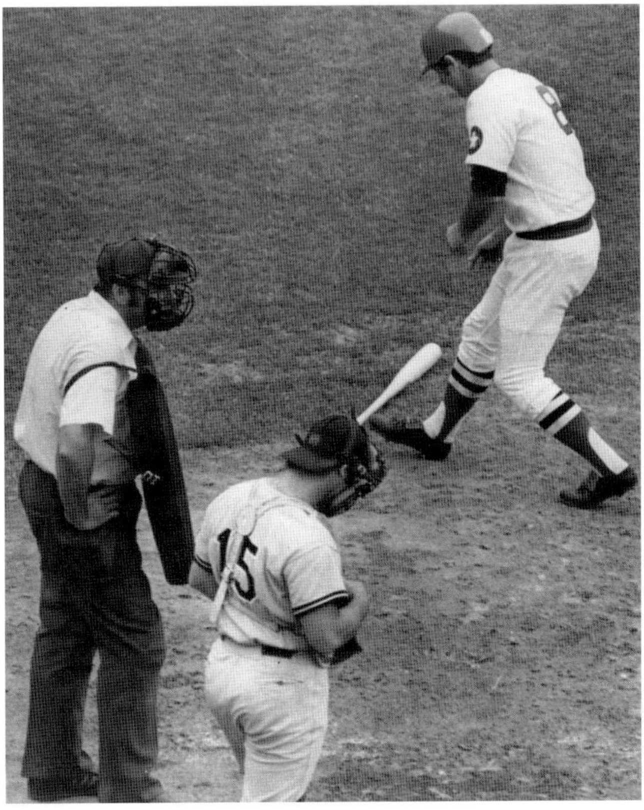

Carl Yastrzemski picks up his bat in the sixth inning of the June 28 game against the Yankees. Yaz had homered in the fourth inning off pitcher George "Doc" Medich. It was now the sixth, and the Yankees led 6-3 with two runners on base. Medich threw a brushback pitch, and Yastrzemski deposited the next pitch in the center field bleachers to tie the game.

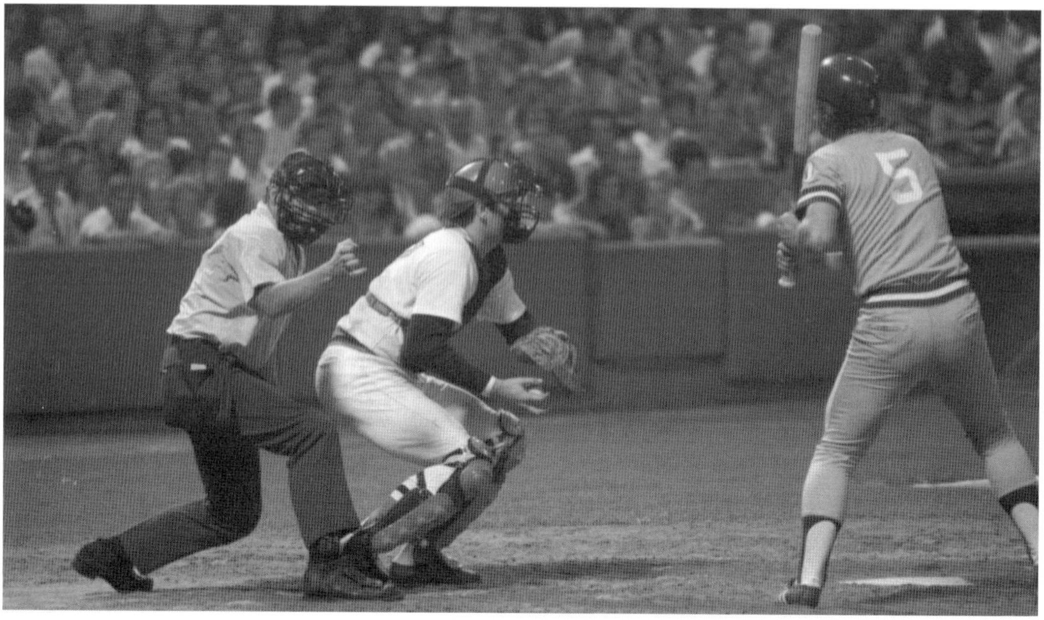

July 18 marked the second game of a two-game set with the Royals. A 22-year-old George Brett, seen here taking a strike from Red Sox pitcher Bill Lee, was in the second season of his Hall of Fame career. That career included three batting titles: the 1980 MVP Award, the 1985 American League Division Series MVP, and a career .337 postseason batting average in nine series (.373 in two World Series).

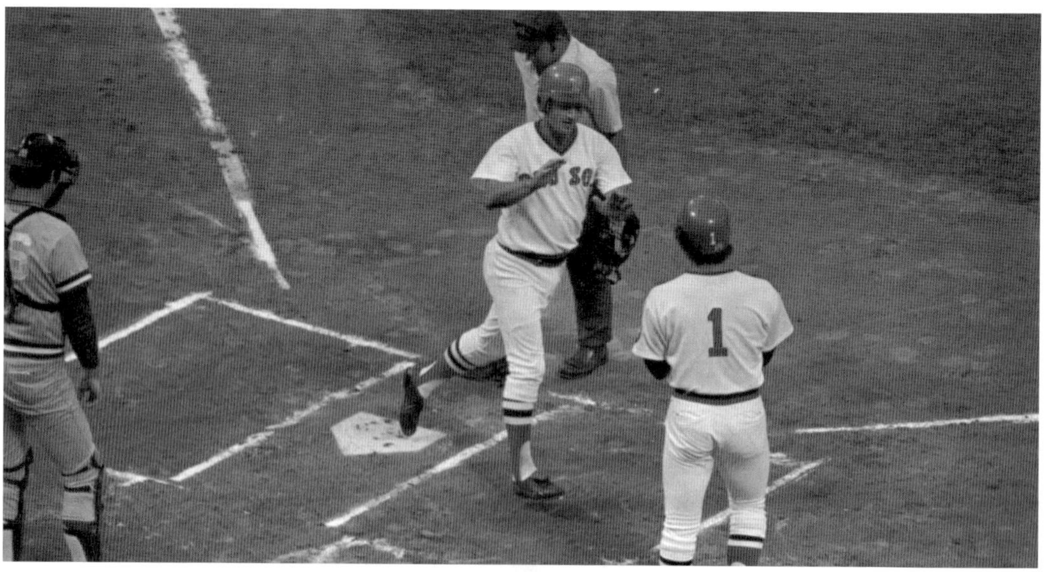

The Royals sent young flamethrower Steve Busby to the mound. The last time he had faced the Red Sox at Fenway was on May 15, and he had fired a four-hit shutout at them. Carl Yastrzemski erased any chance of Busby duplicating that effort when he launched a first-inning, two-run homer, following a single by Bernie Carbo, and a sacrifice by Denny Doyle. Carbo (1) welcomes Yaz home.

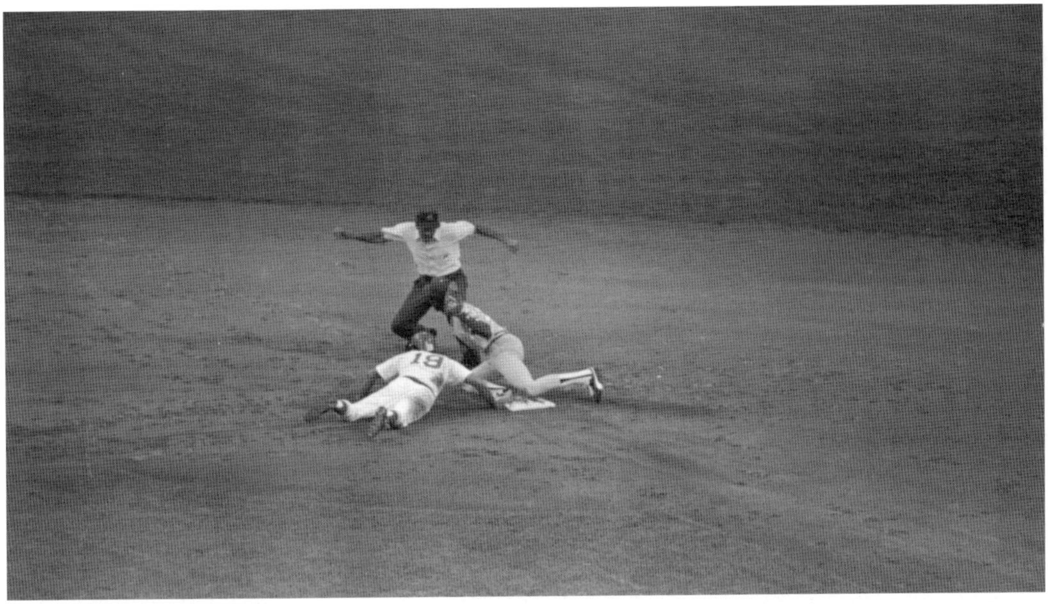

Fred Lynn followed Yaz's homer with a walk and then stole second base, his fifth of the year. Here, umpire Lou DiMuro flashes the safe sign as Frank White applies the tag too late to get the head-first sliding Lynn. Lynn was stranded at second, and the Sox led 2-0 after one.

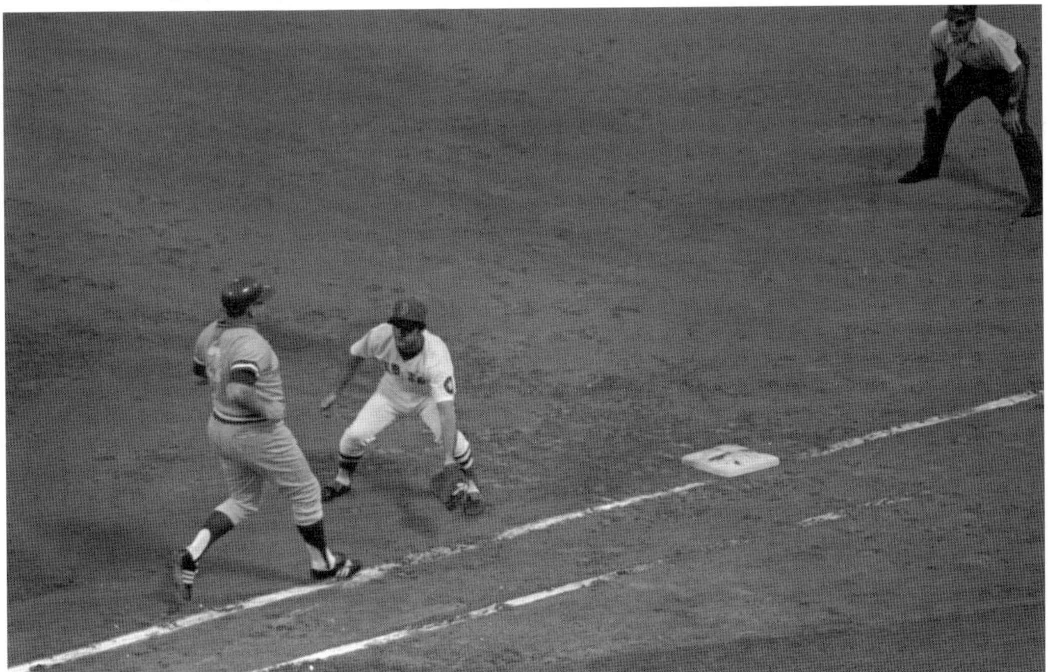

Yaz showed some defensive prowess in the Royals second inning, when he made a nice play moving up the first-base line on a wide throw by shortstop Rick Burleson. He applied the tag, getting Harmon "Killer" Killebrew. Killer was in the last year of his career, and on this night, he would hit career home run No. 570, his 37th and last at Fenway Park.

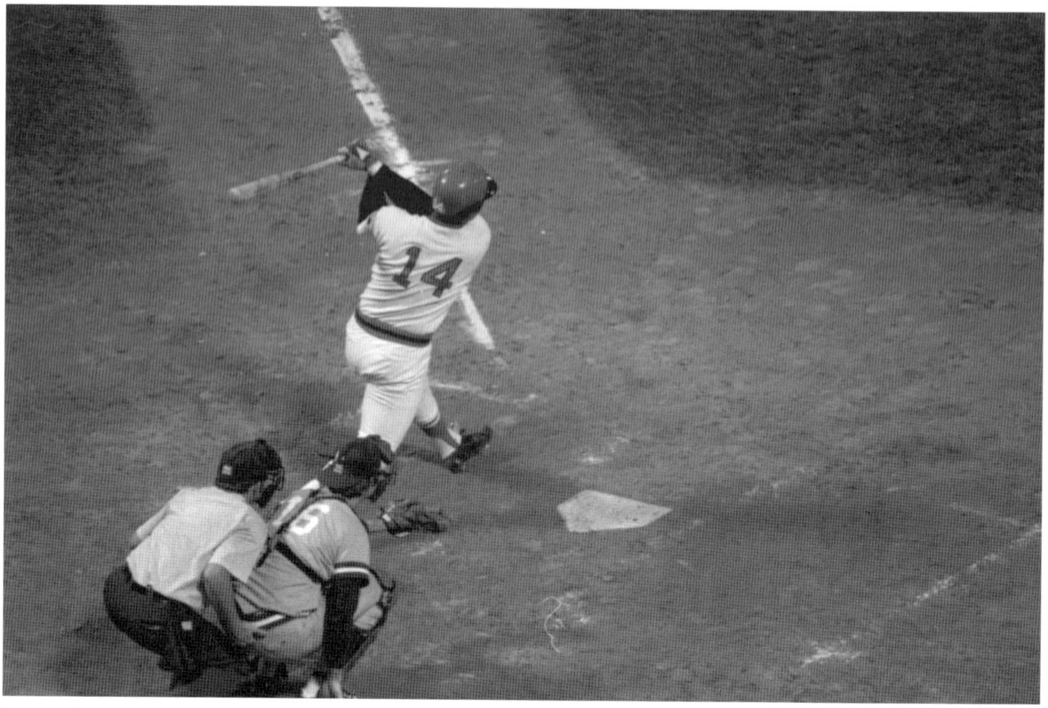

In the May 15 game, Busby had struck out Rice four times. He got him again in the first inning of this game. Leading off the third inning, Rice exacted his revenge when he launched a Busby fastball over the screen in left field (above), giving the Red Sox a 6-0 lead. Coach Don Zimmer extends a well done as Rice rounds third (below) on the lap of his 15th home run of the year. In their careers, Rice faced Busby 18 times. Rice walked twice and mustered only three hits against him; however, two were homers. Busby fanned Rice seven times, five of them in a row. On this night, Busby was gone in the fourth inning of a 9-3 Sox win, their ninth in a row.

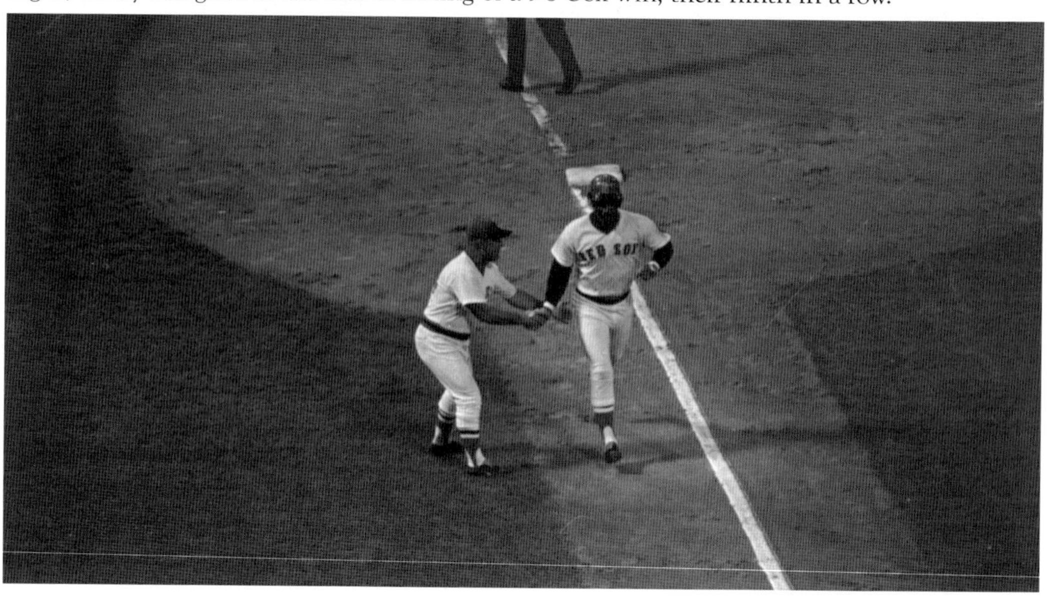

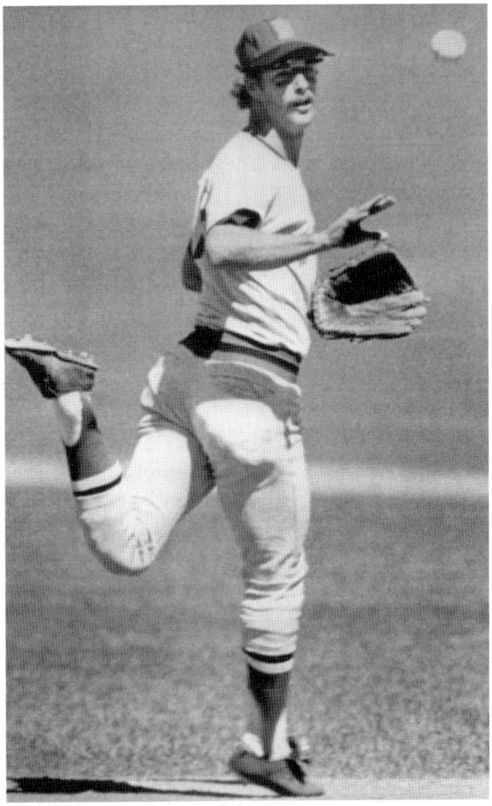

Rick Burleson applies a ballet move as he forces Yankee pinch runner Fred Stanley at second to end the fifth inning in a game at Shea Stadium on July 26. The Yankees were playing at Shea Stadium while Yankee Stadium was being renovated. The Red Sox won this game 4-2 with a three-run ninth, extending their lead in the American League East to eight games over the Yankees and Orioles.

Darrell Johnson throws some batting practice, and Johnny Pesky (35) hits infield fungos before the Red Sox–Tiger doubleheader on July 31. July was the Sox's best month, as they won 22 of 33 games. When the Tigers arrived for this five-game series, the Sox were enjoying a comfortable eight-game lead in the American League East.

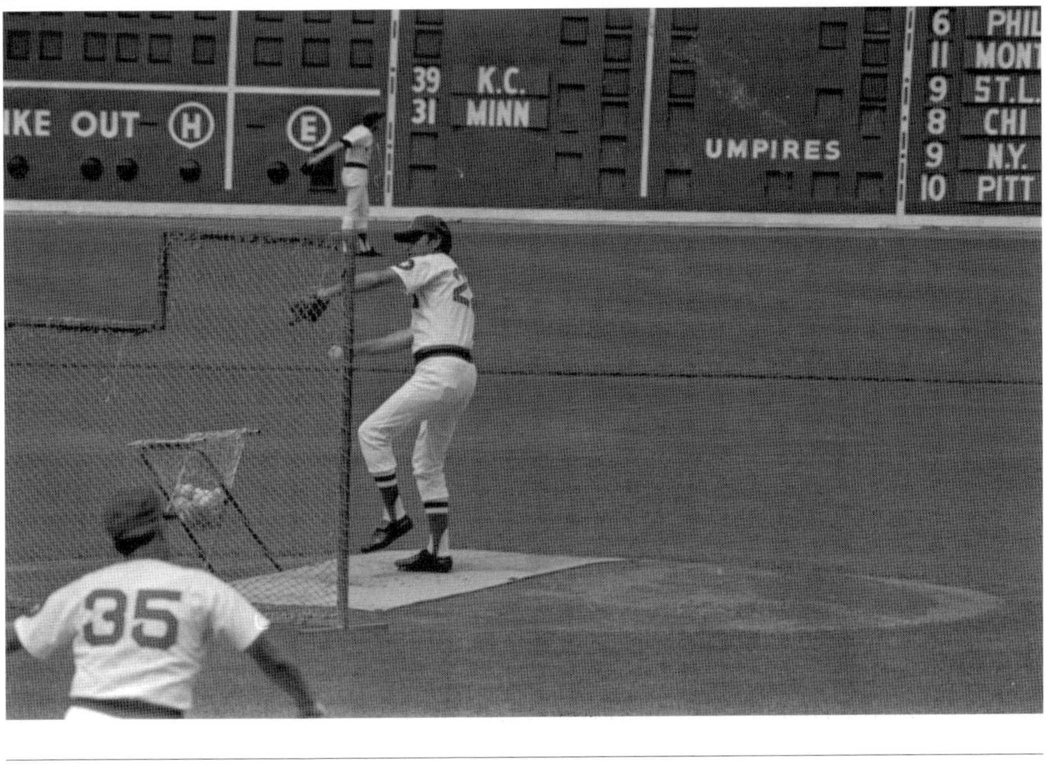

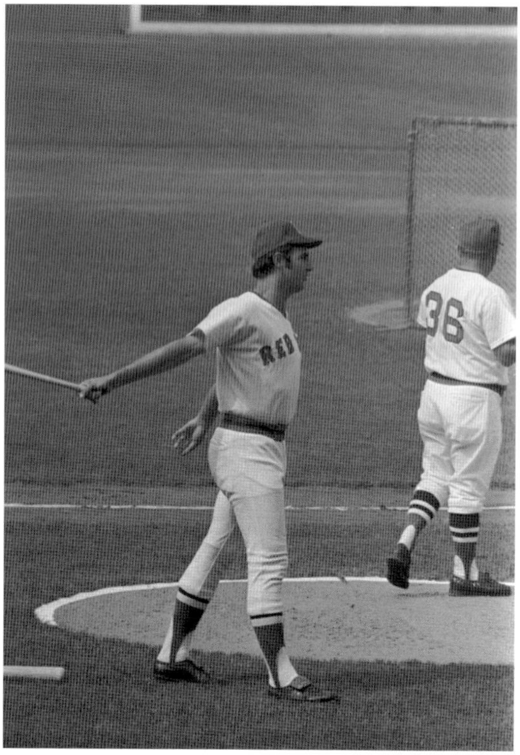

Here, Fred Lynn loosens up, preparing to get in the cage for his round of batting practice. The rookie center fielder was hitting .329 with 18 home runs and 75 RBI. This was the first time he faced the Tigers since his three home run, 10-RBI night at Tiger Stadium in June. Coach Eddie Popowski (36) is standing in the fungo circle.

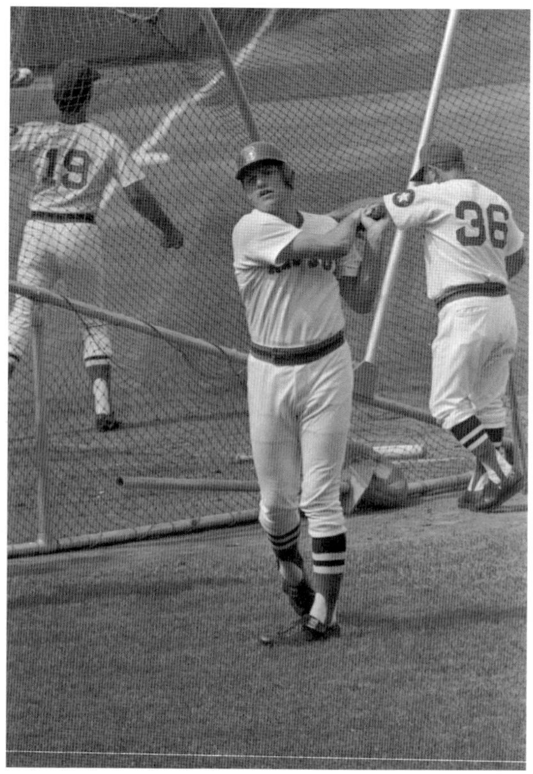

Carlton Fisk prepares for his turn in the cage as Fred Lynn (19) throws a ball back to the pitcher and Eddie Popowski (36) leans on the frame. Fisk had rejoined the team on June 23, having broken an arm in spring training. The New Hampshire native was a welcome addition to the Red Sox offense, as he was hitting .333 with four homers and 21 RBI in 34 games.

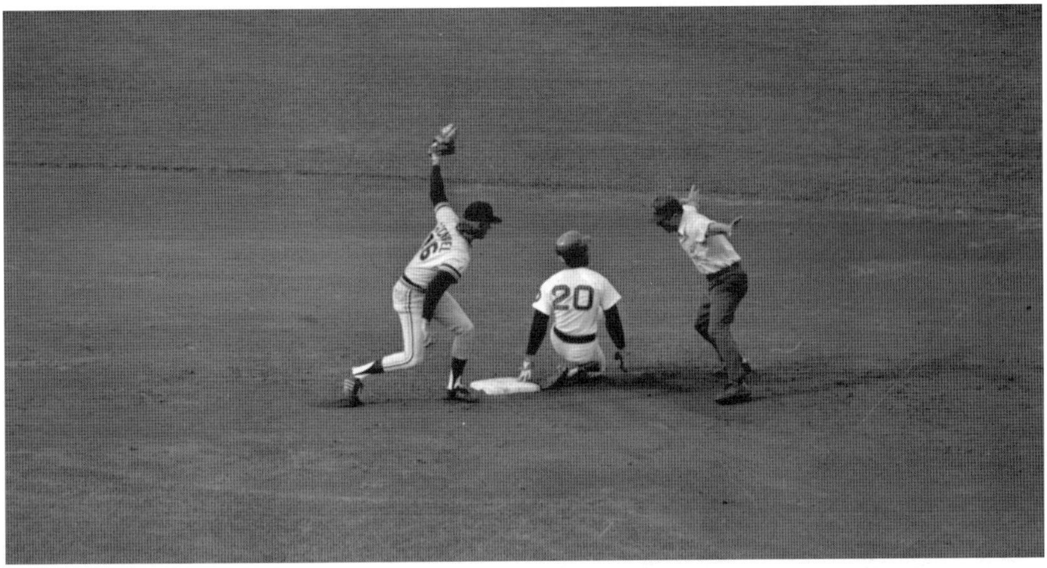

Juan Beníquez (20) slides safely into second ahead of catcher Bill Freehan's throw for his sixth steal of the season. Beníquez had singled to lead in the first game of the July 31 doubleheader. Following his steal, he advanced to third on a ground out to second by Denny Doyle. He scored when Carl Yastrzemski also grounded out to second, tying the score at one.

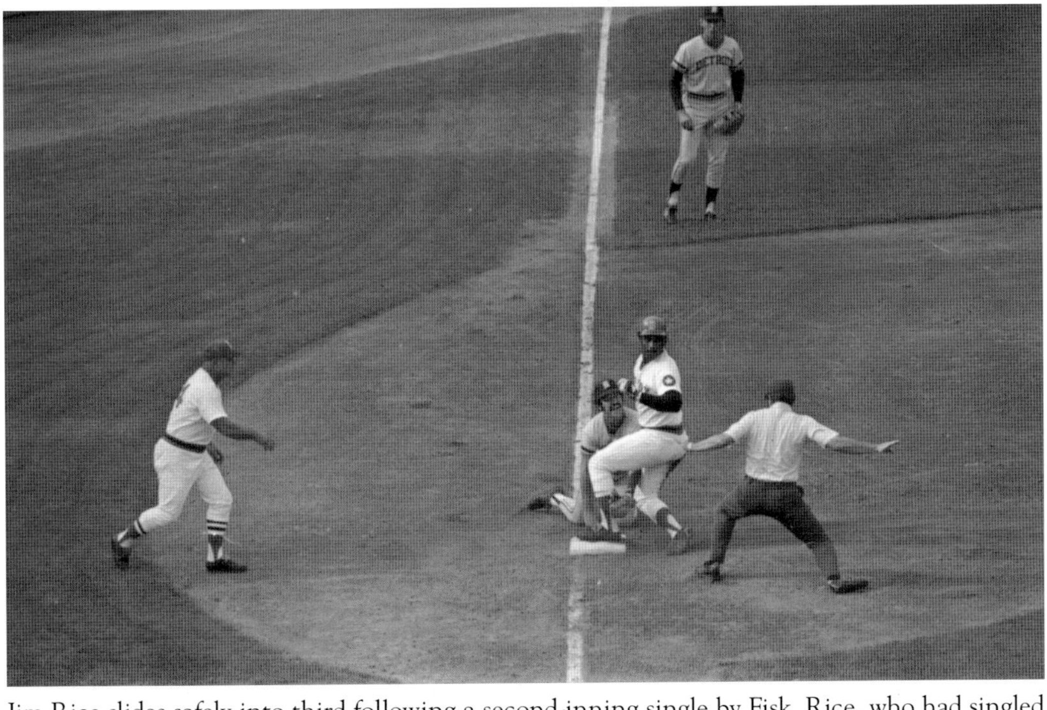

Jim Rice slides safely into third following a second-inning single by Fisk. Rice, who had singled to lead off the inning, looks to umpire Larry McCoy for the call while coach Don Zimmer and shortstop Gene Michael observe. Rice did not score, however, as Evans struck out, and Petrocelli hit into an inning-ending double play.

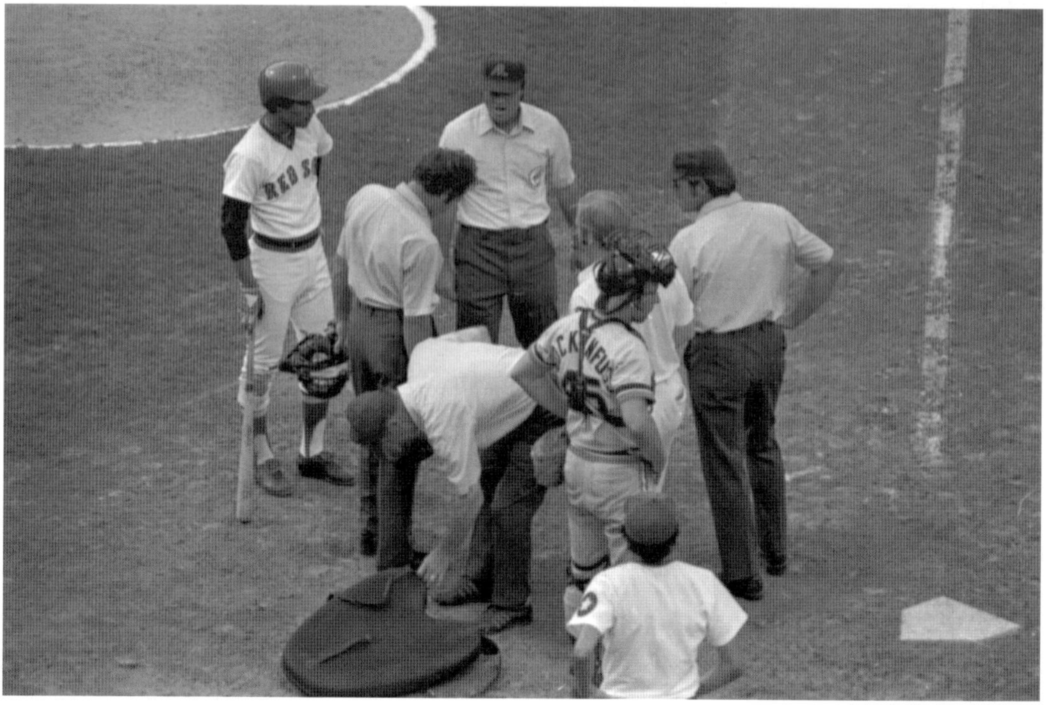

In the third inning, Beníquez doubled with one out, however, he did not score, as both Doyle and Yastrzemski flied out, allowing Detroit to maintain a 2-1 lead. Before his double, Beníquez (leaning on bat) fouled a pitch back that struck umpire Joe Brinkman in the mask, requiring a visit from Red Sox trainer Dick Moss (center) and his entire umpiring crew. Brinkman remained in the game.

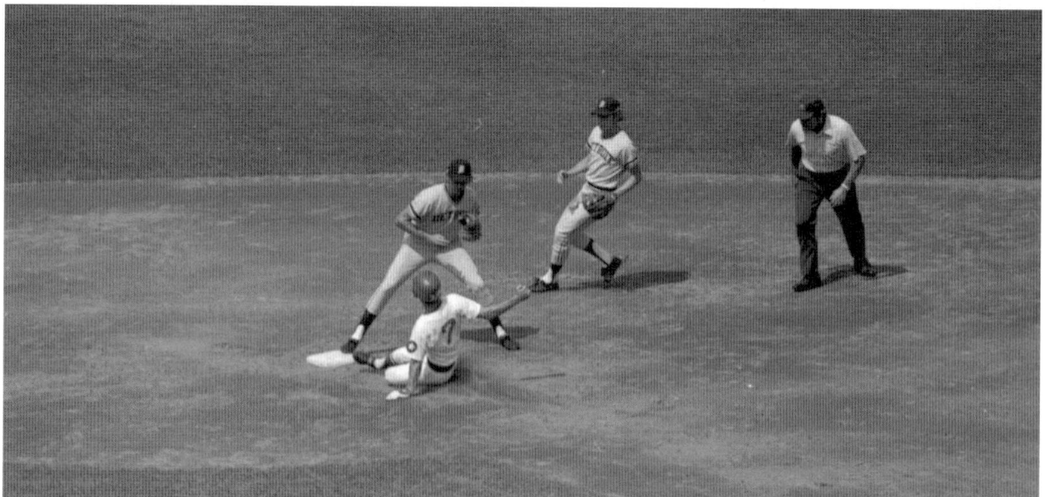

Rick Burleson slides safely into second following a sacrifice bunt by Juan Beníquez. Burleson walked, leading off the eighth with the score still 2-1 to Detroit. Fiery and intense, Bill Lee once said of him, "Some guys didn't like to lose, but Rick got angry if the score was even tied . . . and he had the greatest infield arm of anyone I had ever seen."

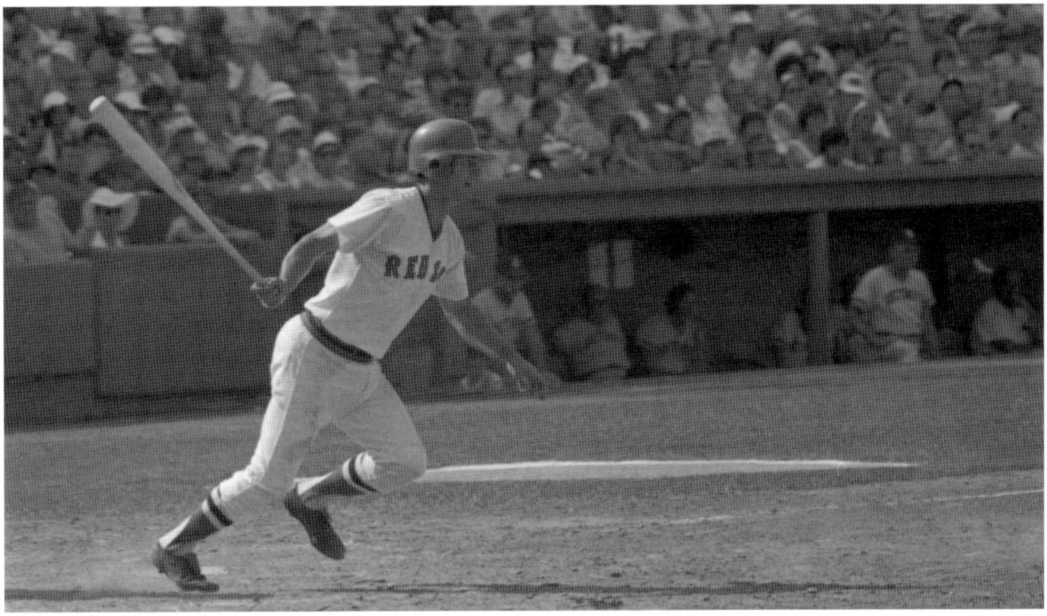

Following a fly out by Denny Doyle, Yastrzemski stepped in and promptly singled in the Rooster to tie the game at 2-2. In situations where Yaz came to bat in the seventh inning or later with his team tied or within a run either way, the 36-year-old captain hit an astounding .351 with four homers and 15 RBI.

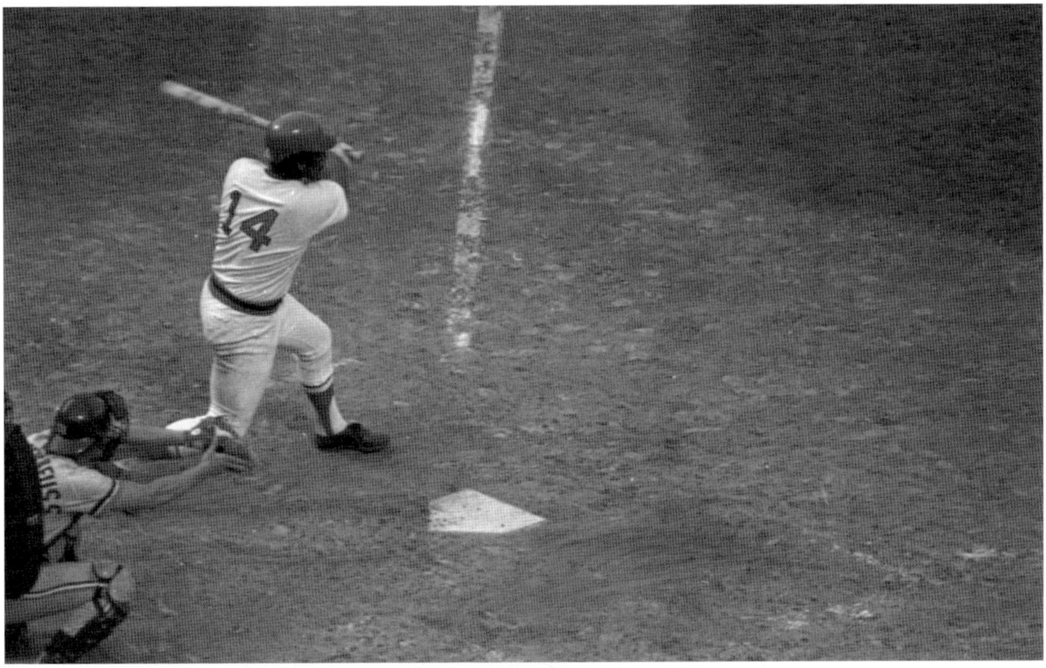

The Red Sox loaded the bases in the ninth on three walks, but they could not push the winning run across. However, in the 10th, Doyle opened up with a single and stole second; after an intentional walk to Fred Lynn, Jim Rice singled, scoring Doyle to end the game.

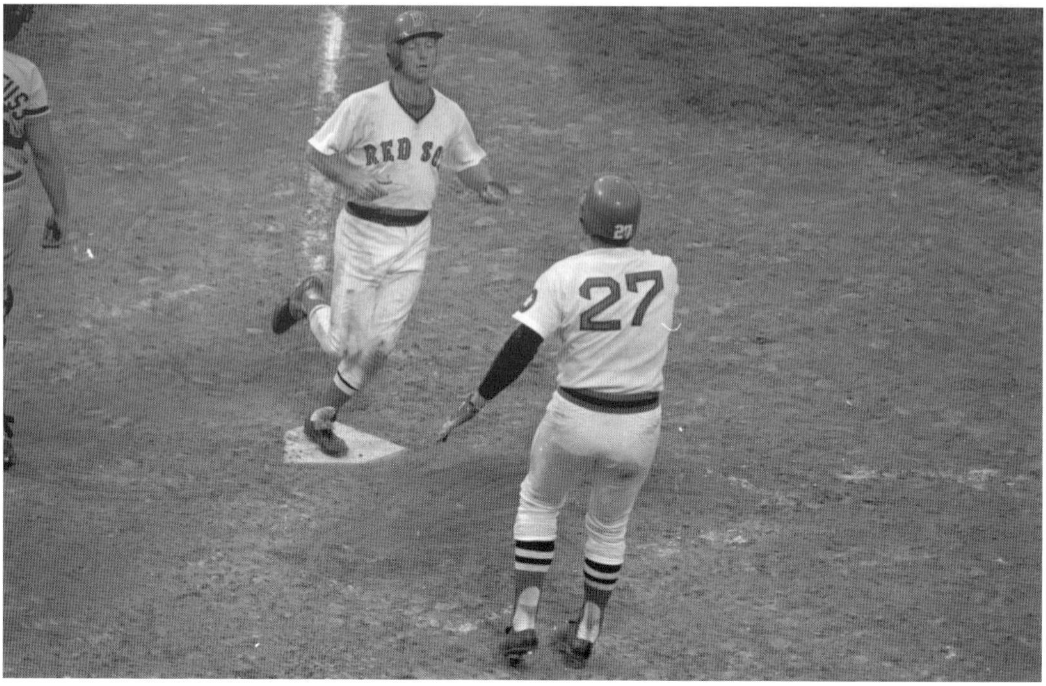

On-deck hitter Carlton Fisk welcomes home Doyle with the winning run as Tiger catcher John Wokenfuss heads for the Tiger dugout. Acquired at the trading deadline in June from the Angels, Doyle became entrenched at second base for the remainder of the year, hitting the best he had his entire career while playing a solid second base. His base hit leading off the 10th inning extended his hitting streak to 18 games.

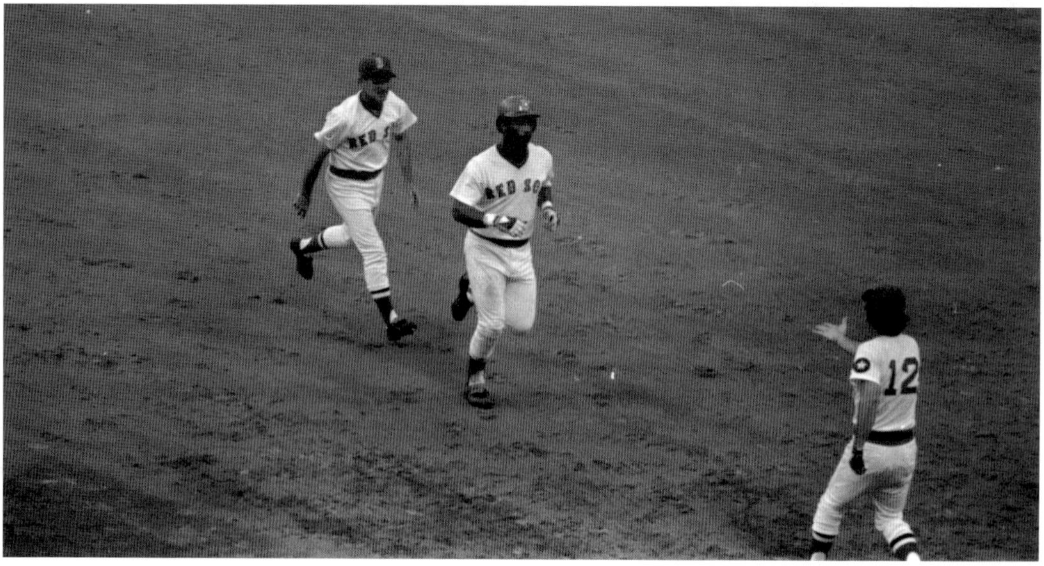

Red Sox utility infielder Bob Heise (12) extends a congratulatory hand to Rice as he heads back to the dugout, followed by Johnny Pesky. The 3-2 comeback, walk-off win gave the Red Sox a nine-game lead over the Orioles—their largest lead of the season.

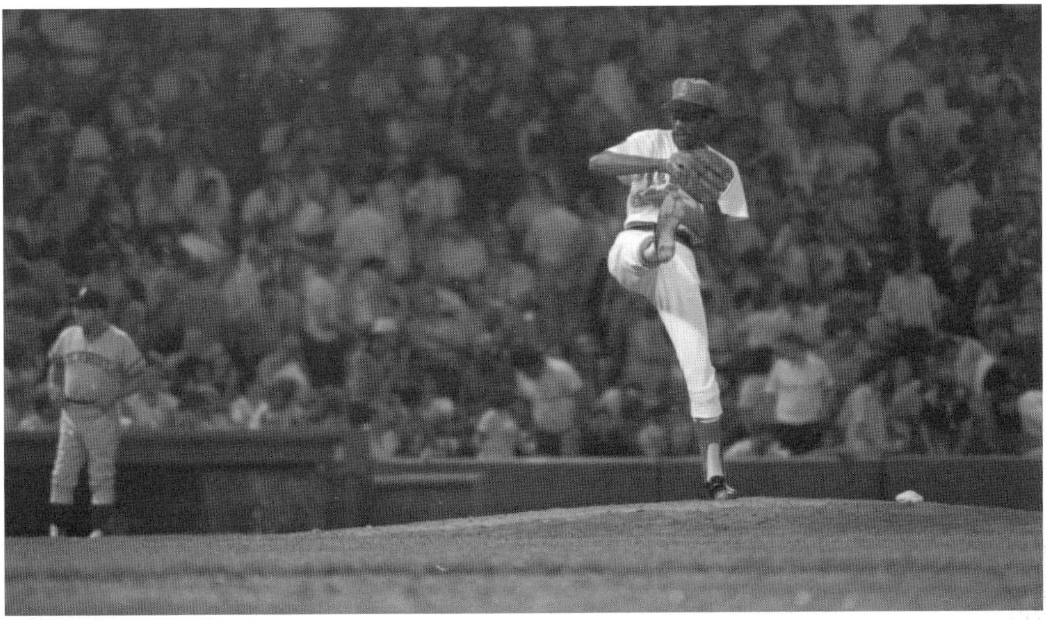

The nightcap of the doubleheader belonged to Rogilio Moret and the Red Sox. The slender lefty bent but never broke, battling through nine Tiger hits to win 6-1, while striking out eight and walking but one. The rising star had 36 appearances for the 1975 Sox, 20 out of the bullpen. Moret's 14-3 record was enough to lead Major League Baseball, with an .824 winning percentage.

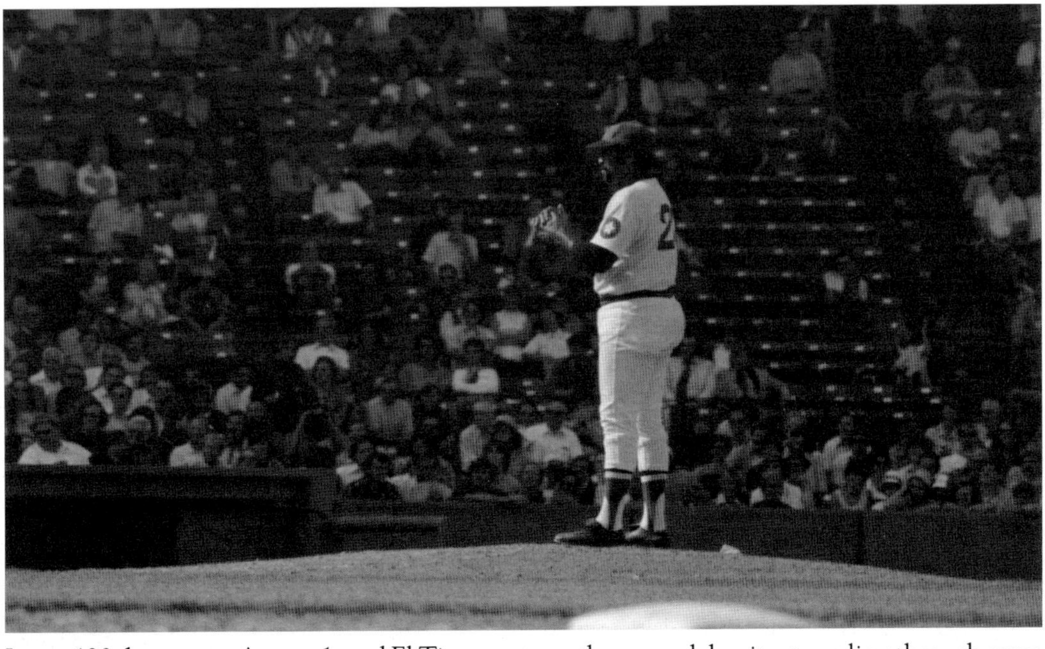

It was 100 degrees on August 1, and El Tiante was on the mound despite struggling through some shoulder problems and having surrendered 10 earned runs in his last 13 innings. He was leading 6-3 in the ninth when he surrendered a three-run home to Willie Horton, gave a solo shot to Bill Freehan, and left having served up seven runs and 14 hits. The Red Sox were now behind 7-6.

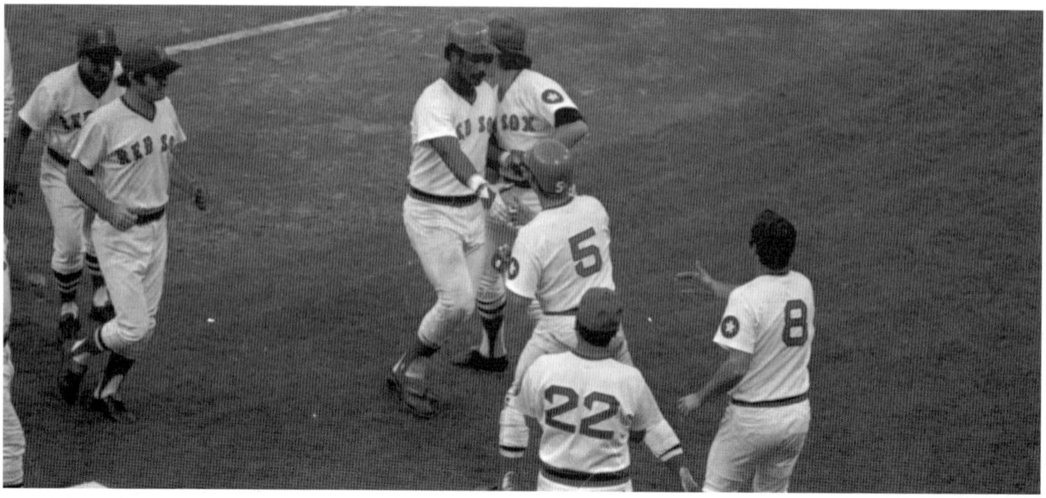

In the Sox's 10th, Denny Doyle led with a single and ultimately scored on a Yastrzemski game-tying single. Yaz took second on the throw home, prompting an intentional walk to Lynn. Jim Rice laid down a bunt, which he beat out for a hit, and Yaz scored when the pitcher threw the ball away. Rice receives kudos following his walk-off bunt from Doyle (5), Yaz (8), Darrell Johnson (22), and others.

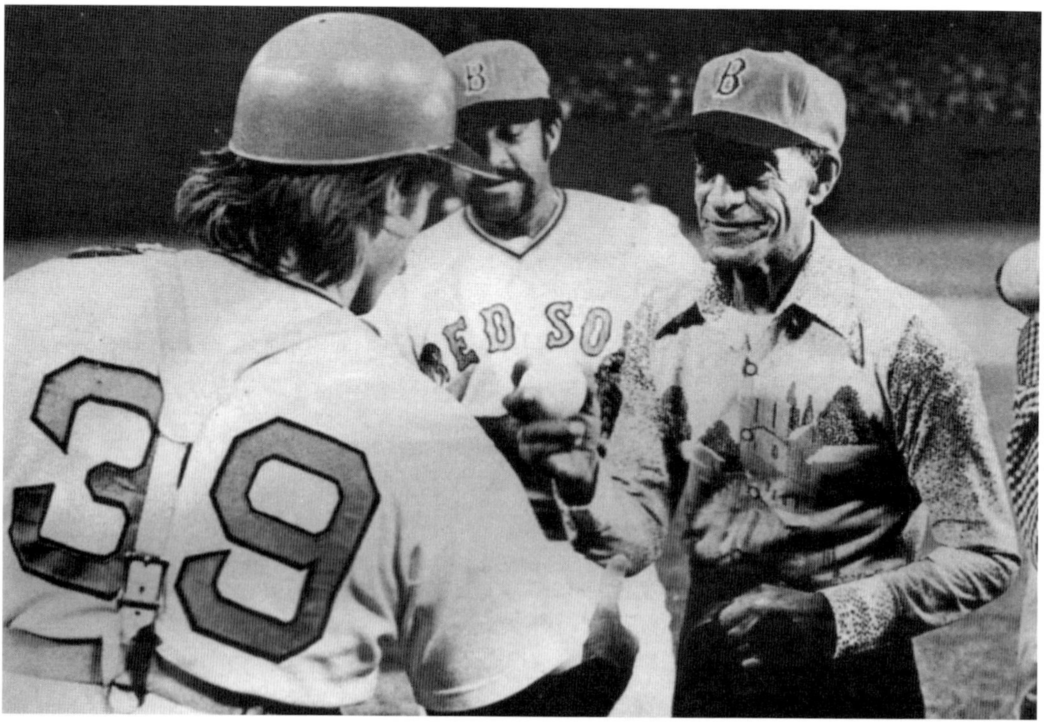

On Tuesday, August 26, Luis Tiant Sr. and Jr. took the mound at Fenway. Reunited with his father for the first time in 15 years just days earlier, Luis Jr. watched as El Tiante Sr. threw out the first pitch to Red Sox catcher Tim Blackwell (39). The former Negro League star pitcher threw out two pitches because the first one was not a strike.

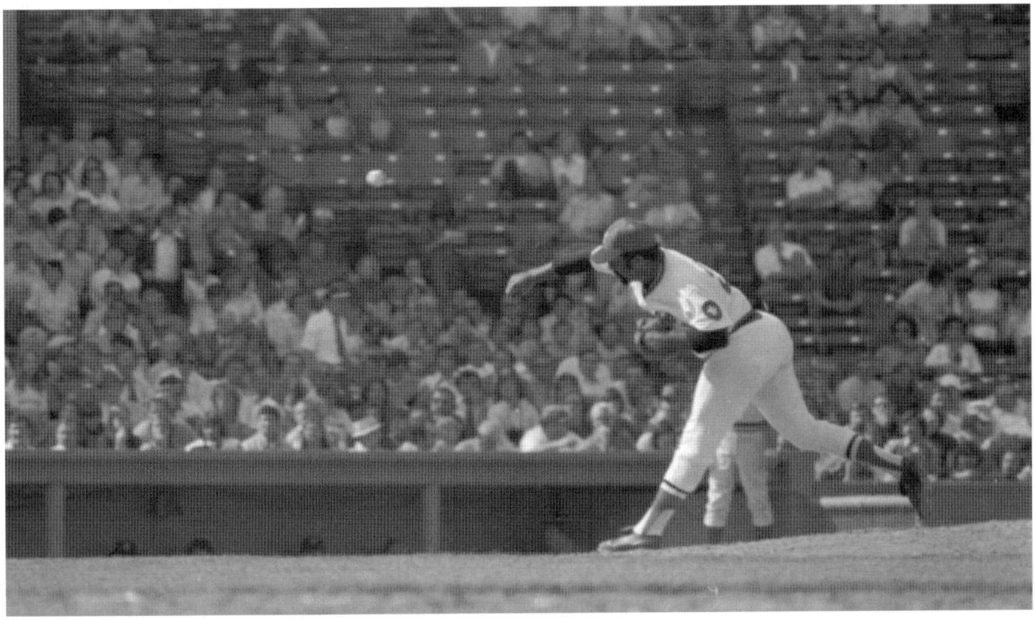

Luis Tiant came into his August 30 start versus Oakland battling a bad back and still spent from the emotion of his parents' arrival from Cuba just nine days earlier. He had not been sharp in his previous outing, and it was the hope of Tiant and fans that the pitcher would return to form as the Red Sox geared up for the stretch drive.

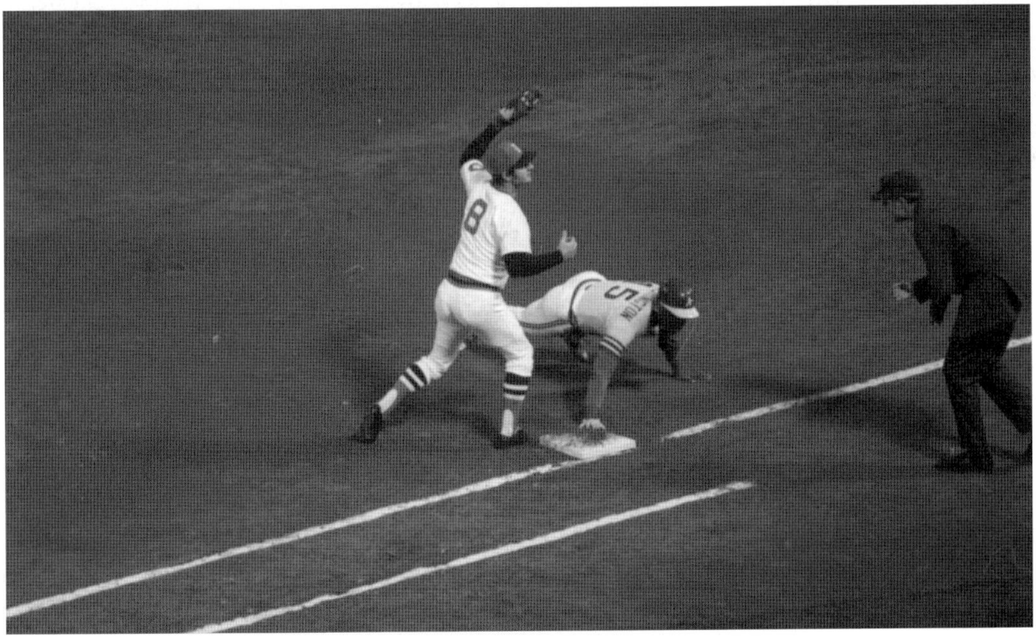

In the first inning, Claudell Washington, Oakland's left fielder, singled with one out. After several throws to first, Tiant picked him off for the inning's second out. In this photograph, Sox first baseman Carl Yastrzemski gives first-base umpire Bill Haller a thumbs-up sign as Haller calls Washington out.

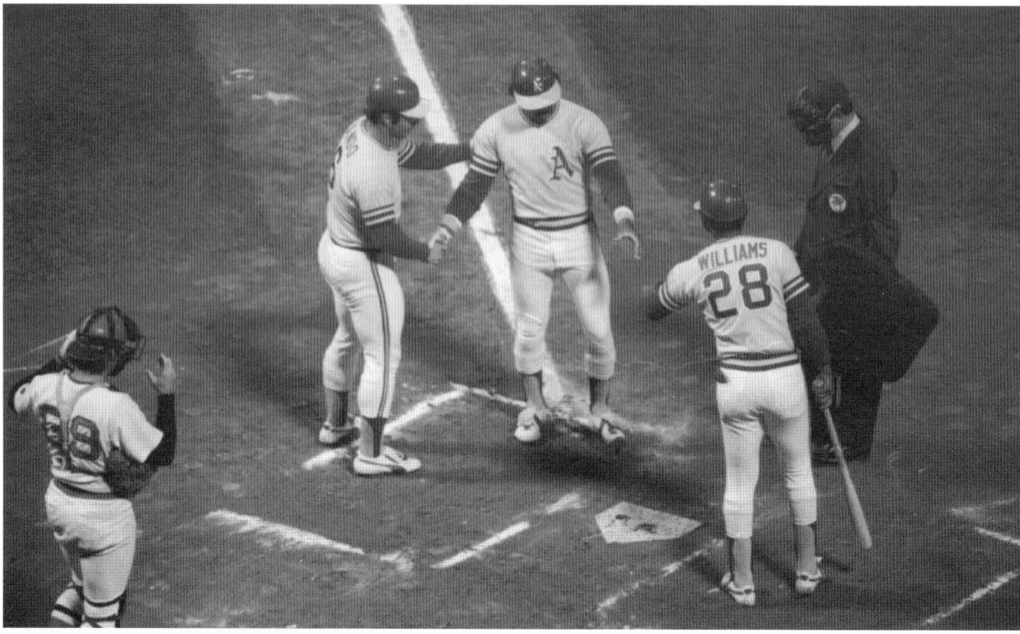

After Tiant walked Sal Bando, Reggie Jackson hit a home run to give the A's a 2-0 lead. Here, Reggie is welcomed by Bando and on-deck hitter Billy Williams (28). Red Sox catcher Tim Blackwell looks on as home plate umpire Armando Rodriquez makes sure Jackson touches home.

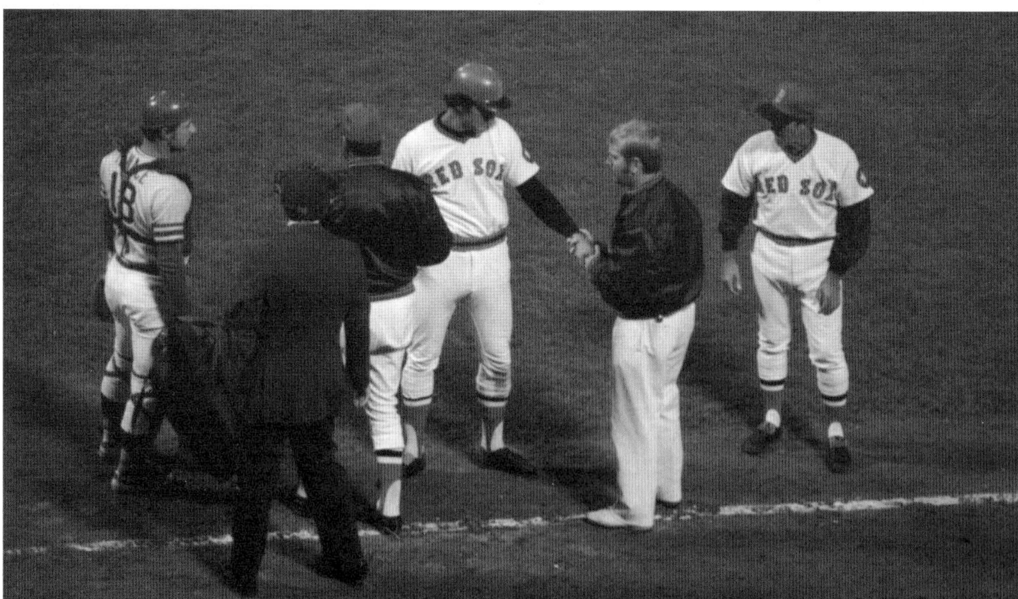

The Red Sox went ahead 3-2 in the bottom of the first inning on a double, an error, a walk, a single, and a double play. Dwight Evans was hit by a Glenn Abbott pitch in the first inning. Here, he is tended to by trainer Charlie Moss, while catcher Gene Tenace (18), Armando Rodriquez (umpire), Red Sox manager Darrell Johnson, and first-base coach Johnny Pesky look on. Evans stole second but did not score.

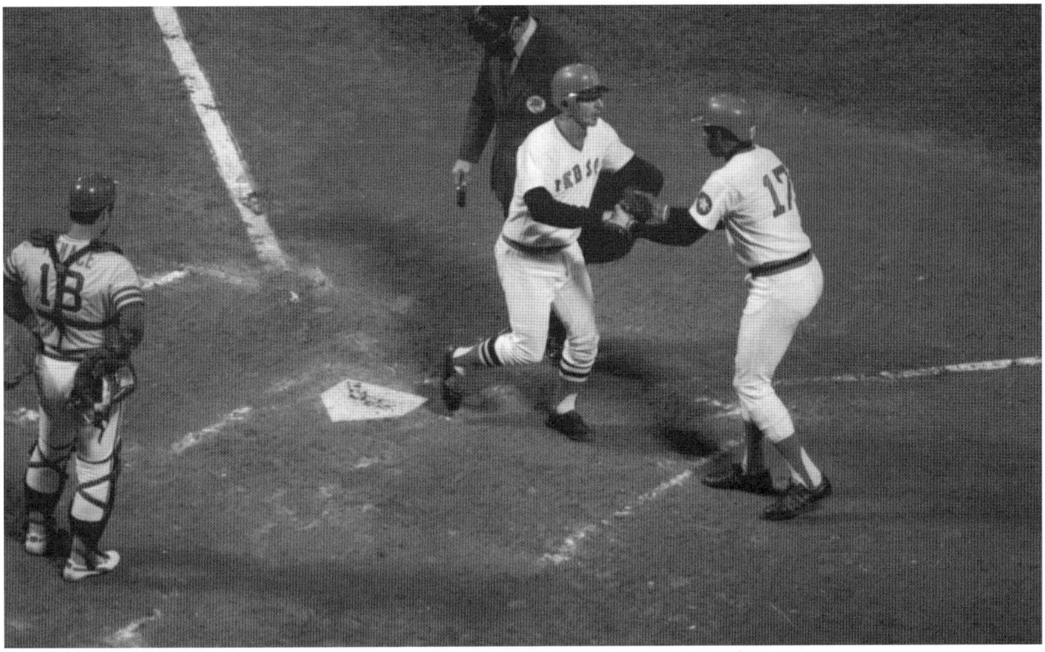

The Red Sox tied the game in their second inning when Carl Yastrzemski homered, scoring Cecil Cooper, who had walked. Here, Cooper welcomes Yaz home as A's catcher Gene Tenace and umpire Armando Rodriquez look on. After only two innings, the score was knotted at five.

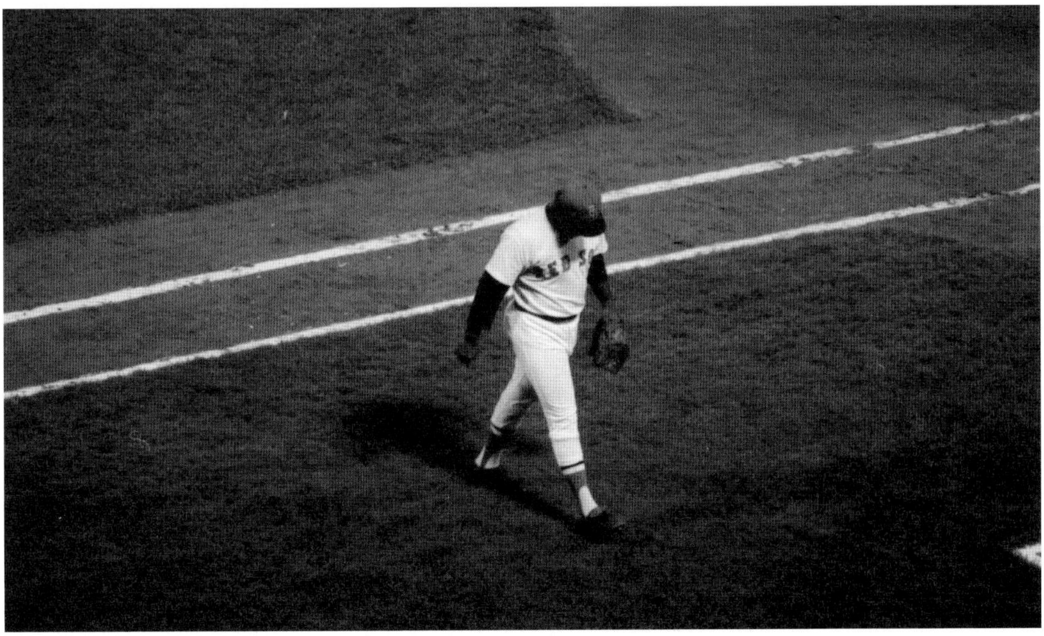

Luis Tiant left the game after just a little over two innings, his shortest outing of the season. In successive outings, he had pitched a total of 8.66 innings, giving up eight runs and 14 hits while walking five and striking out only three. The concern about his back injury heightened, and some even suggested it might be the end of the line for the great Cuban hurler.

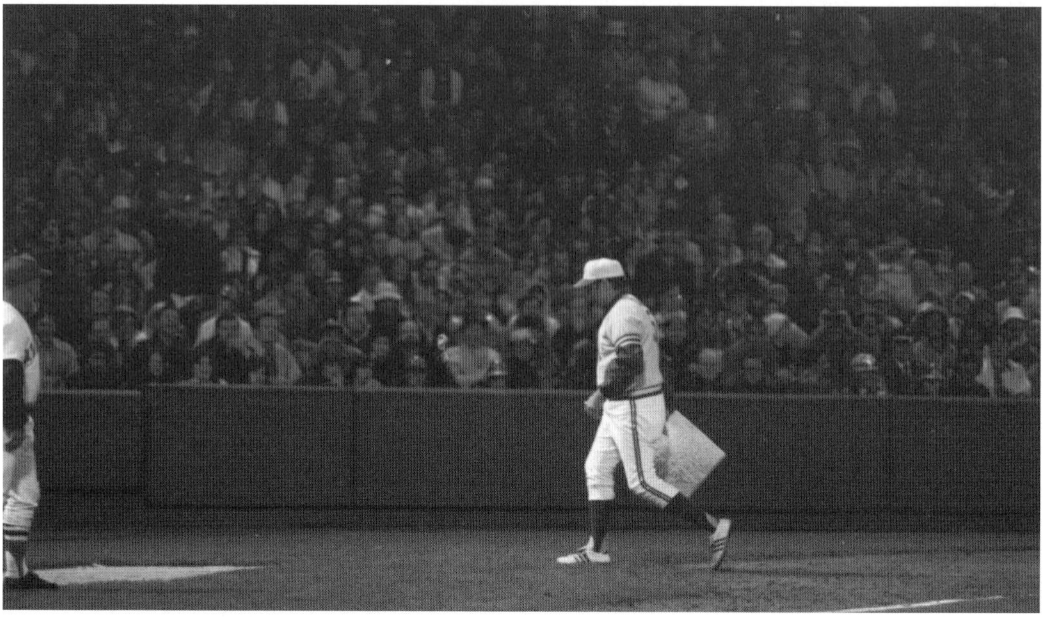

Oakland A's skipper Al Dark was not convinced that second-base umpire Rich Garcia had made the correct call on a Jim Rice steal in the ninth. Garcia ejected Dark, who was so infuriated he removed third base and flipped it into the stands before stalking into the dugout. The A's won it in the 10th inning.

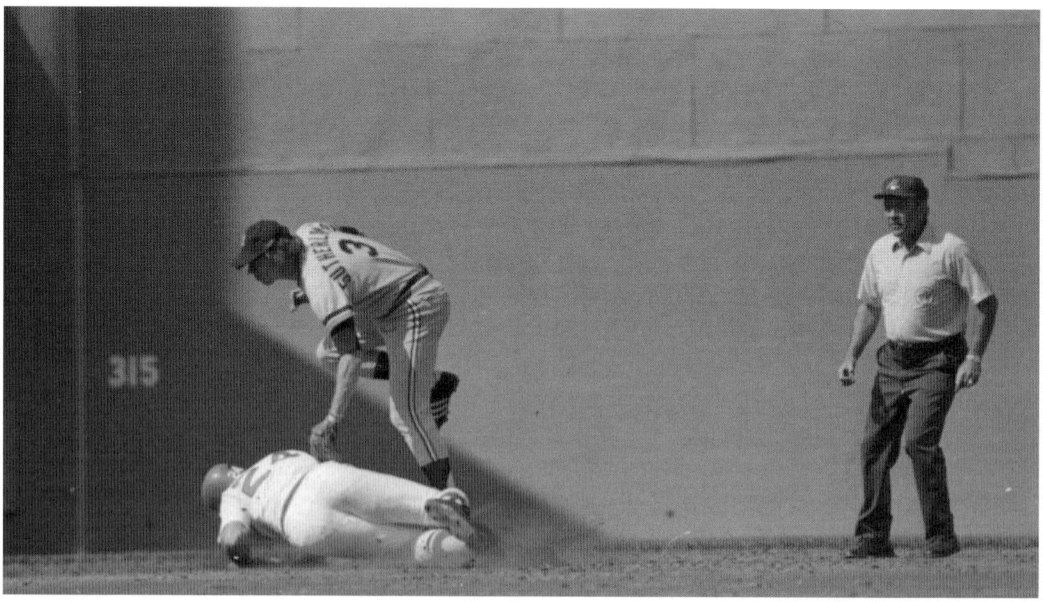

In September 11 action, the Red Sox scored in the second inning on a triple by Rice, who then scored on a ground out by Fisk. Following singles by Dwight Evans and Rico Petrocelli, Rick Burleson grounded to shortstop Tom Veryzer, who threw the ball past second baseman Gary Sutherland (3), as Dwight Evans (24) slid in safely. Petrocelli scored, and Evans moved to third on the play, giving the Red Sox a 2-0 lead.

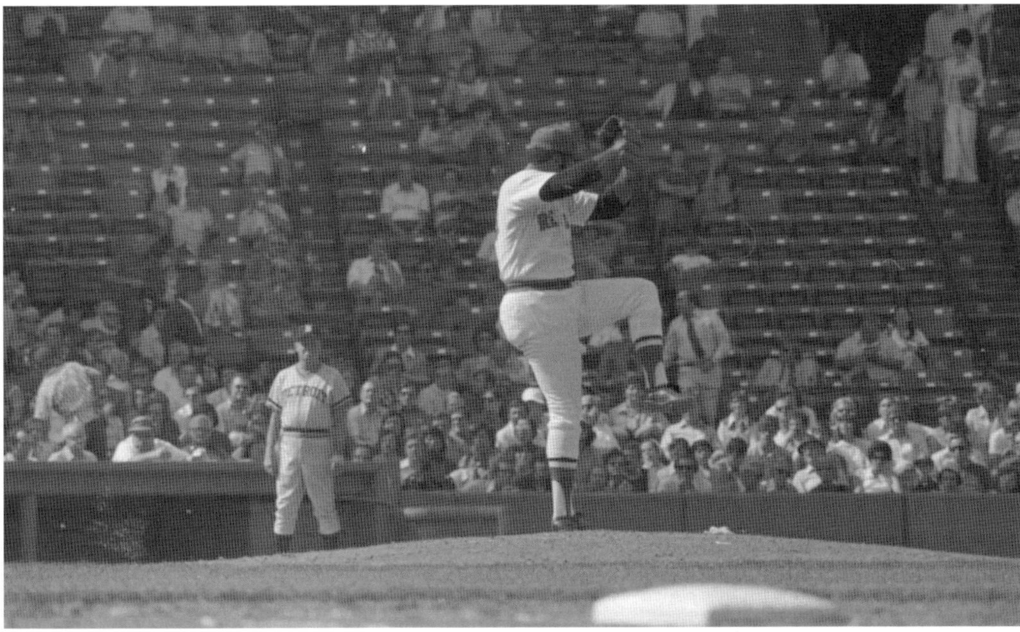

On Thursday, September 11, Luis Tiant took to the mound to close out a series with the Tigers. The Sox had lost four of their last five games, and although they still possessed a five-game lead, there was trepidation within the Fenway Faithful, mindful of September 1974. Adding to their trepidation was the fact that El Tiante had not won in a month, was battling a bad back that had shelved him for two weeks, and in his last outing he was shelled by Oakland, lasting only 2.33 innings. However, it took but one inning, and the 9,508 in attendance could see that the twisting, turning, head bobbing El Tiante was back. He rctired the first 14 Tigers in order, and the faithful sensed they were in the midst of something special.

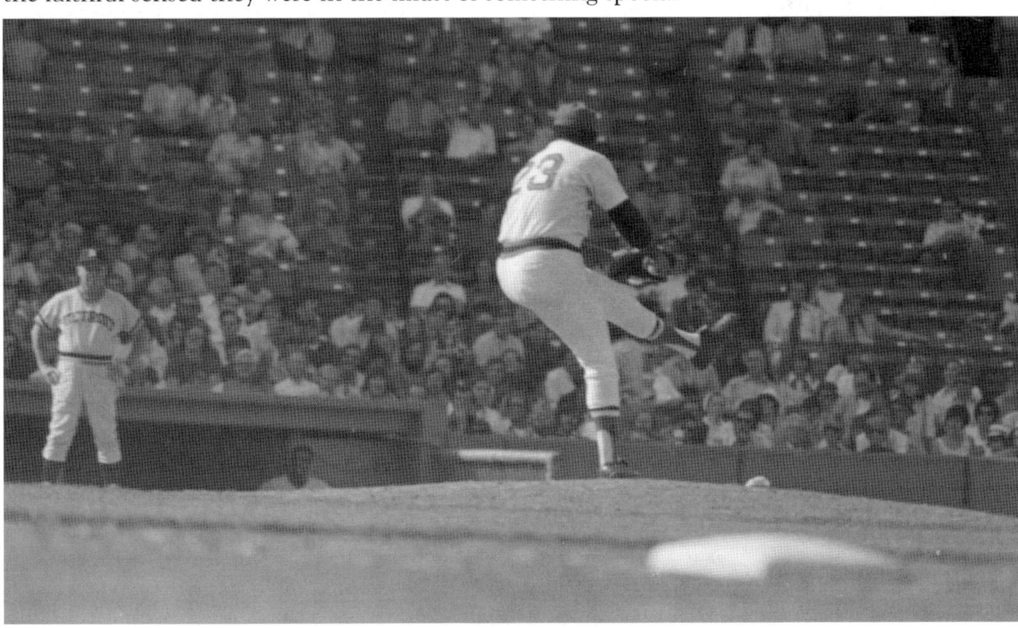

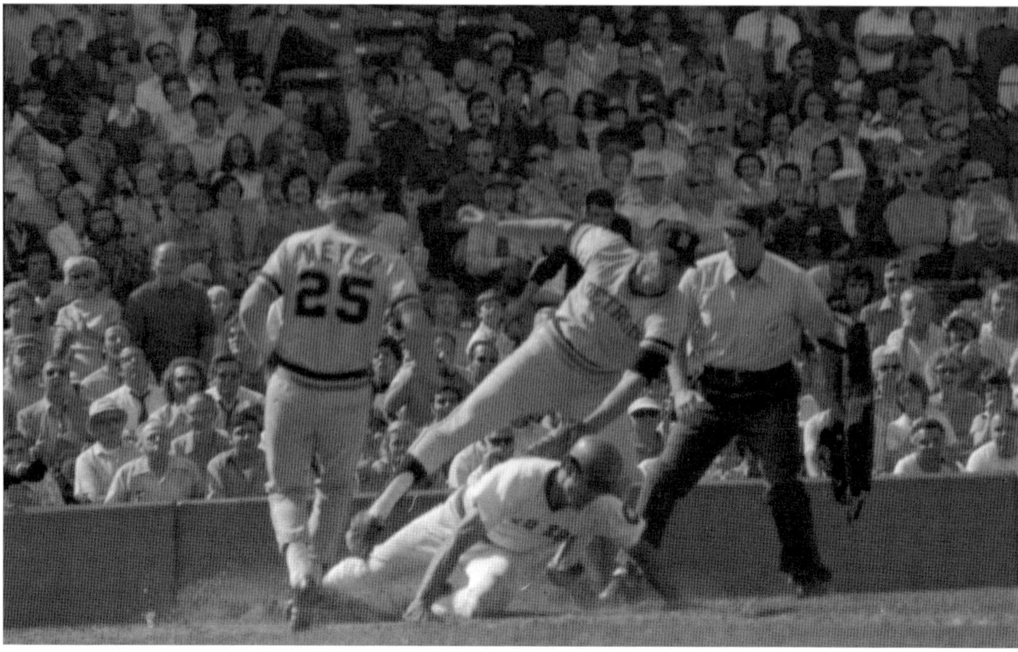

Dwight Evans is tagged out by Tiger pitcher Dave Lemaczyk, seen here having just made the tag, in a second-inning rundown, where the throws went from catcher to third base to Lemaczyk. Meyer (25) is in place and ready to receive a throw that was not needed. The third-base umpire is Nick Bremigan.

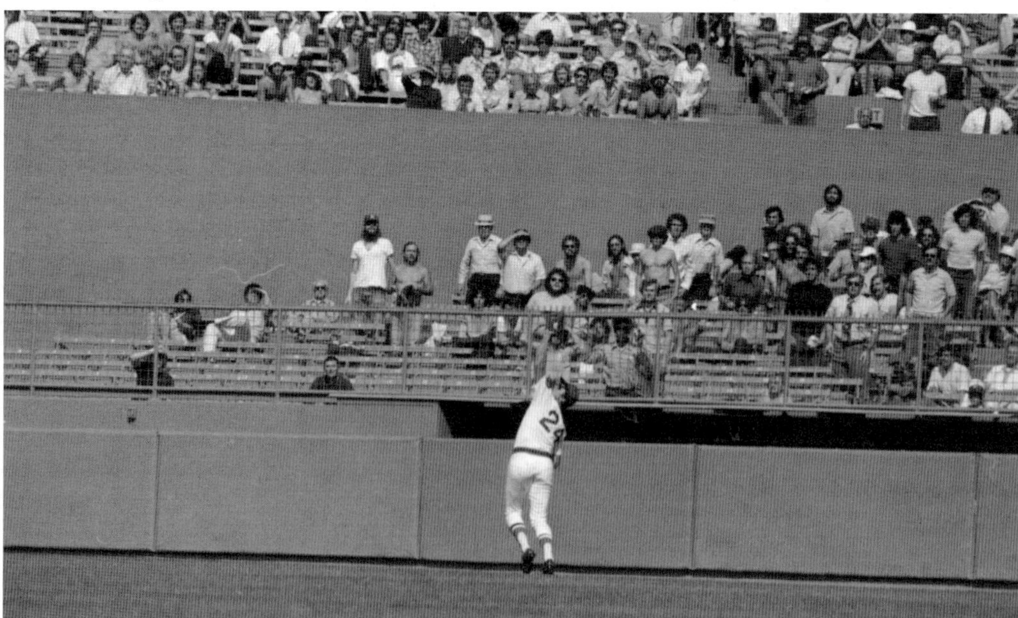

Dwight Evans makes a nice running catch of a fly ball off the bat of Tiger shortstop Tom Veryzer. Veryzer was the second out of the third inning; it was Tiant's eighth straight out and the hardest hit ball of the day up to that point.

Tiant heads to the dugout, having just struck out Ron LeFlore to end the third inning. It was his third one, two, three inning in a row and his second strikeout of the game. He was just getting warmed up.

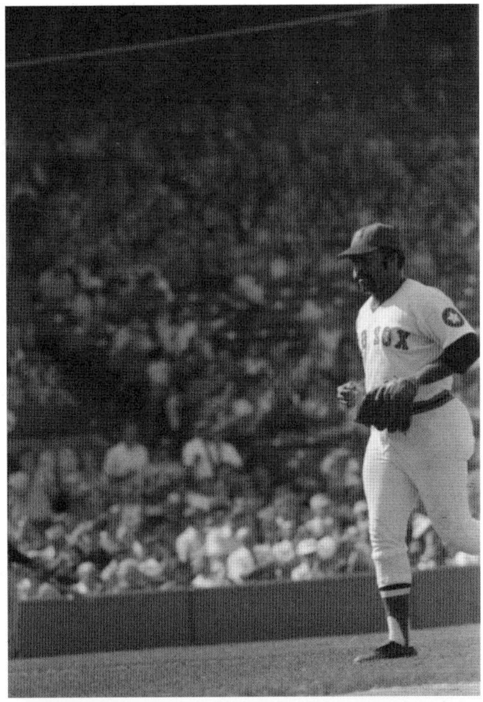

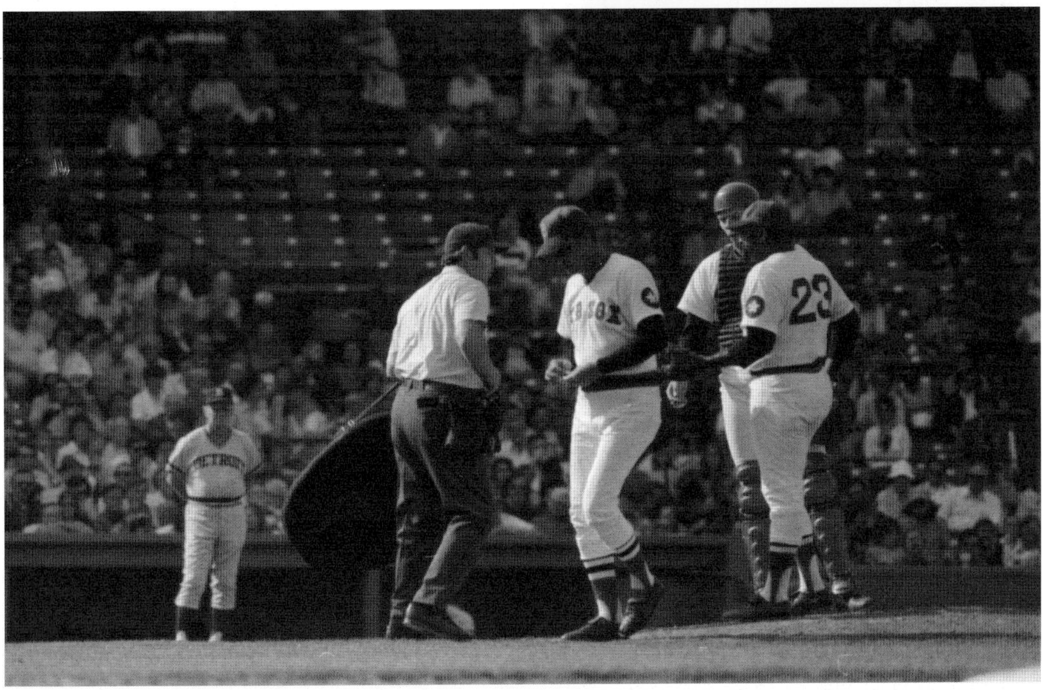

Tiant entered the eighth inning with a 3-0 lead, his only blemish being a walk to Bill Freehan in the fifth. With two outs in the eighth, Aurelio Rodriquez lined a Tiant fastball up the middle for the Tigers first hit of the game. This prompted a visit from manager Darrell Johnson (center), who is chased from his chat with Fisk (catcher) and Tiant (23) by umpire Jim McKean.

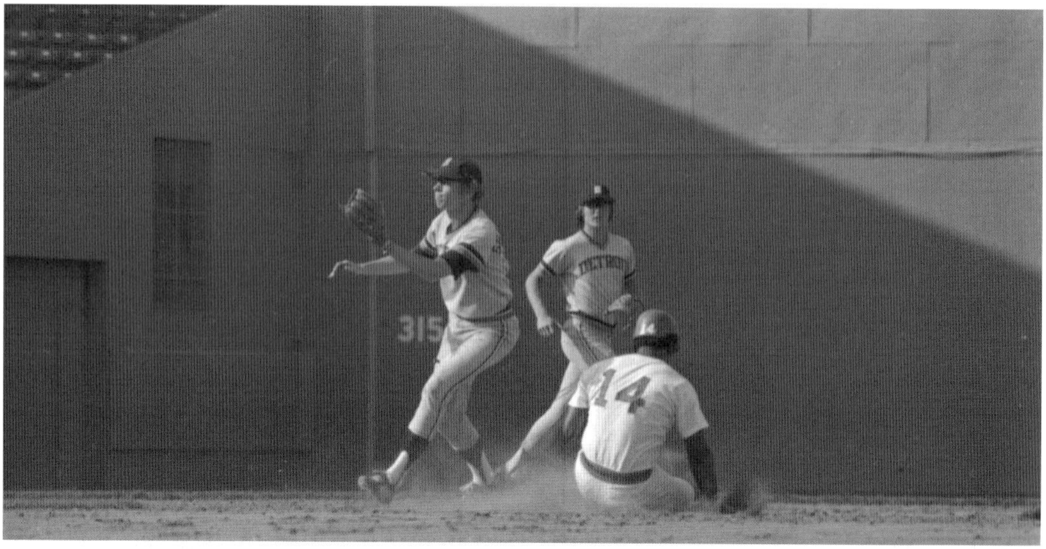

Jim Rice (14) led off the eighth inning and stole second. Here, he slides in safely as second baseman Gary Sutherland takes the throw and shortstop Tom Veryzer moves to back up the play. Rice moved to third on a fly to right by Petrocelli but died there when Dwight Evans lined out to center to end the inning.

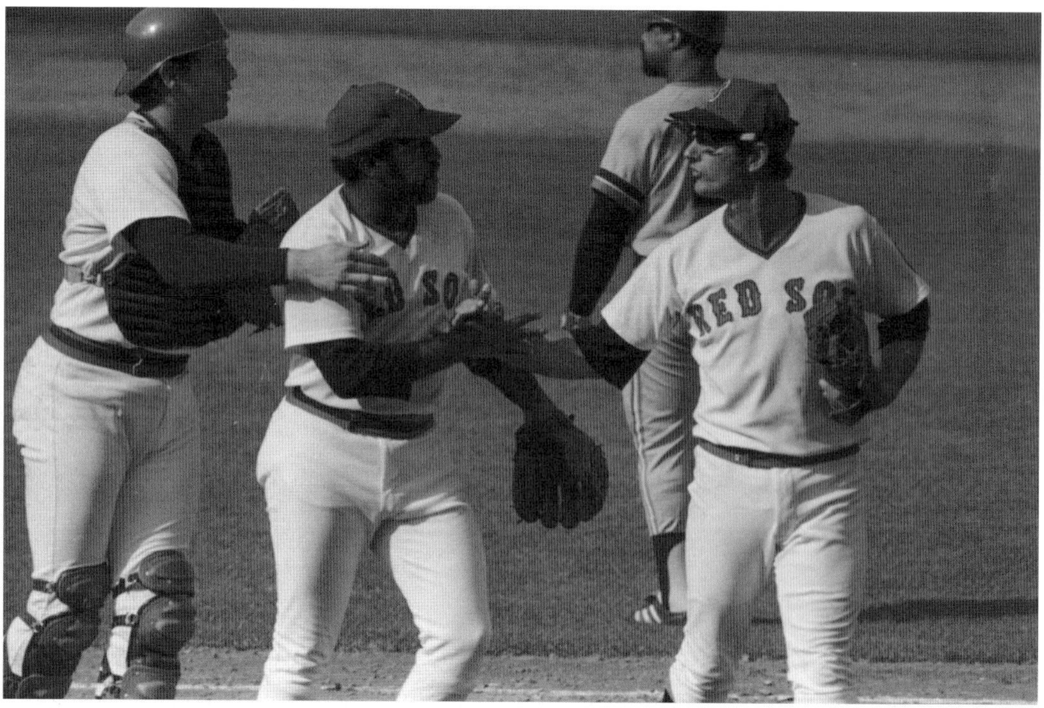

Tiant surrendered a solo homer in the ninth, ending the game with a 3-1 win on a three-hitter with 10 strikeouts. Here, he is congratulated by catcher Carlton Fisk (left) and first baseman Carl Yastrzemski (right). In the background is Willie Horton, who flew out to right to end the game. His critics and skeptics were silenced.

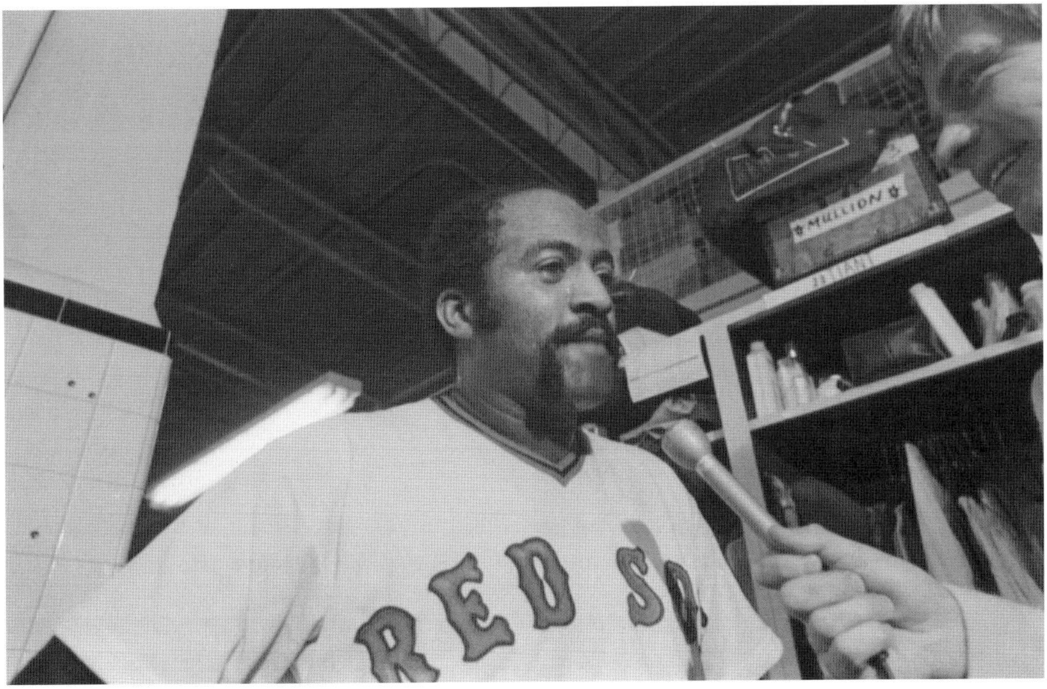

In the postgame clubhouse, Tiant gave his interviews and then joined his father as they lit up cigars from their native Havana, Cuba. It was the first time his parents had seen him win. His mother, who watched in the stands, deeply moved by the adoration from the Fenway Faithful, said, "This is all I want out of life . . . He is all we have and all that's important to me is that happiness and goodness come to him."

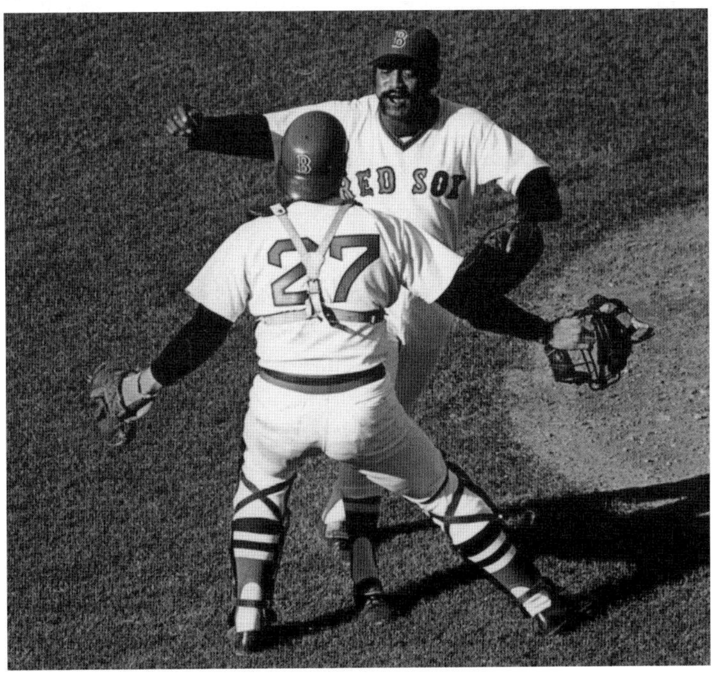

It was September 16, and the second-place Orioles were in town, 5.5 games behind Boston. Jim Palmer was pitching against Luis Tiant. The lead seemed secure, with only 10 games left, but the memories of the 1974 debacle were vivid. Tiant put the Fenway Faithful at ease by throwing a 2-0 shutout, scattering five hits. Carlton Fisk (27), embracing Tiant, homered, as did Rico Petrocelli, to account for the runs. (Courtesy of the Boston Red Sox.)

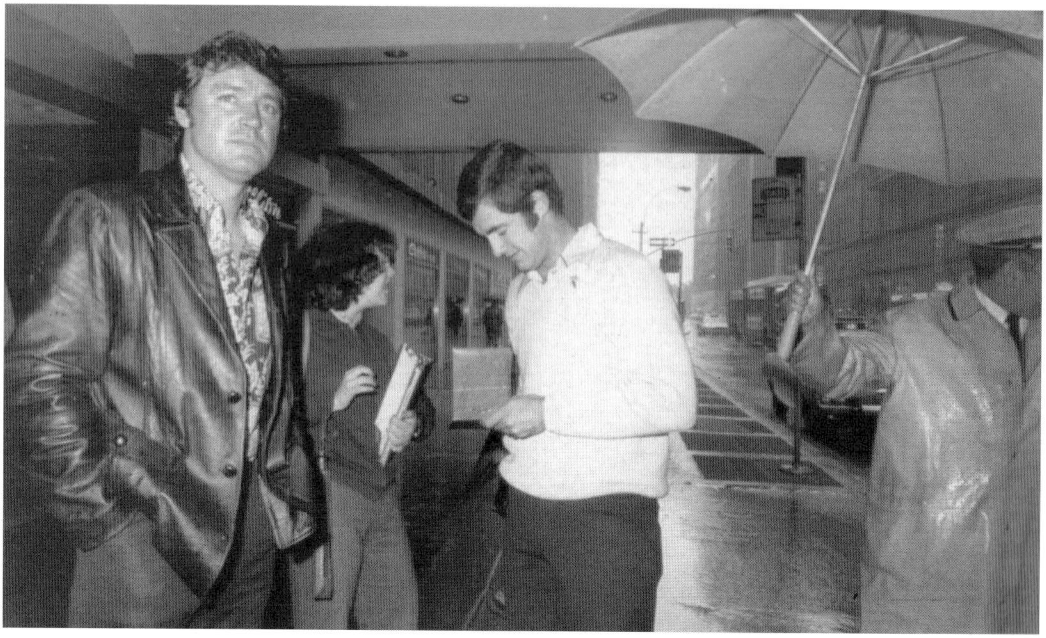

Fred Lynn signs an autograph for a fan outside a New York hotel while Deron Johnson (left) waits with him for a cab to take them to Shea Stadium. Their scheduled twi-night doubleheader was rained out, and the Red Sox headed home to Boston, where they clinched the American League East crown two days later.

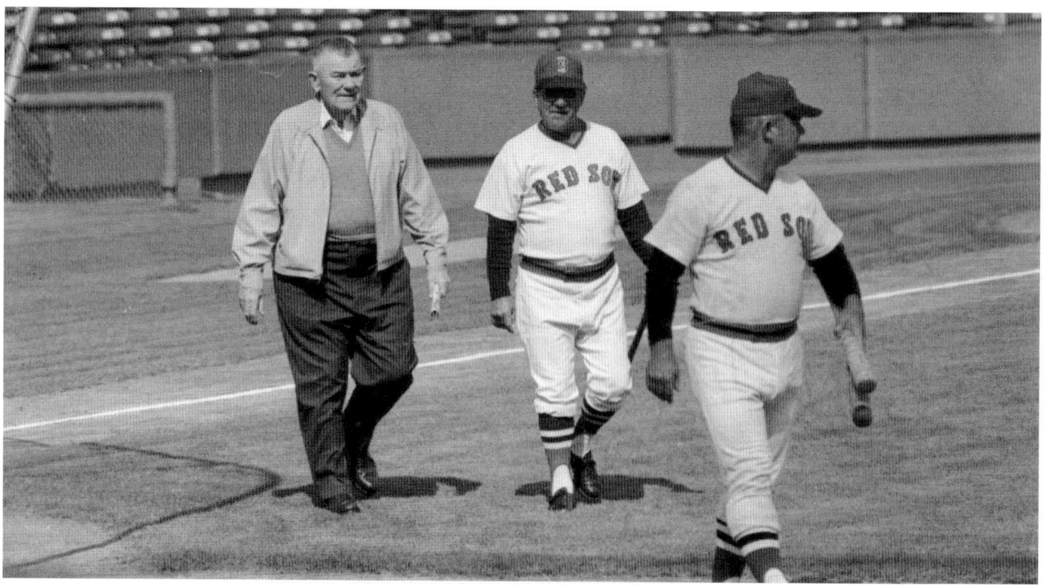

With Hurricane Eloise wiping out the final two games between the Red Sox and Yankees in New York and the opening game of Cleveland's final series in Boston, it was not until Friday, September 26, when play was ready to resume at Fenway. From left to right, owner Tom Yawkey and coaches Eddie Popowski and Don Zimmer check out the field before the Red Sox twi-night doubleheader against the Indians.

On September 22, the Red Sox beat the Yankees 6-4, with Rick Wise besting Yankee rookie southpaw Ron Guidry. It increased their lead to four games over the Orioles. The Sox had six to play, and Baltimore had eight to go. Any combination of Red Sox wins and Oriole losses totaling four would clinch the American League East for Boston. However, Mother Nature was about to intervene, and her name was Hurricane Eloise. Smashing into the Florida Panhandle, Eloise wreaked havoc and destruction through the South and up the East Coast into New England. It brought the American League East race to a screeching halt and taxed the Fenway Park ground crew (right) while forcing some innovative drying methods for the Red Sox organization. Eloise killed 31 Americans, caused $500 million in damages, and dropped over five inches of rain on Fenway Park.

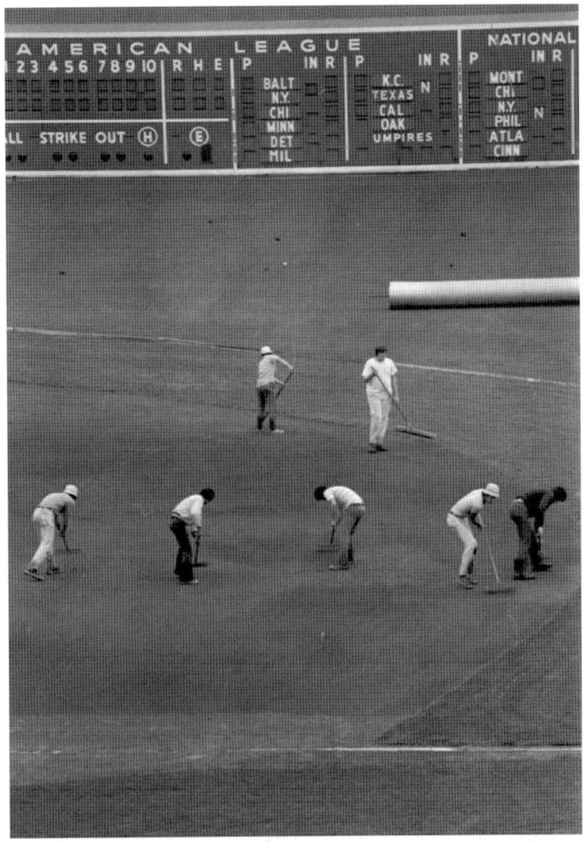

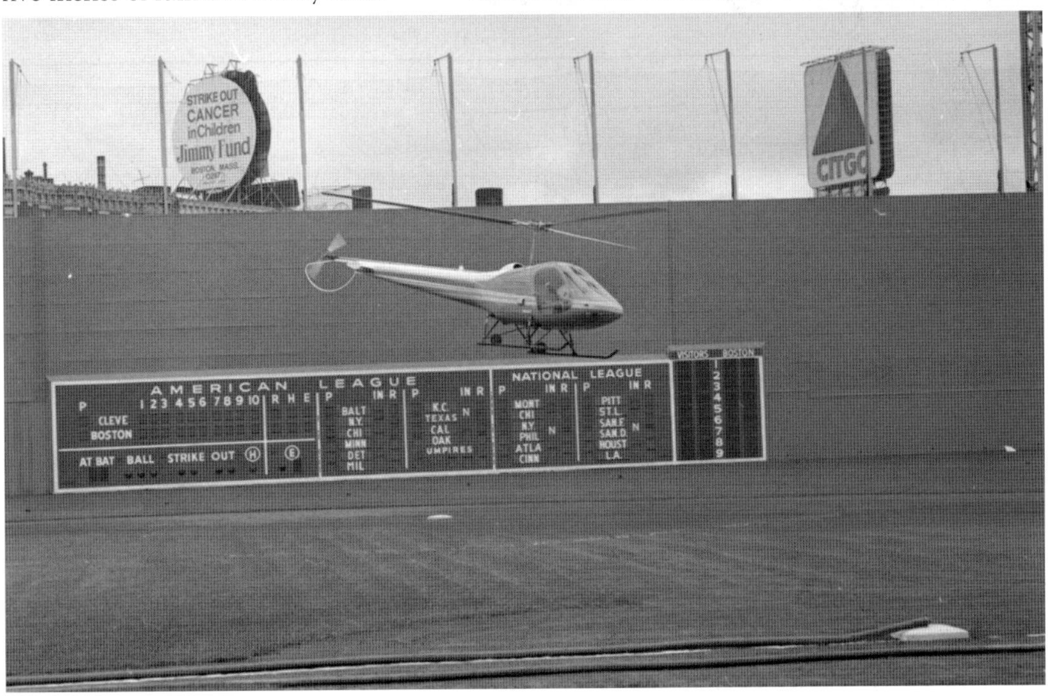

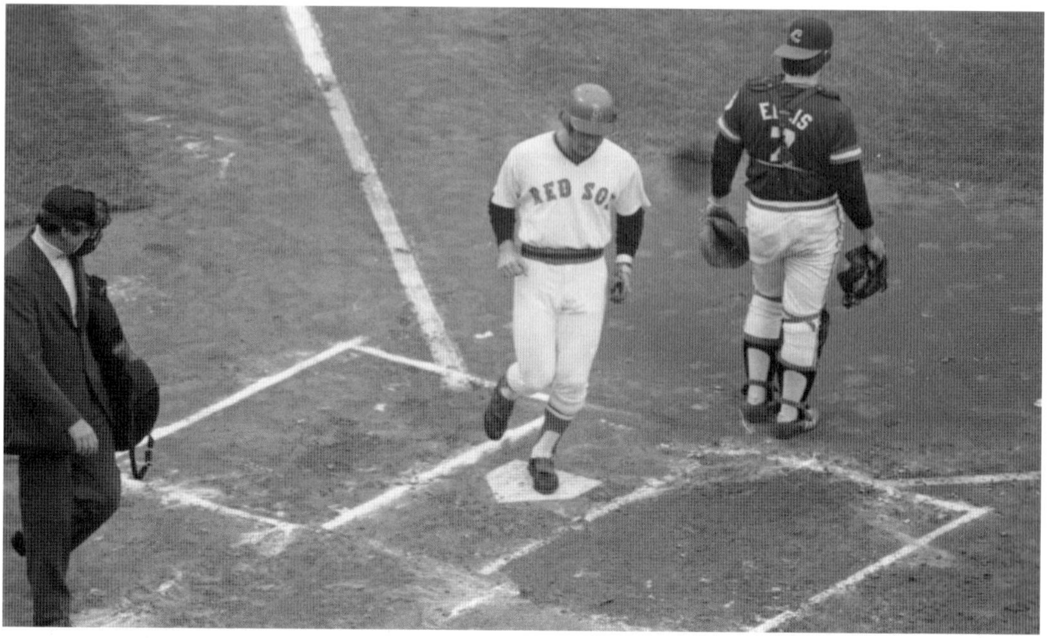

Bernie Carbo is shown here scoring the first run of the first game of the September 26 doubleheader. It came across on a sacrifice fly by Fred Lynn. Carbo walked to lead off the game, advanced to second on a walk to Doyle, and went to third on a fly to right by Yastrzemski. Unbeknownst to the 22,067 Fenway Faithful who braved the chill and the fog, it was the only run Luis Tiant would need on the night.

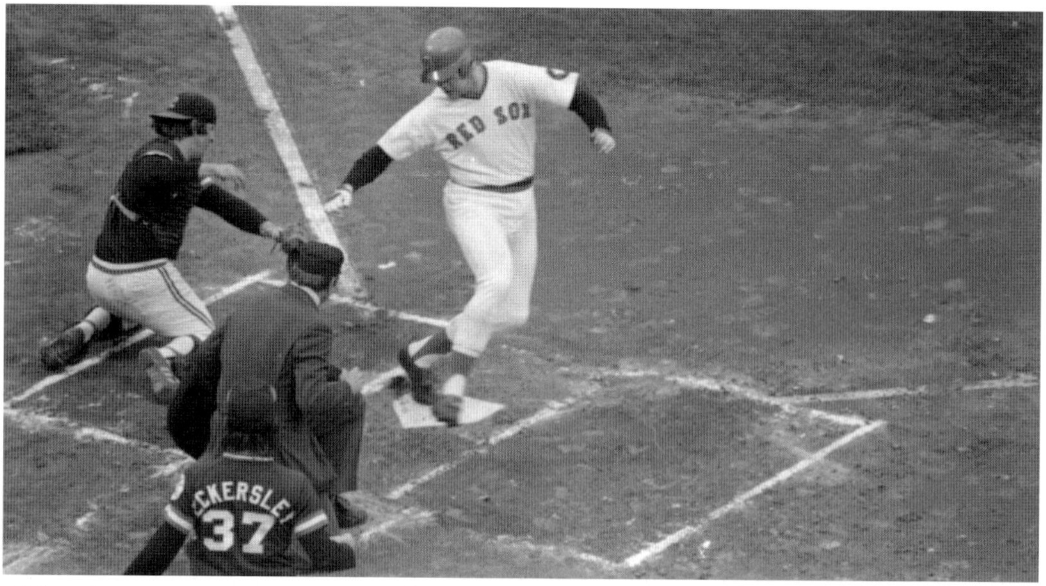

Although appearing safe, Carlton Fisk is thrown out at home to end the first inning of the first game of the doubleheader. Fisk doubled in Denny Doyle to give the Red Sox a 2-0 lead and attempted to score on a single to left by Rico Petrocelli. Oscar Gamble threw to catcher John Ellis, who applied the tag. Umpire Bill Haller makes the call while Dennis Eckersley backs up the play.

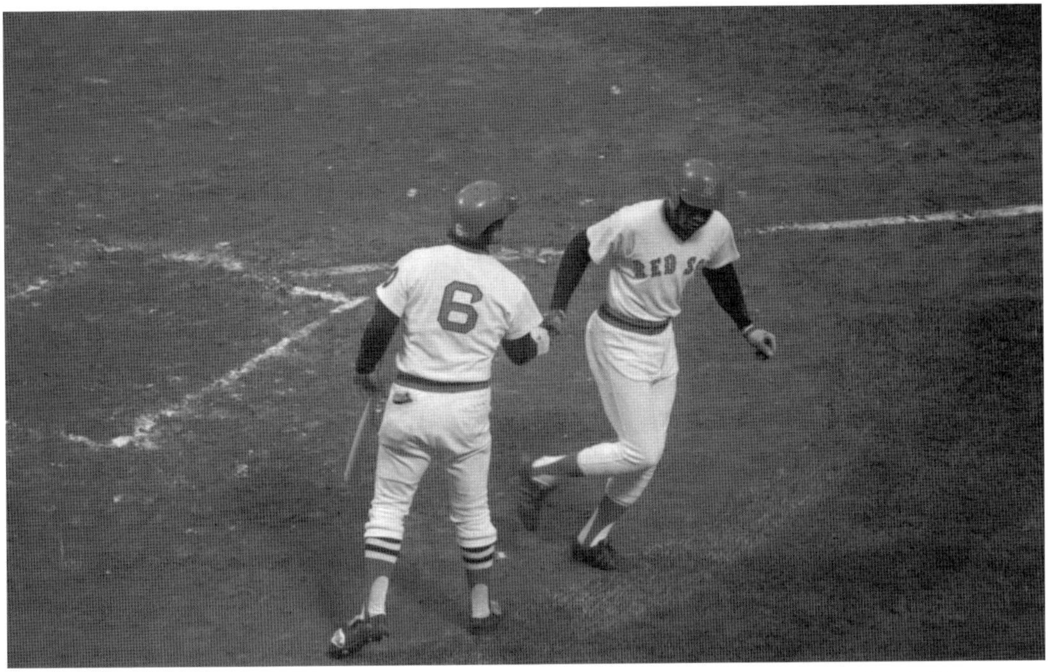

Rico Petrocelli (6) welcomes home designated hitter Cecil Cooper following a leadoff homer in the fourth inning. Cooper's home run off the Indians' 20-year-old rookie Dennis Eckersley was his 14th of the year and gave the Sox a 3-0 lead. Eckersley was 13-7 in 1975 with a 2.60 ERA and did not receive one vote for Rookie of the Year. The reasons? Fred Lynn and Jim Rice.

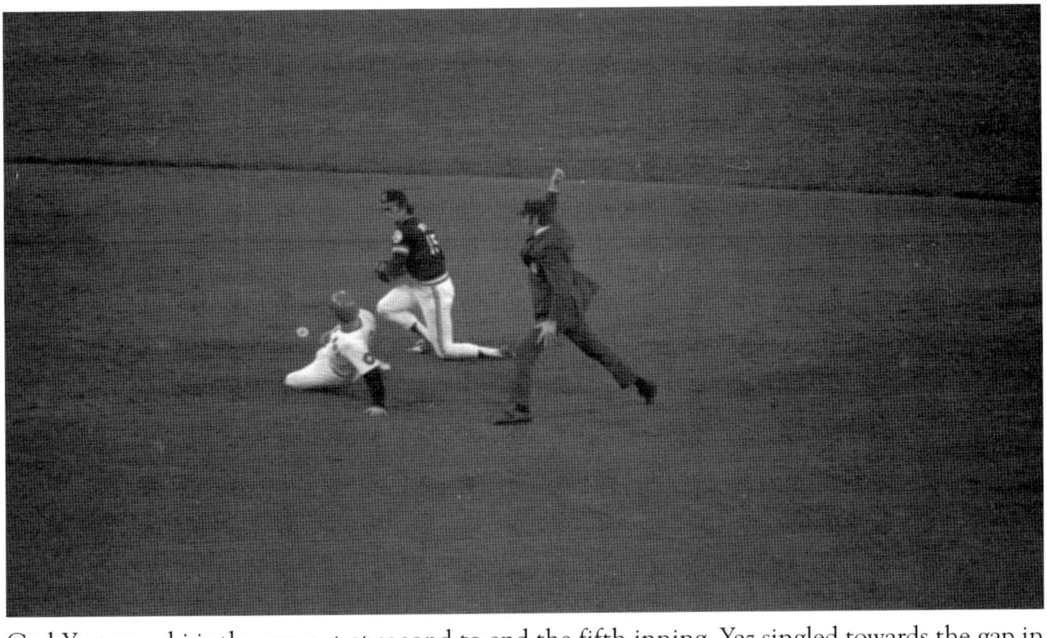

Carl Yastrzemski is thrown out at second to end the fifth inning. Yaz singled towards the gap in left-center field and was attempting to stretch it into a double. Center fielder Rick Manning cut the ball off and threw to shortstop Frank Duffy, who applied the tag called by Don Denkinger.

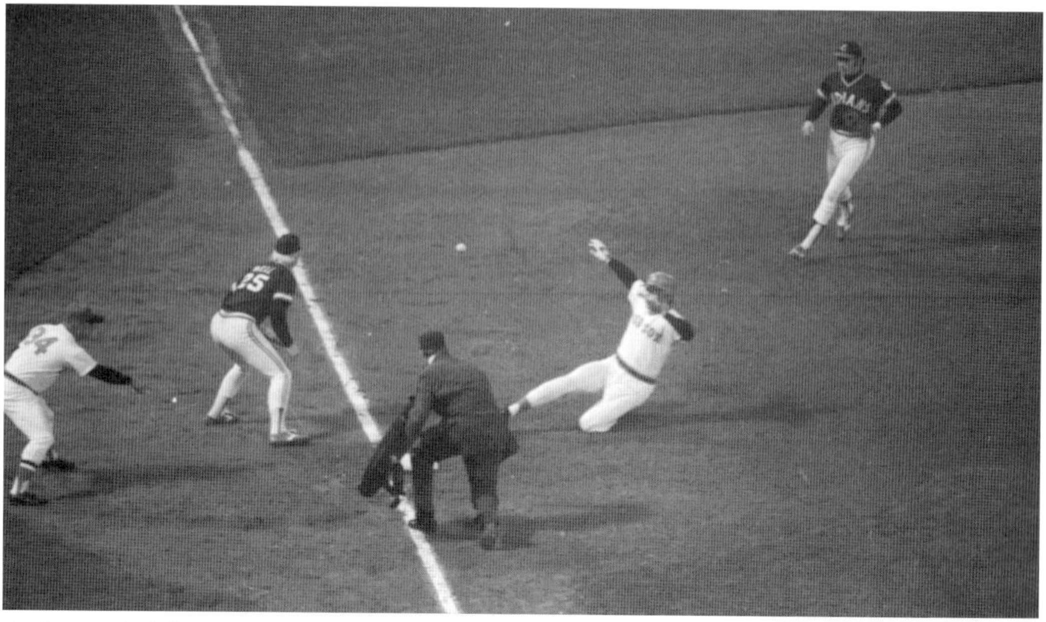

Carlton Fisk slides safely into third as he tripled with one out in the sixth inning. Third baseman Buddy Bell is receiving the ball from left fielder Oscar Gamble as third-base coach Don Zimmer implores Fisk to slide and shortstop Frank Duffy looks on. Home plate umpire Bill Haller has moved into position to make the call.

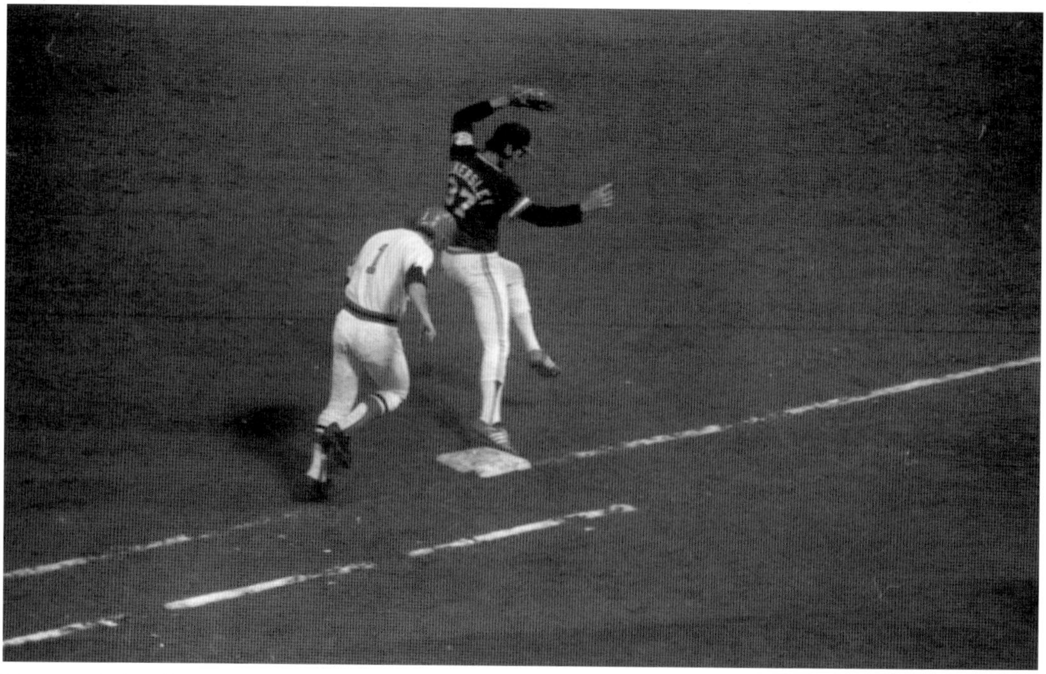

Bernie Carbo (1) is out at first, leading off the seventh inning. Carbo was robbed of a hit when Indians second baseman Duane Kiper made a nice play ranging to his left and made the throw to pitcher Dennis Eckersley, who displays the grace of a ballerina while covering the bag.

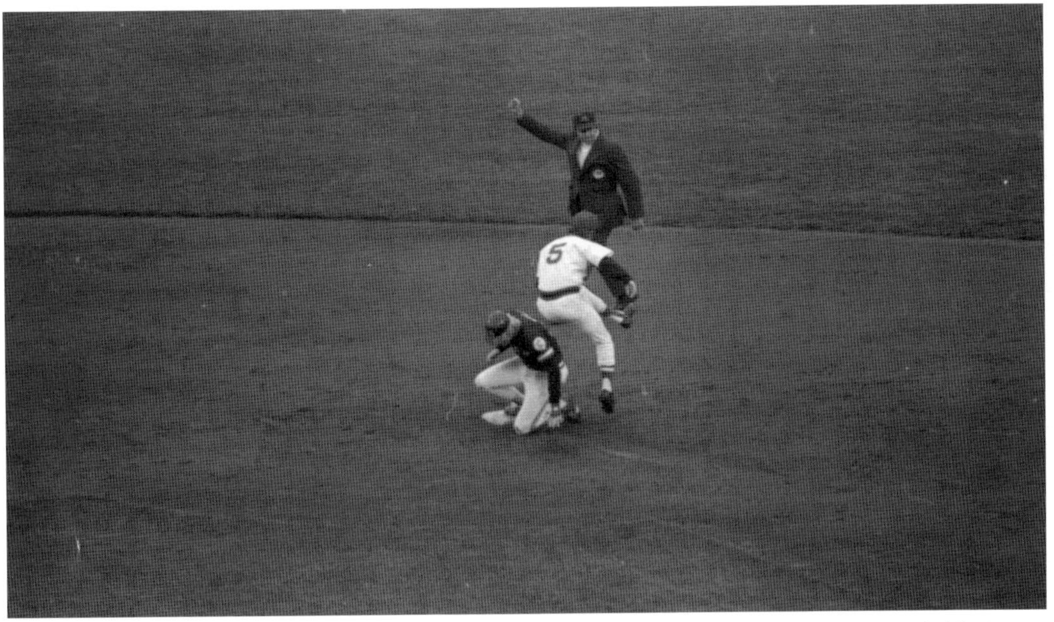

Cleveland third baseman Buddy Bell became the third runner to fall victim to an outfielder's arm in the first game of this twin bill. Bell led off the eighth with a single to left and was gunned down by left fielder Rick Miller. Denny Doyle made the tag, and Don Denkinger made the call.

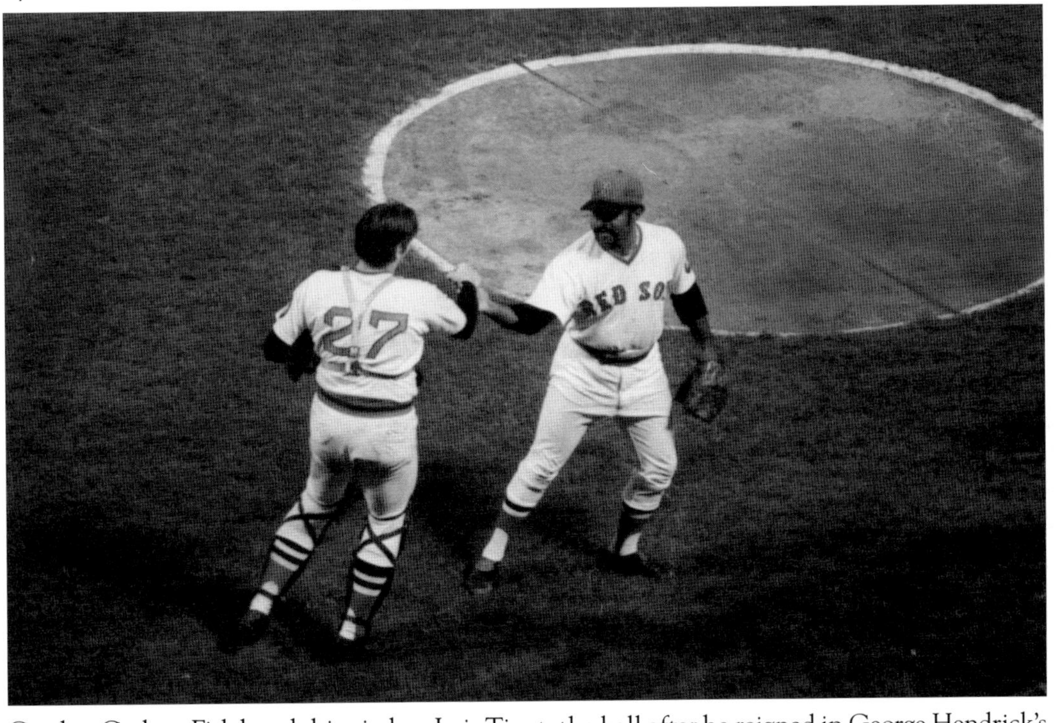

Catcher Carlton Fisk hands his pitcher, Luis Tiant, the ball after he reigned in George Hendrick's pop foul behind the plate to end the game. The Red Sox took the opener of the doubleheader 4-0 behind Tiant's 18th win and his second shutout in his last three starts.

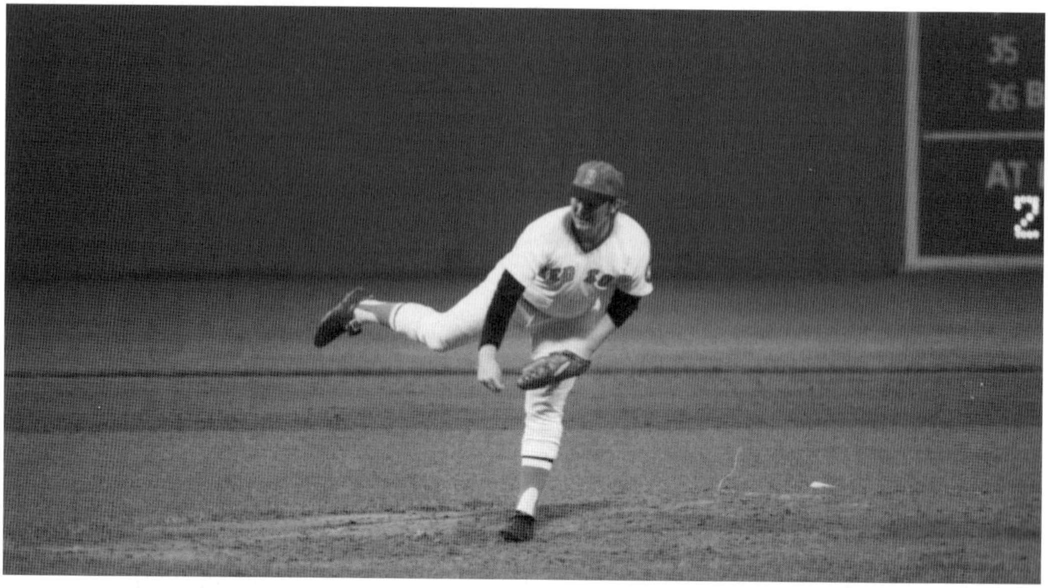

Reggie Cleveland got the nod for the second game of the September 26 doubleheader. Cleveland had an excellent September, going 4-0 with a 2.20 ERA to finish the year 13-9. He, like Tiant in the first game, only allowed one batter to reach third as he completed the first Red Sox back-to-back shutouts since 1956. It was Cleveland's only shutout of the year.

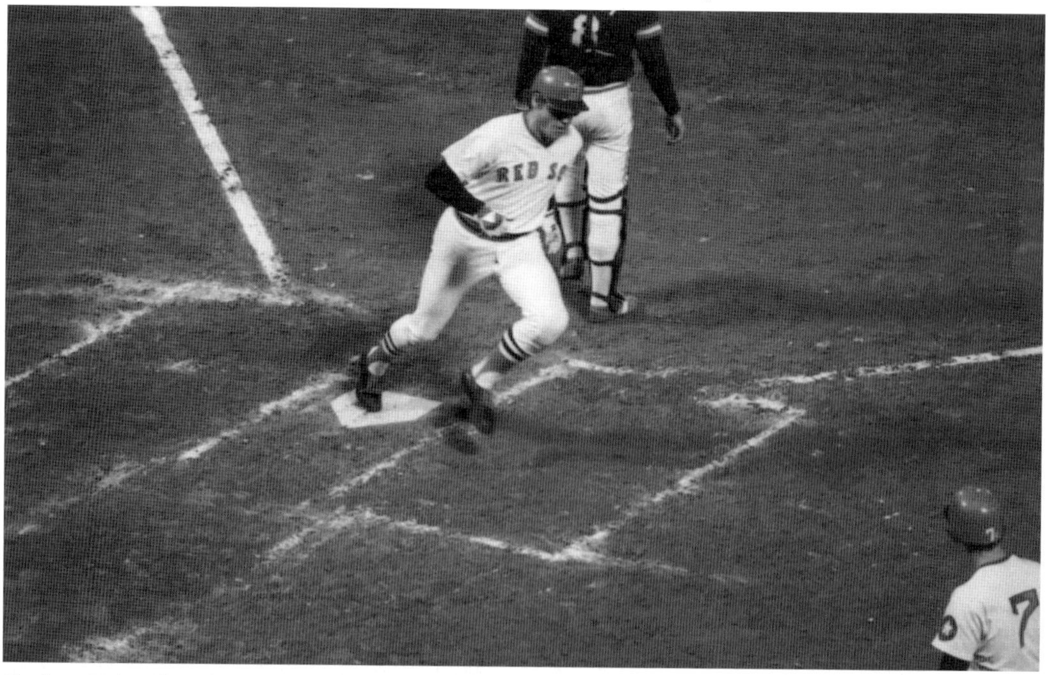

Carlton Fisk, who was the designated hitter in the nightcap of the doubleheader, crosses home with the Red Sox's first run on a sacrifice fly by catcher Bob Montgomery. It was the only run Reggie Cleveland would need on this raw, foggy September night. The fog was so thick that during the radio broadcast, Ned Martin uttered, "I've just lost downtown Boston."

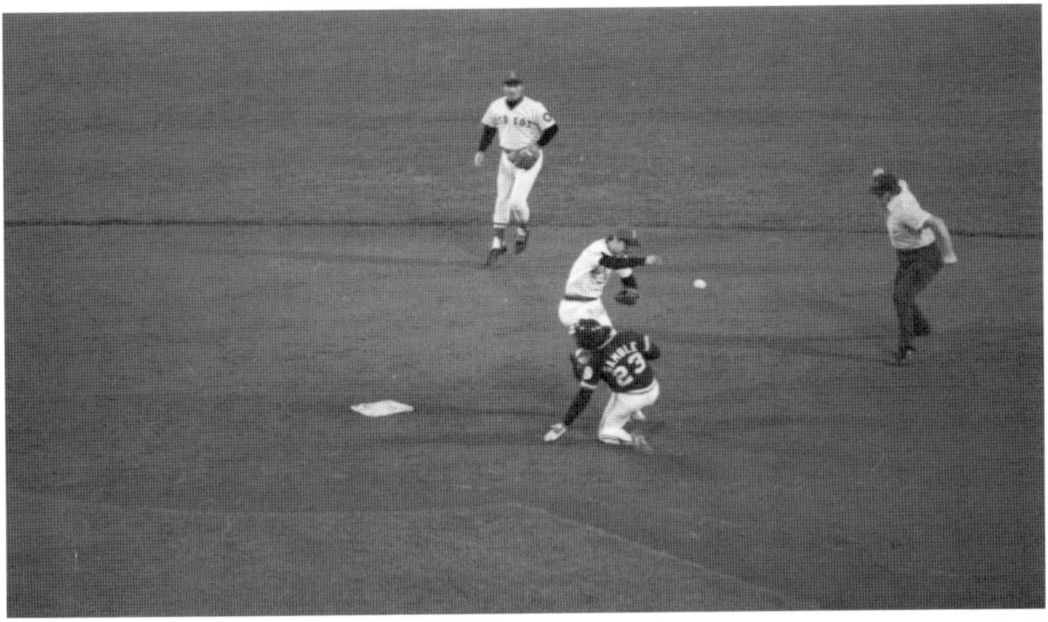

After Oscar Gamble (23) led off the fifth inning with a walk, Cleveland induced George Hendrick to fly out to right, bringing up Buddy Bell. Bell hit a one-hopper back to Cleveland, who fired to Burleson at short, forcing Gamble at second. The Rooster completed the double play with a bullet to first.

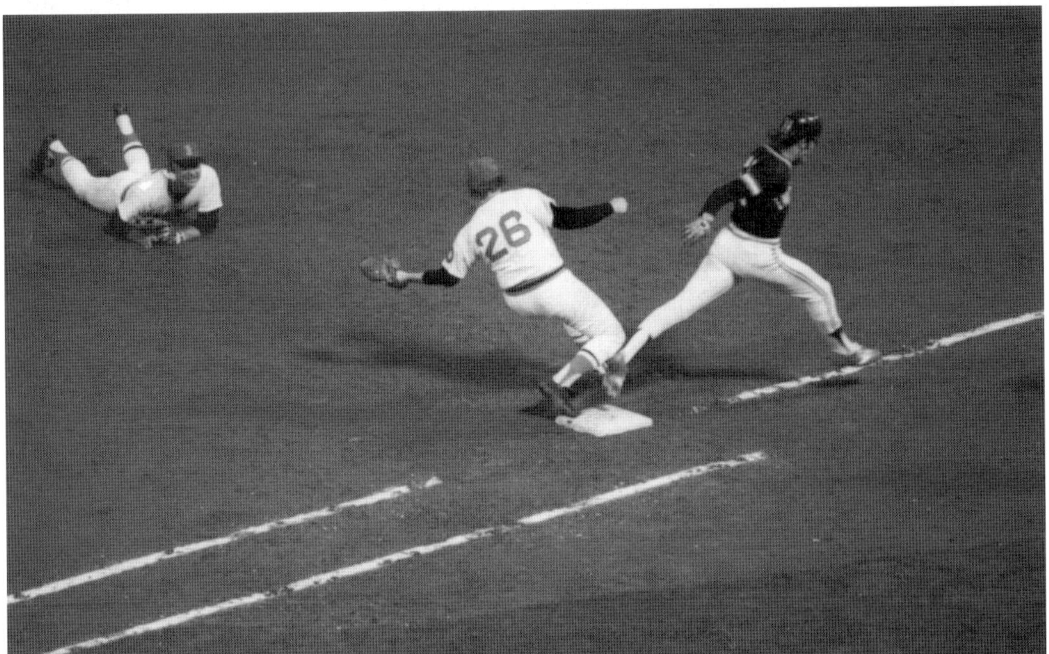

Indians shortstop Frank Duffy beat Reggie Cleveland to the bag for an infield hit with one out in the top of the sixth. Duffy hit a shot to Red Sox first baseman Deron Johnson (prone) and just beat Johnson's throw.

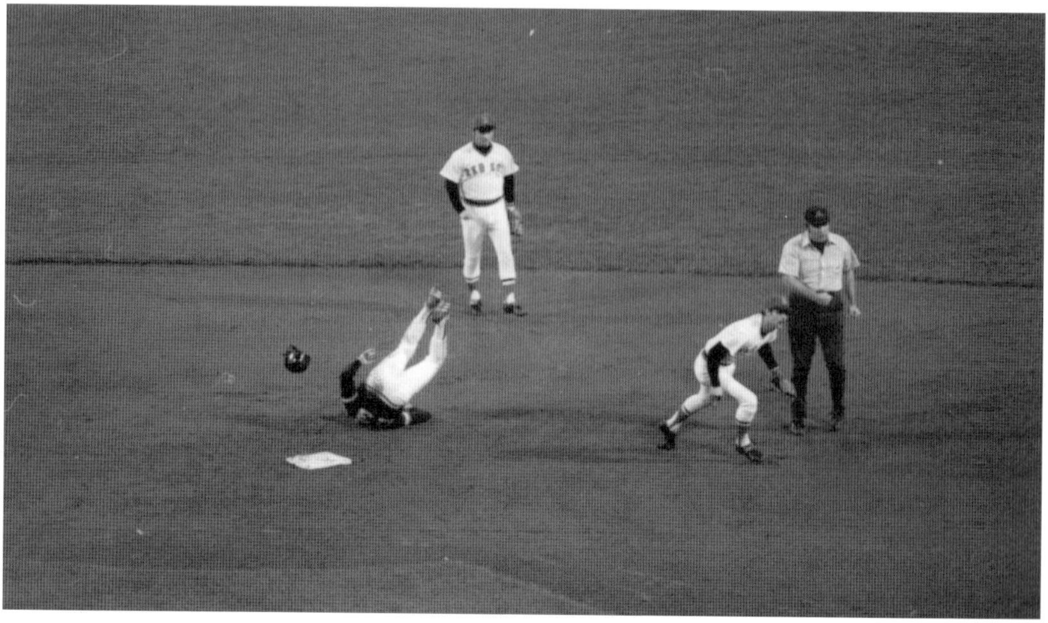

Following a pop out to short by John Lowenstein, Duffy attempted to steal second to put the tying run in scoring position. Duffy was upended by the tag of Rick Burleson (right), which ended the inning. Backing up the play is second baseman Denny Doyle and umpire Larry Barnett.

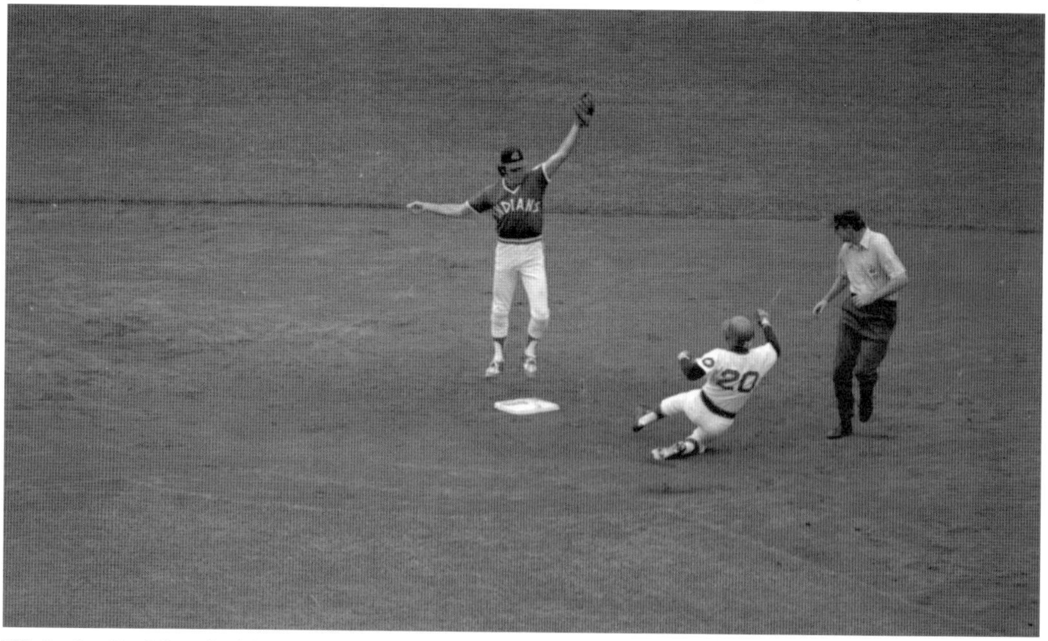

With the Red Sox holding a 1-0 lead in the bottom of the seventh, Denny Doyle doubled with one out. This brought up Juan Beníquez (20), who hit one to the gap in right-center field, scoring Doyle. Right fielder George Hendrick gunned the ball to Frank Duffy at short, trying to cut down Beníquez. Beníquez would score when Dwight Evans followed with a two-run homer, accounting for the final score of 4-0.

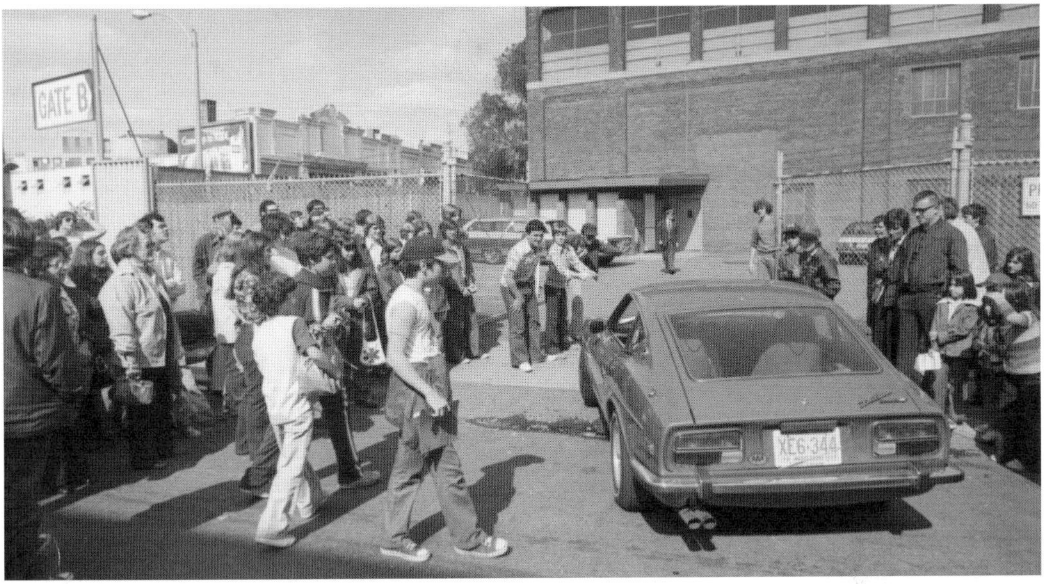

Saturday dawned warm and sunny, and members of the Fenway Faithful took advantage of the beautiful weather, gathering outside the players' parking area to welcome them to the park. This day could bring them the American League East crown. Baltimore was scheduled to play a doubleheader in New York, and if they split and the Sox won, the race would be over. Friday's high temperature was 46 degrees; it would reach 81 on this September Saturday.

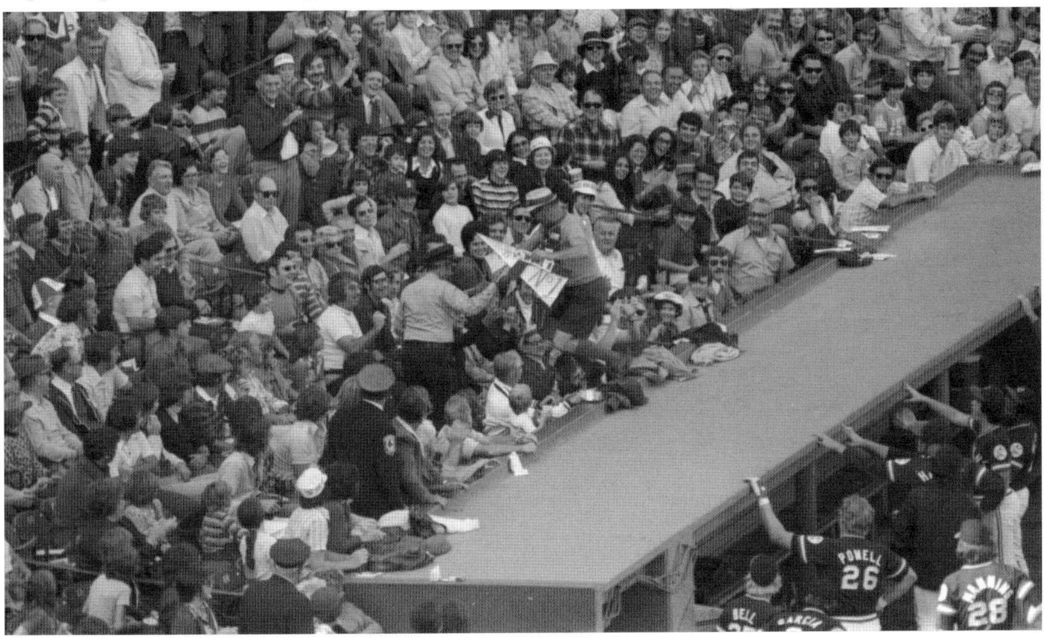

There was a festive mood in the park as the Fenway Faithful reveled in the in the joy of returning to what was now called postseason play. Here, one of Boston's finest assists an overzealous fan who was dancing on the Cleveland dugout, as the inevitability of claiming the American League East title drew near. It was made official when all had gone home, and the Yankees lost to Baltimore.

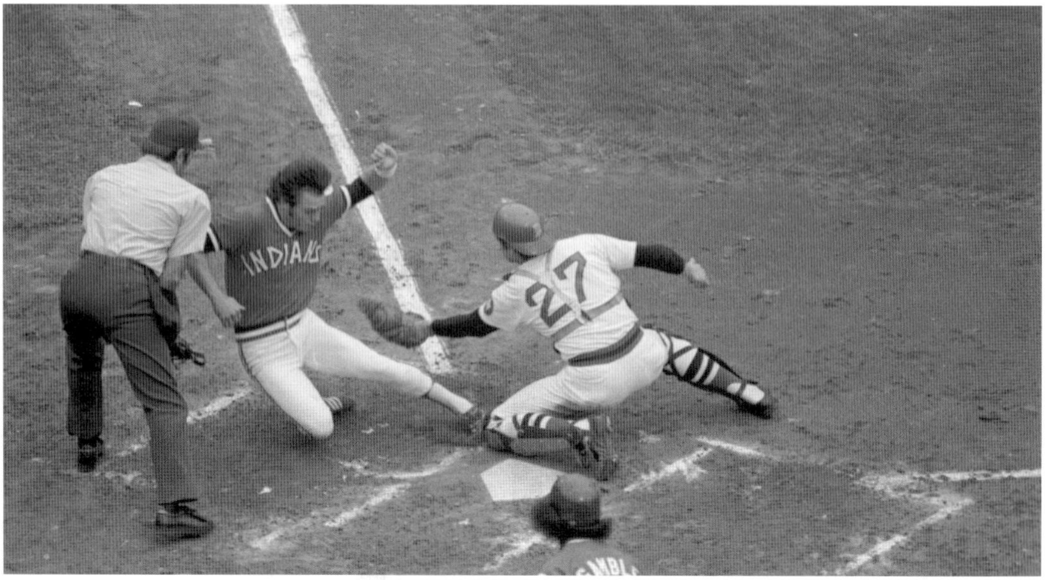

Rick Wise was on the mound for the Sox, and he fell behind 1-0 as a result of his own throwing error in the second inning. In the third inning, Rick Manning reached on a bunt single with one out, which brought John "Boog" Powell to the plate. Powell hit a double off the left field wall and the fleet-footed Manning scored all the way from first. In these two photographs, Manning avoids Fisk's tag while umpire Don Denkinger and on-deck hitter Oscar Gamble look on. Below, Manning tumbles backward in front of Rick Wise (40) and Gamble (23) as Denkinger calls him safe. Wise had gone behind the plate to back up the play.

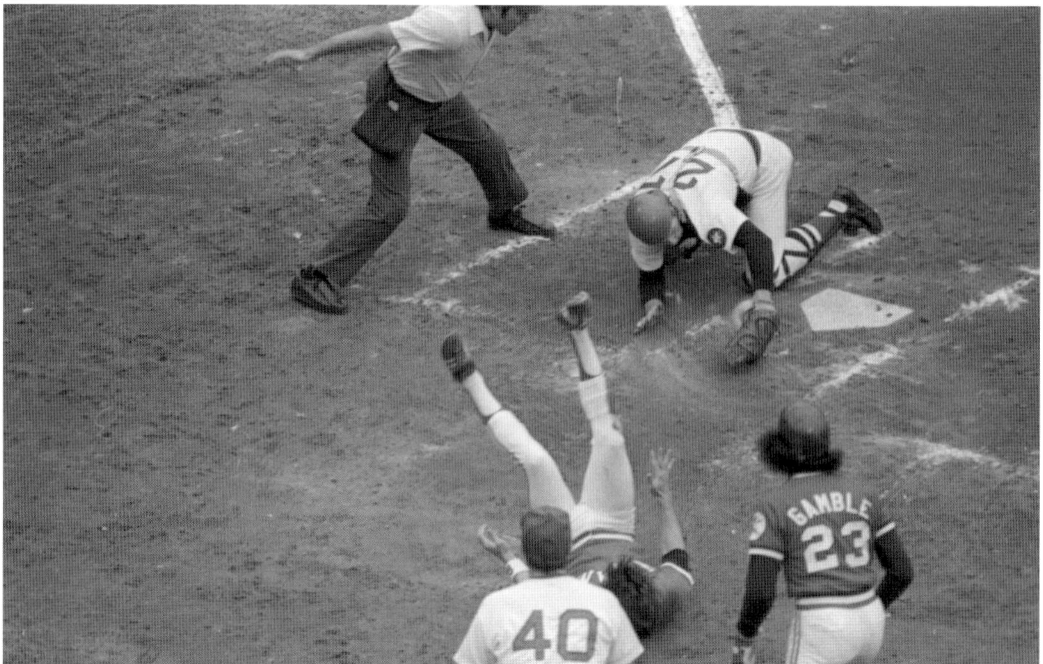

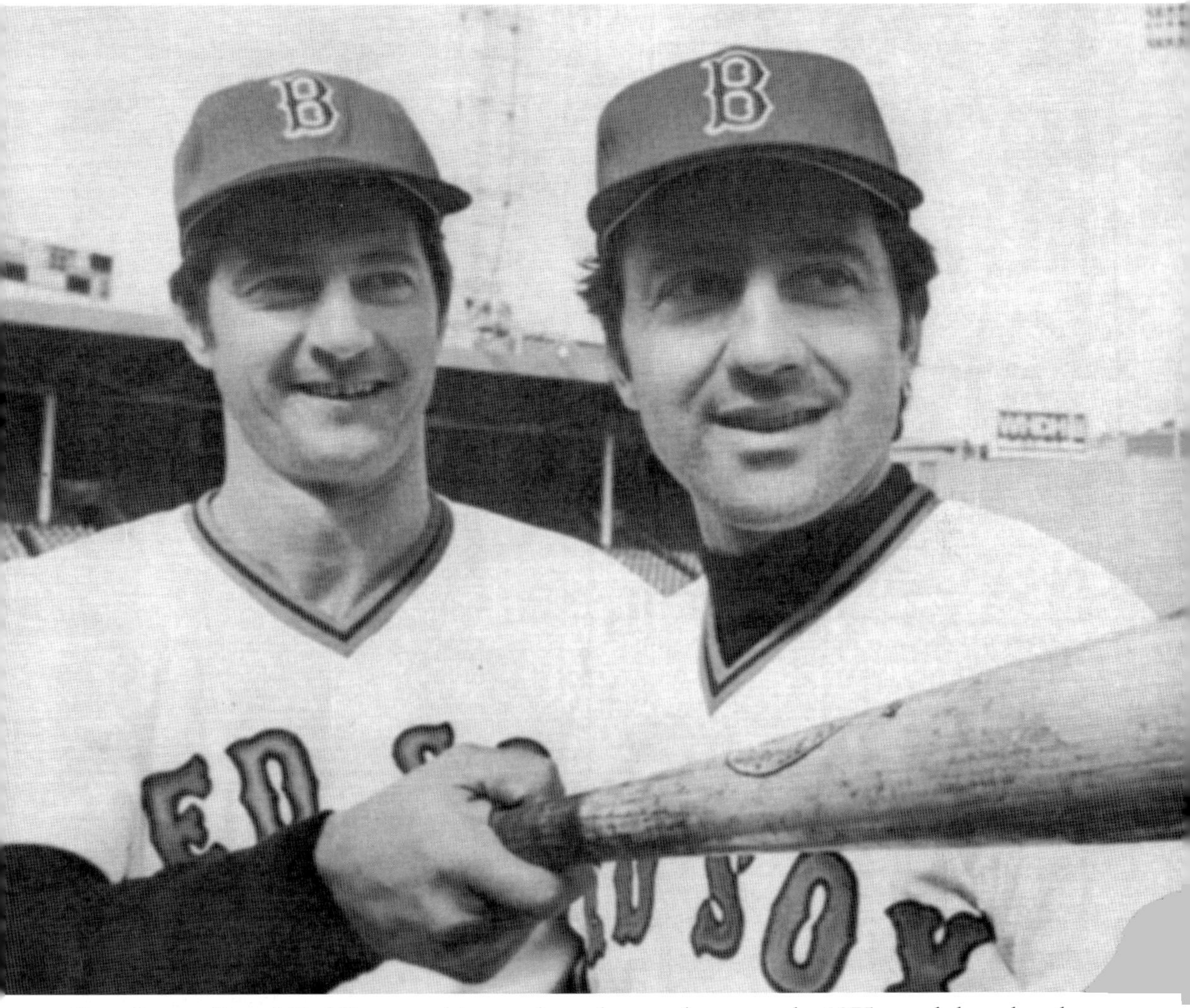

Rico Petrocelli and Carl Yastrzemski were the only two players on the 1975 squad that played on the 1967 Impossible Dream team. Petrocelli battled inner-ear problems throughout the season and retired following the 1975 campaign. An all-time Red Sox favorite, he was inducted into the Red Sox Hall of Fame in 1997. New England rekindled their love affair with Yaz in the 1975 postseason. His performance in the 1975 postseason invoked memories of 1967 in the hearts of the Fenway Faithful. He rose to iconic status in 1978 when he registered his 3,000th hit. Yaz retired in 1983 and was inducted into Cooperstown five years later. His number, 8, was the fourth Red Sox number to be retired, in 1989.

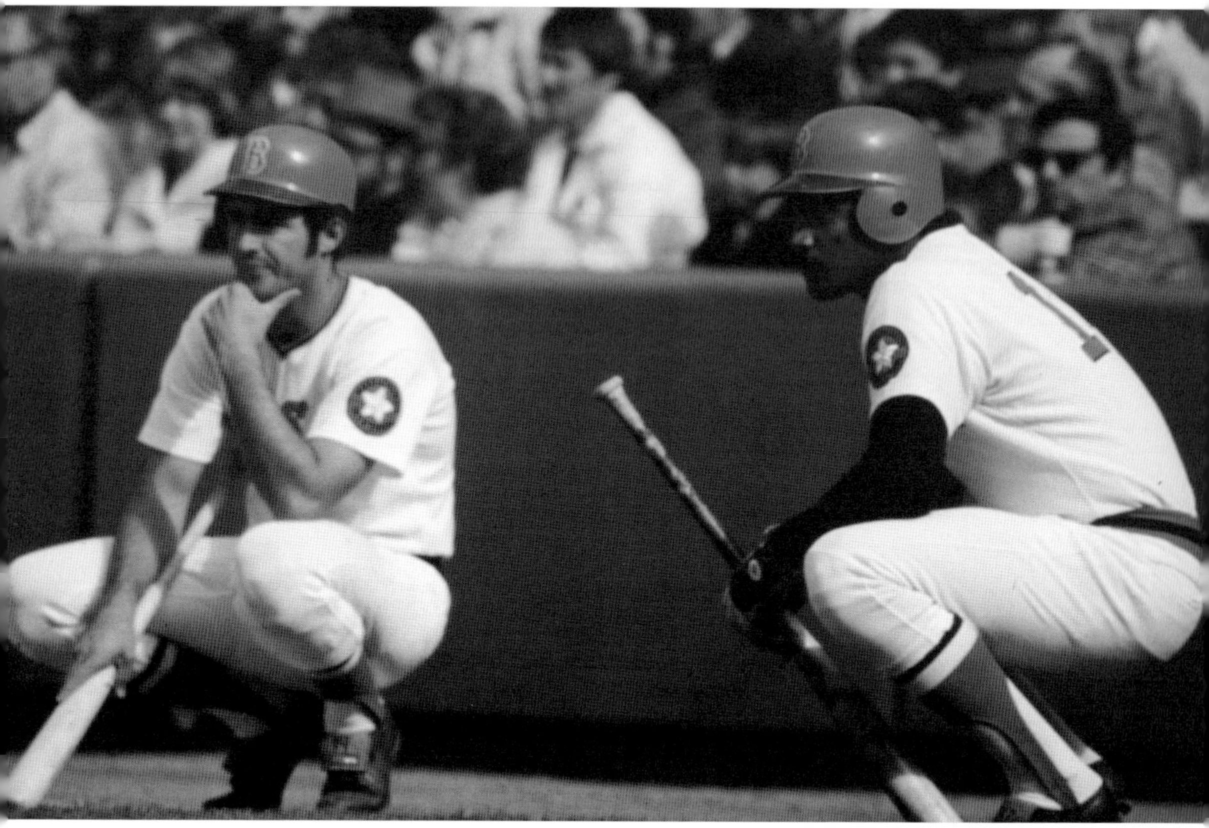

Fred Lynn (left) and Jim Rice arrived upon the scene within days of each other at the end of the 1974 season. Within weeks of the onset of the 1975 season, they were the engines pulling the Red Sox train. They took the city and the American League by storm. Lynn hit .331 with 21 homers and 105 RBI and became the first player in major-league history to garner MVP and Rookie of the Year Awards in the same season. Jim Rice hit .309 with 22 homers and 102 RBI. The Gold Dust Twins were and remain the greatest pair of rookie teammates in baseball history. Lynn was the MVP while Rice finished third in the voting. Both are members of the Red Sox Hall of Fame, and Jim Rice joined 1975 teammates Yaz and Fisk in Cooperstown in 2010. (Courtesy of the Boston Red Sox.)

3

Toppling the A's and Restoring the Game

The Red Sox upset the Oakland A's in the American League Division Series, dethroning the three-time defending World Champions. Cincinnati, on the other hand, struggled a bit in April but from the first of May went 96-43, playing nearly .700 baseball. They moved into first place in the National League West on June 7 and never looked back. They clinched the National League West on September 7 and finished the year 20 games up on the second-place Dodgers. They then rolled through the Pirates in three straight, and Vegas gamblers and just about everyone else expected them to roll through the Red Sox as well.

Everyone, that is, except the Red Sox themselves.

Baseball was limping. It was still attempting to come back from the strike of 1972, while the NFL was growing exponentially in popularity among the American sporting public. There were many who felt that baseball had been deposed by football as America's pastime. The television ratings supported the claim, as the top-five most-watched sporting events in history were Super Bowls.

What transpired between the Red Sox and Reds was a World Series for the ages: beginning with a Red Sox shutout by Luis Tiant in Game 1 and ending with Joe Morgan's bloop single in the ninth inning of Game 7, which made Cincinnati champions. In between came a ninth-inning comeback win by the Reds; a ninth-inning tie by Boston, which eventually was won by the Reds; a 169-pitch game win by Tiant; and what Major League Baseball itself calls the "Greatest Game Ever Played."

That Greatest Game Ever Played (Game 6) was watched by more people than any other baseball game in history. The following night, Game 7 became the most-watched sporting event in the history of American television.

Baseball was back!

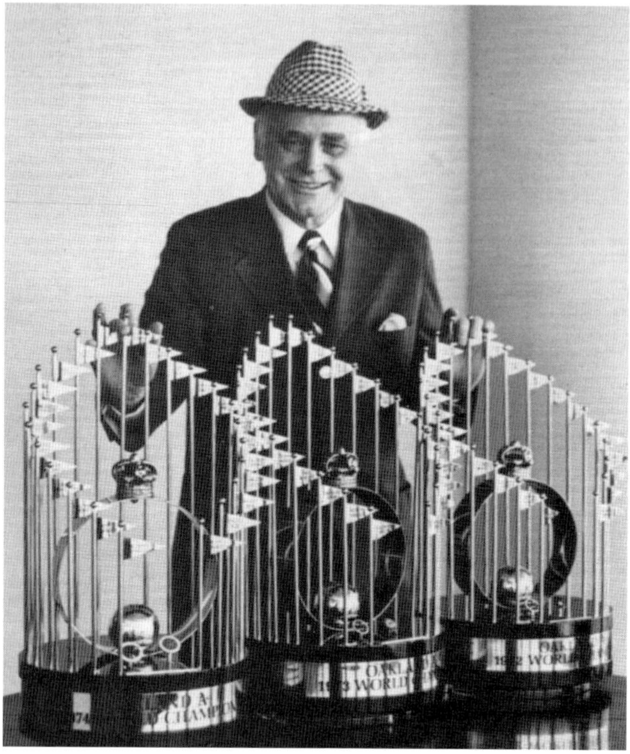

Vegas odds maker "Jimmy the Greek" instilled the Oakland A's a 6-5 favorite to win its fourth straight World Championship. Here, Oakland owner Charlie Finley poses with his team's three trophies, signifying their baseball supremacy. Oakland is the only other team in baseball history, besides the Yankees, to captured three straight World Series.

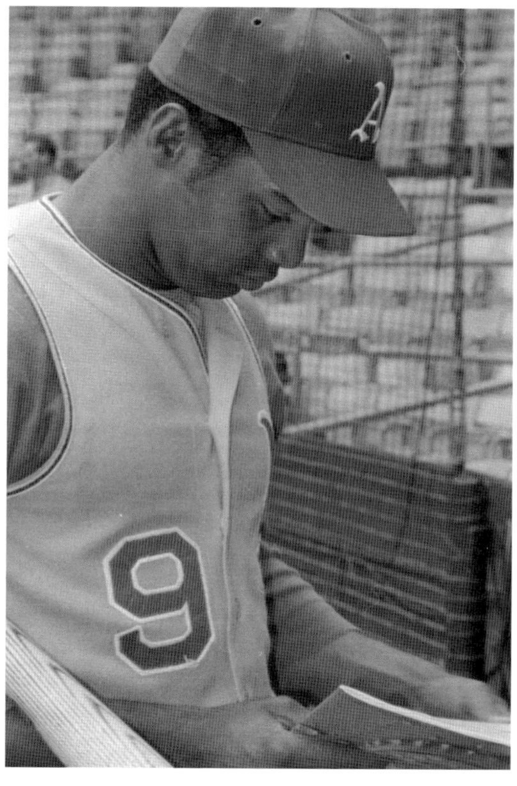

Reggie Jackson was the straw that stirred the Oakland drink. Although he was not yet know as "Mr. October," he was the MVP of the 1973 World Series when he hit .310 with a homer and six RBI. He came into Fenway the 1975 American League home run champ, having hit 36 bombs and knocking in 104 runs. Here, he signs an autograph for a member of the Fenway Faithful before the first game of the playoffs.

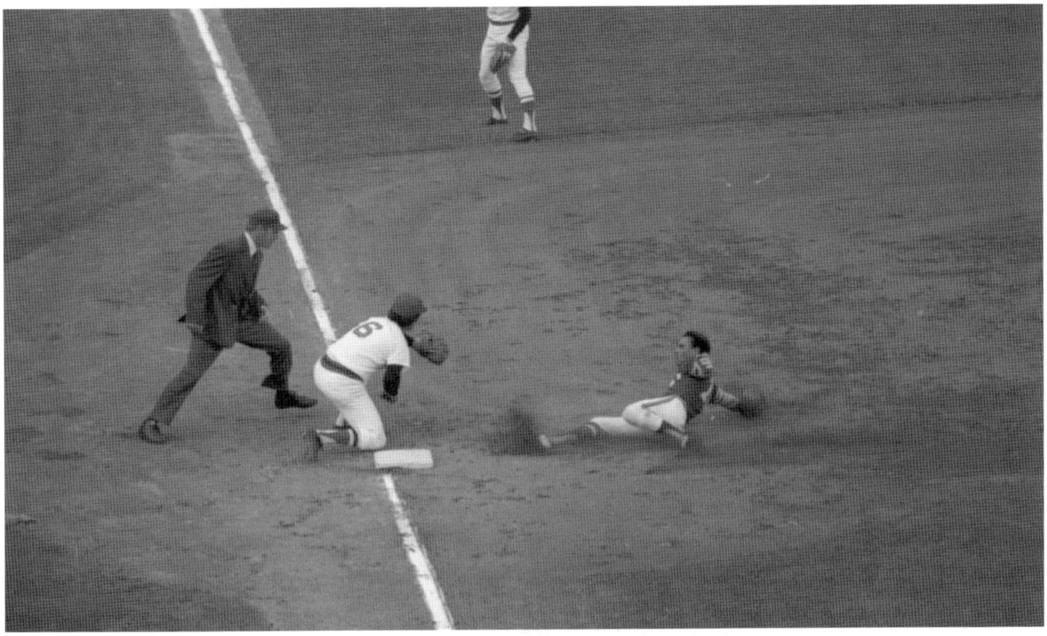

The only Oakland run came across when the A's shortstop Bert "Campy" Campanaris scored on an error by Cecil Cooper in the eighth inning. Campy, seen here sliding safely into third on a double by Jim Holt, had reached on an error by Rick Burleson leading off the inning. Burleson went into the dugout and apologized to Luis Tiant for "blowing his shutout." "Don't worry about it," came the reply. "We're going to win the game and that's all that matters."

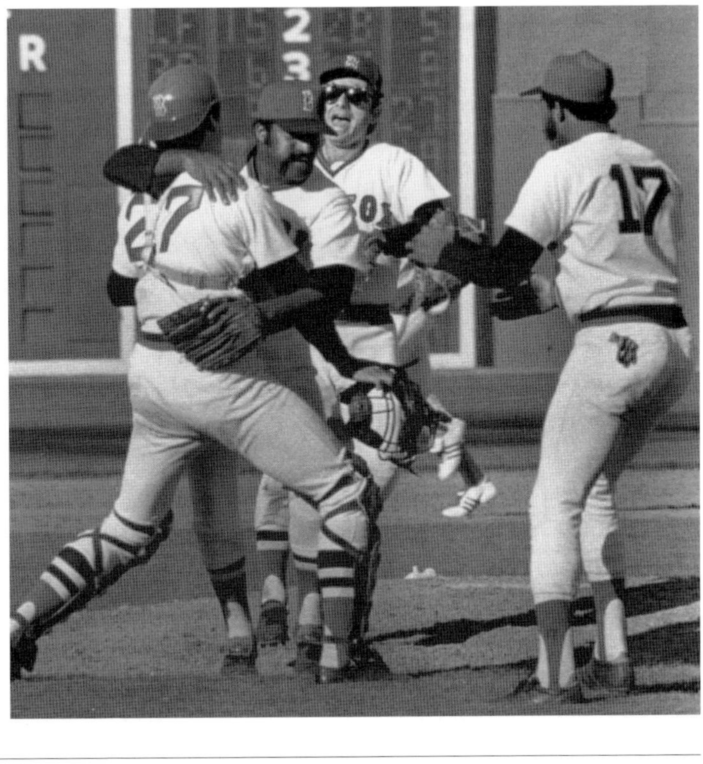

Carlton Fisk (27) and Luis Tiant embrace after their Game 1 win against the A's as first baseman Cecil Cooper (17) and Denny Doyle are about to join in the celebration. Oakland stumbled in this game, as the Sox scored two runs in the first of three Oakland errors. It was all Tiant would need as he shut the defending World Champions down on three hits in the 7-1 win.

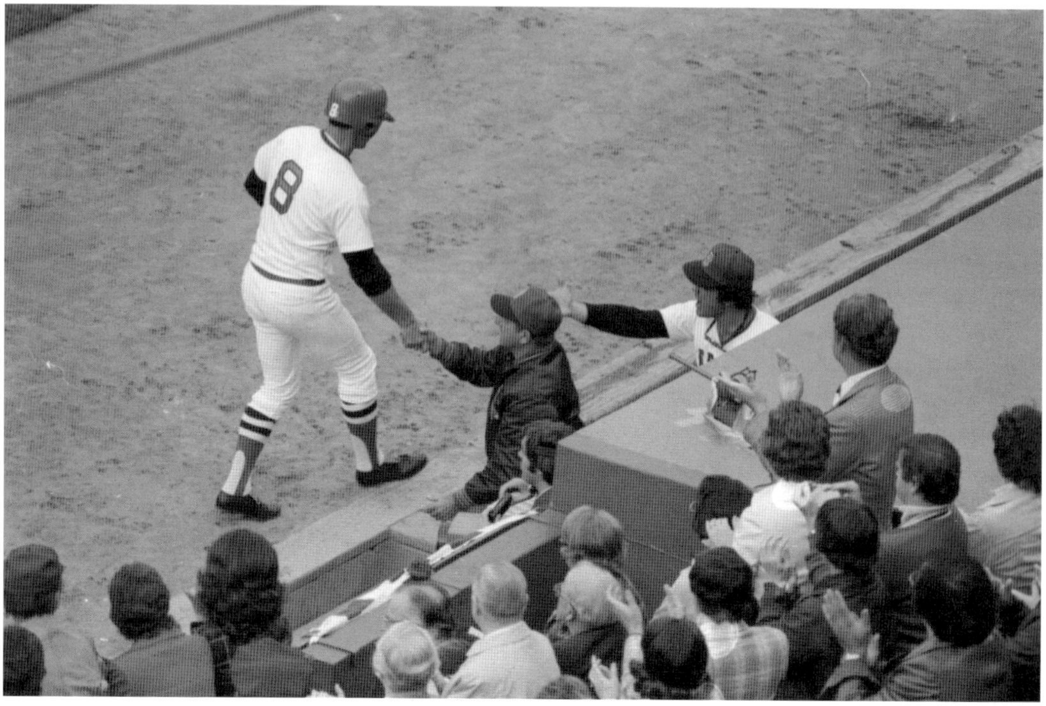

Reggie Jackson's two-run homer in the first inning staked the A's to a 2-0 lead in the second game. Oakland added another run in the top of the fourth; however, Carl Yastrzemski got two of them back with a two-run homer in the bottom of the fourth, making it 3-2. He is welcomed back to the dugout by manager Darrell Johnson (left) and Dwight Evans (right).

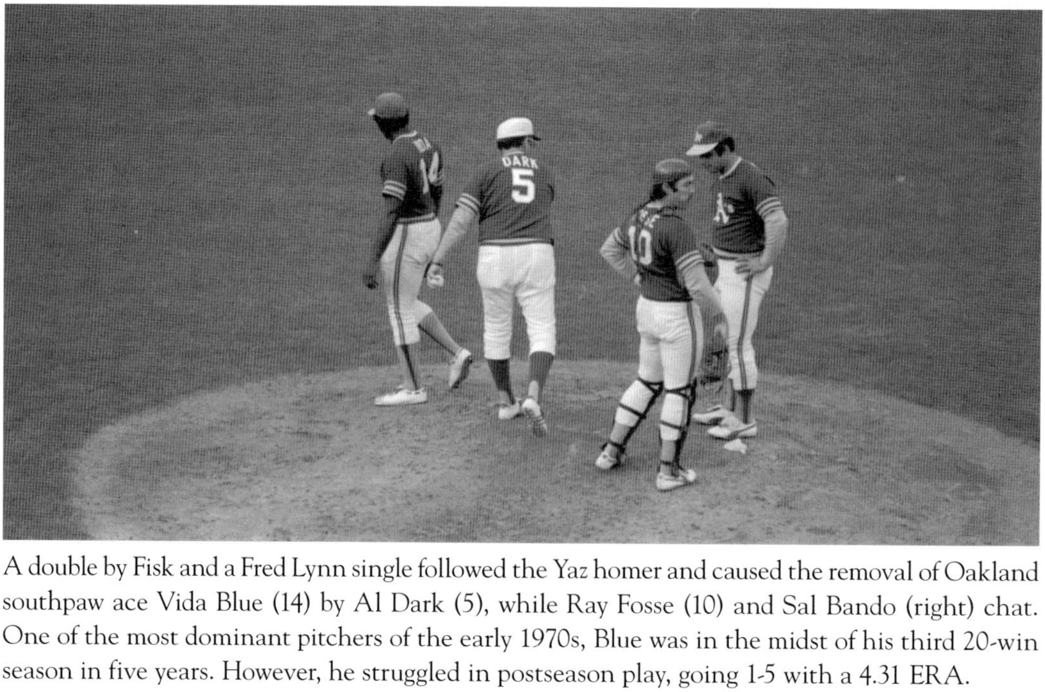

A double by Fisk and a Fred Lynn single followed the Yaz homer and caused the removal of Oakland southpaw ace Vida Blue (14) by Al Dark (5), while Ray Fosse (10) and Sal Bando (right) chat. One of the most dominant pitchers of the early 1970s, Blue was in the midst of his third 20-win season in five years. However, he struggled in postseason play, going 1-5 with a 4.31 ERA.

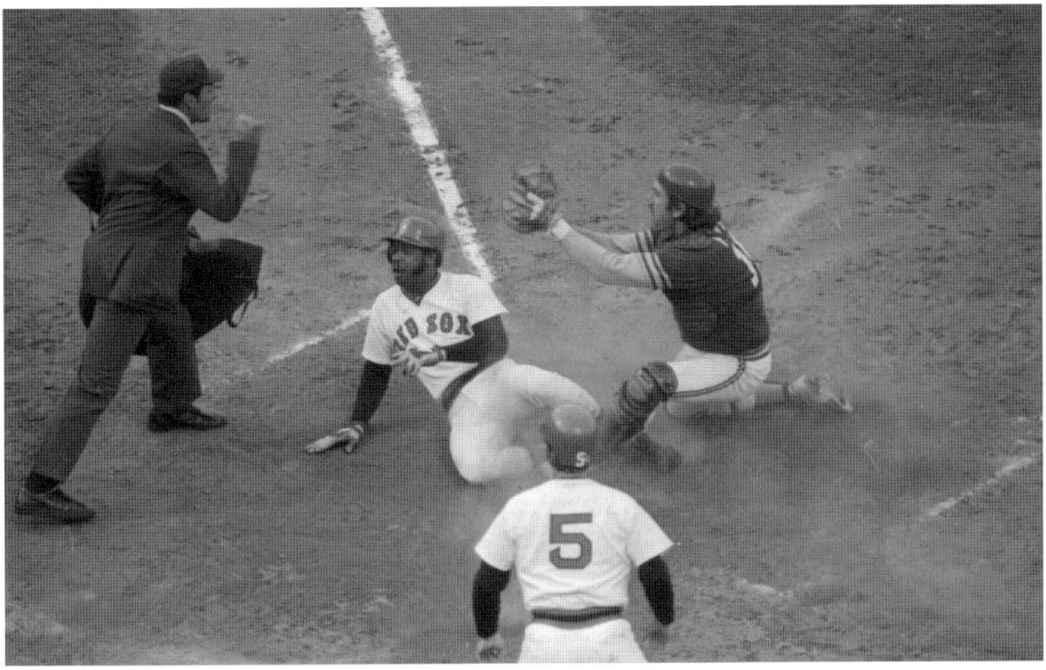

With the score tied in the fifth, Cecil Cooper led off with a double and was sacrificed to third by Rick Burleson. Juan Beníquez followed with a fly ball to right field. Reggie Jackson made the catch and then threw Cooper out at the plate. Ray Fosse (10) makes the catch and the tag, keeping the sliding Cooper off the plate. Home plate umpire Lou DiMuro makes the call.

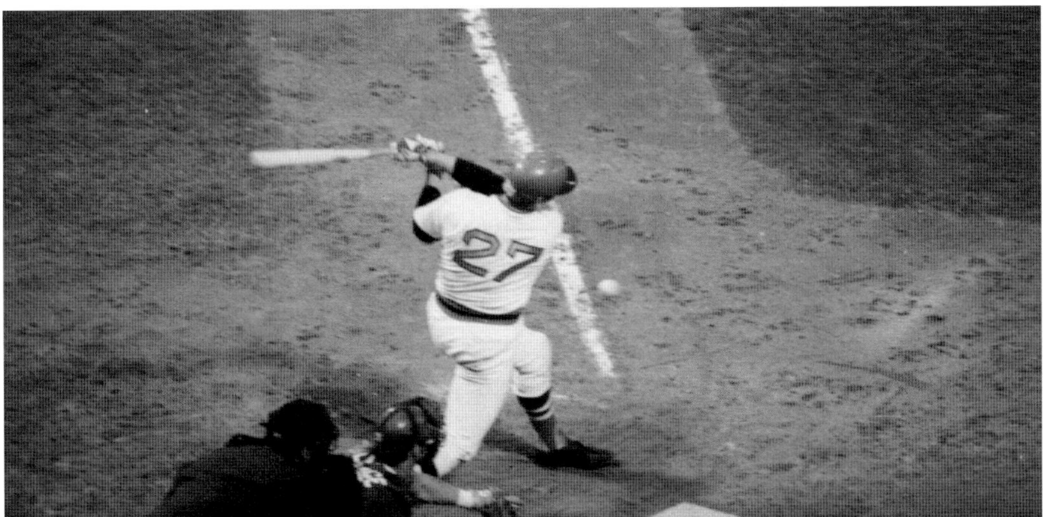

In the sixth inning, the Red Sox took the lead for keeps when, with one out, Carl Yastrzemski doubled, and Carlton Fisk singled him home. Fisk joined the team in June after recuperating from knee surgery and a broken arm. He proved a valuable offensive addition, hitting .412 with runners in scoring position and .375 with two outs and runners in scoring position. He hit his stride in September, hitting .371.

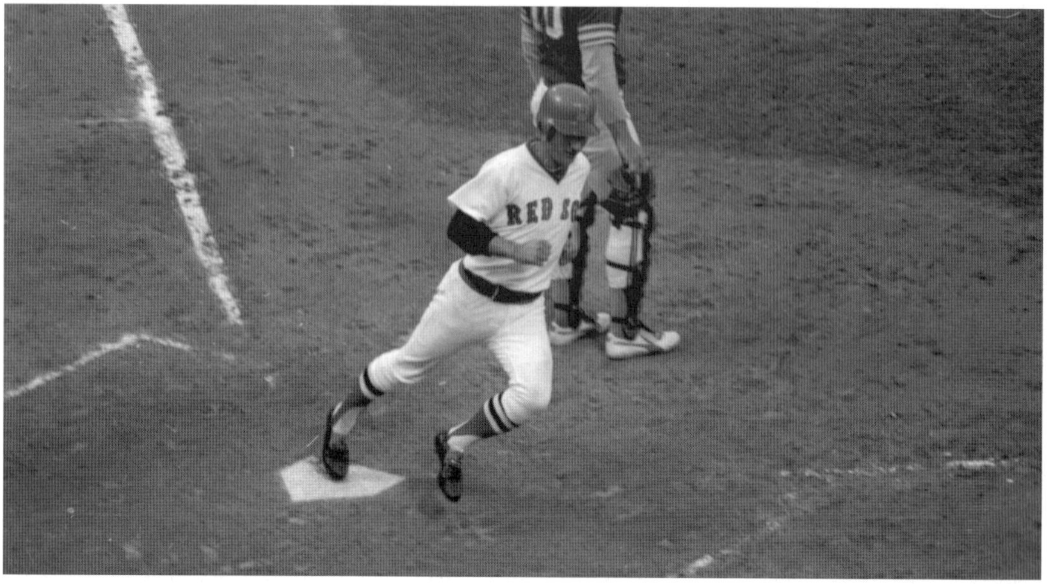

Yastrzemski crosses home with what proved to be the winning run. Yaz had suffered a partially separated shoulder in July, which hampered his swing. He struggled through August and September, hitting only .223. Rejuvenated by the postseason, he hit .455 in the American League Championship Series and .310 in the World Series, while adding two outfield assists in the American League Division Series after playing left field only five times throughout the year.

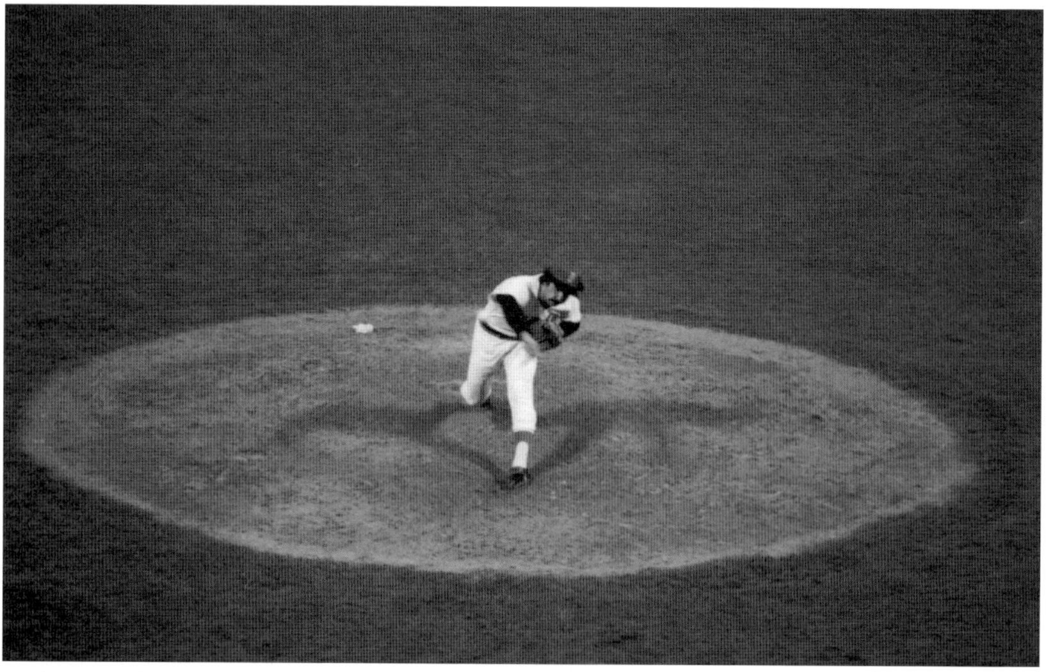

Red Sox relief pitcher Dick Drago throws the final pitch of the second playoff game to Caesar Tovar, who grounded into a force play to end the game. Drago earned a three-inning save, facing 10 batters and surrendering two hits and no runs while striking out two and walking no one.

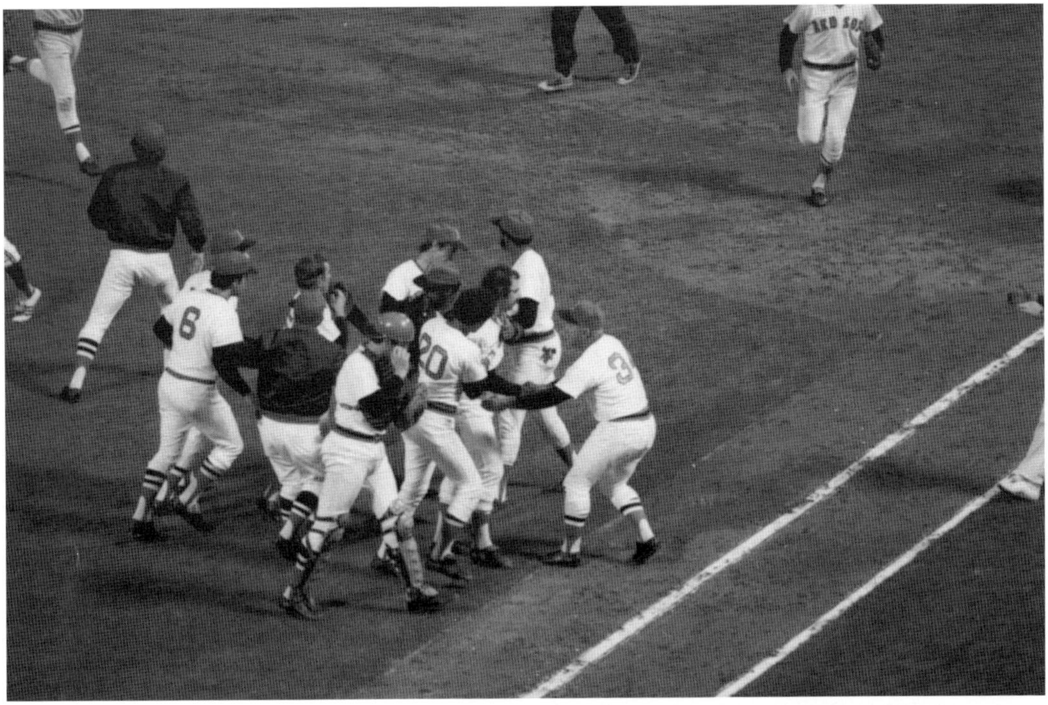

The Red Sox mob Drago after he recorded the final out, bringing the Red Sox to within one win of the 1975 pennant. Drago is hatless between Juan Beníquez (20) and Cecil Cooper to his left. Carlton Fisk is in gear on the left, and Don Zimmer (34) is extending his hand to the pitcher. Rick Burleson is facing Cooper, and Rico Petrocelli (6) is making his way around the pack.

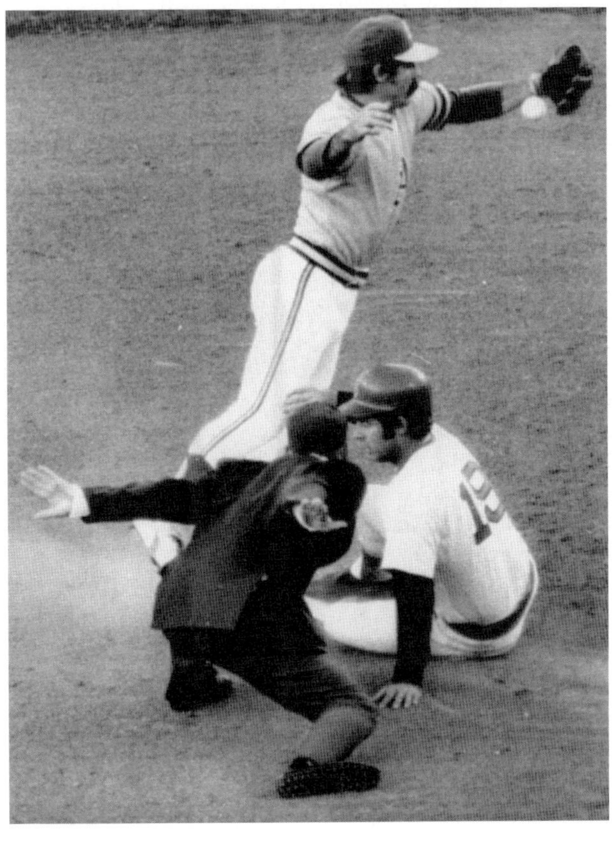

It was on to Oakland, with the Red Sox needing only one win to clinch the pennant. It was the fourth inning when Fred Lynn slid safely into second on an error by left fielder Claudell Washington. Umpire Jim Evans gives an emphatic safe call, and Lynn later scored the first run of the game on a single by Rico Petrocelli.

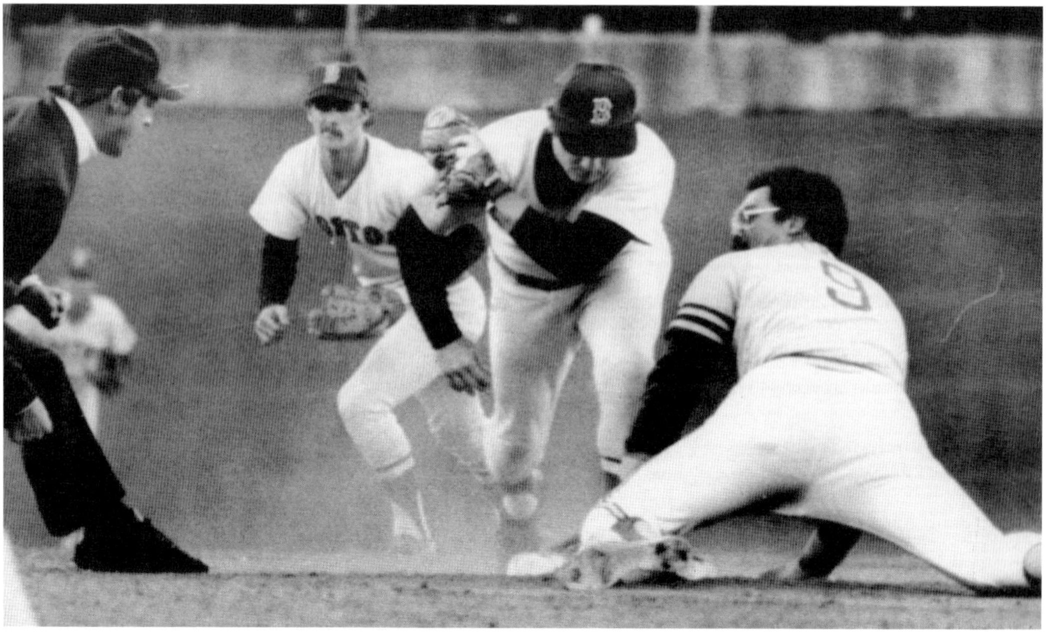

In the bottom of the fourth with two outs, Reggie Jackson singled toward the gap in left-center field. Yastrzemski cut the ball off and fired a laser to Denny Doyle, who applied the tag to end the inning. As Yaz made his way to the dugout, he said to a prone Jackson, "Reggie, you should know better." Jackson and the A's were dead, and it was on to the fall classic for the Red Sox.

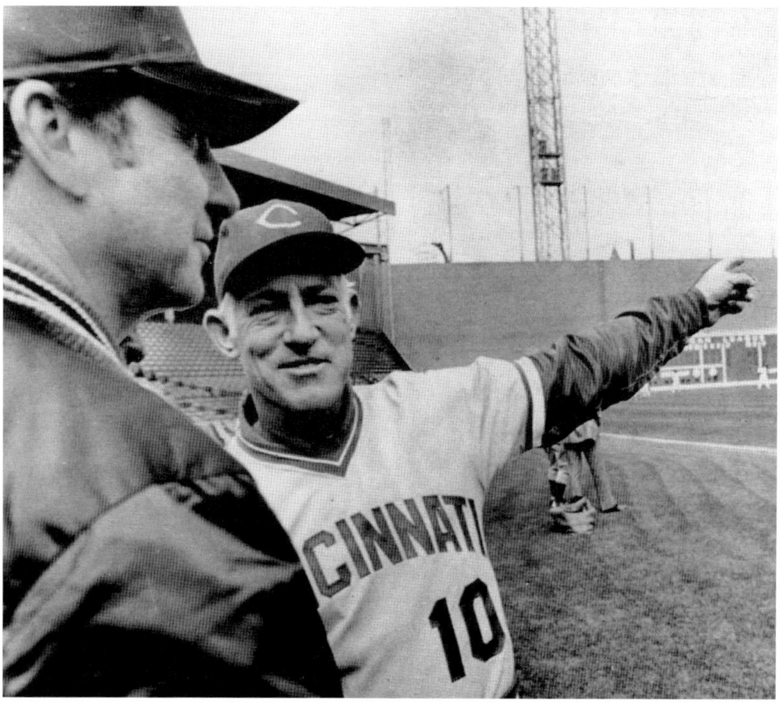

The World Series brought Cincinnati's Big Red Machine to Fenway Park. The Reds had won 108 games and were heavily favored to win the series over the Red Sox, who had won 95 games. Red Sox manager Darrell Johnson (left) shows his Reds counterpart George "Sparky" Anderson around Fenway Park before the start of the first game.

The 1975 Red Sox captured the hearts of New England. Entering first place on June 29 with a win against Catfish Hunter and the Yankees, the Red Sox never trailed again all year. By the end of the World Series, they captured the hearts of baseball fans across the country.

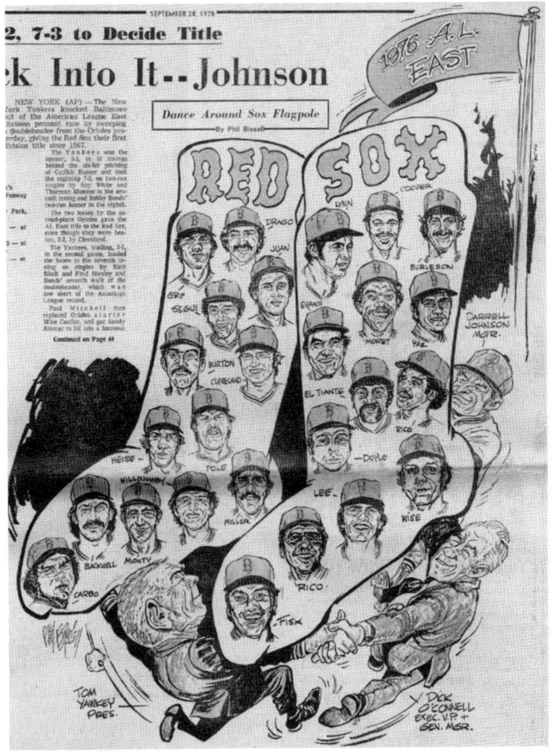
SEPTEMBER 28, 1975

2, 7-3 to Decide Title

k Into It--Johnson

NEW YORK (AP) — The New York Yankees knocked Baltimore out of the American League East Division pennant race by sweeping a doubleheader from the Orioles yesterday, giving the Red Sox their first division title since 1967.

The Yankees won the opener, 3-2, in 10 innings behind the six-hit pitching of Catfish Hunter and took the nightcap 7-3, on two-run singles by Roy White and Thurman Munson in the seventh inning and Bobby Bonds' two-run homer in the eighth.

The two losses by the second-place Orioles gave the AL East title to the Red Sox, even though they were beaten, 5-2, by Cleveland.

The Yankees, trailing, 3-1, in the second game, loaded the bases in the seventh inning on singles by Rick Bladt and Fred Stanley and Bonds' seventh walk of the doubleheader, which was one short of the American League record.

Paul Mitchell then replaced Orioles starter Mike Cuellar, and got Sandy Alomar to hit into a forceout

Continued on Page 44

Dance Around Sox Flagpole

By Phil Bissell

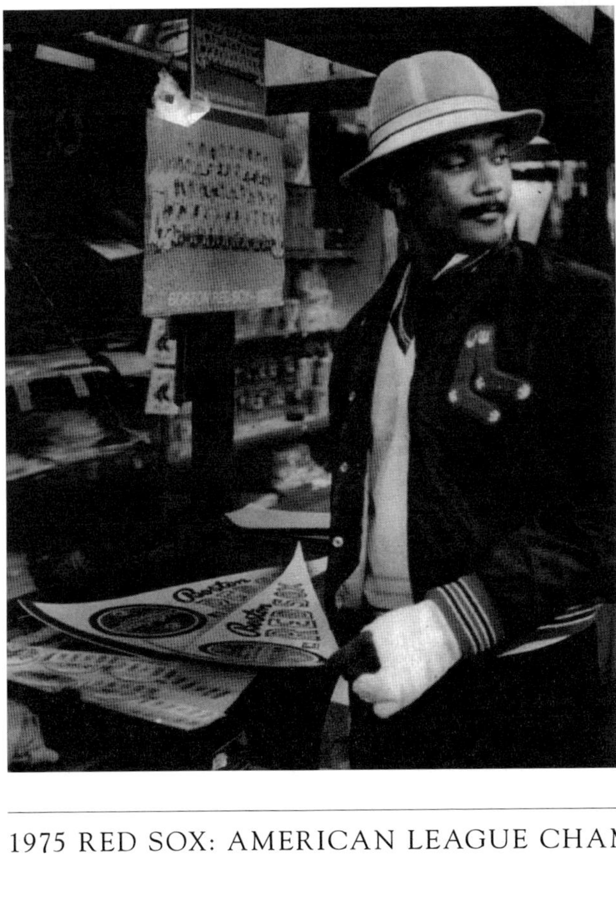

Not in the World Series lineup was Red Sox rookie left fielder Jim Rice. The broken wrist he suffered on September 19 sidelined him for the postseason. Here, he purchases a souvenir pennant at a Fenway Park stand. Fred Lynn asserted 40 years later, "I am convinced if we had Jimmy, we would have won the World Series."

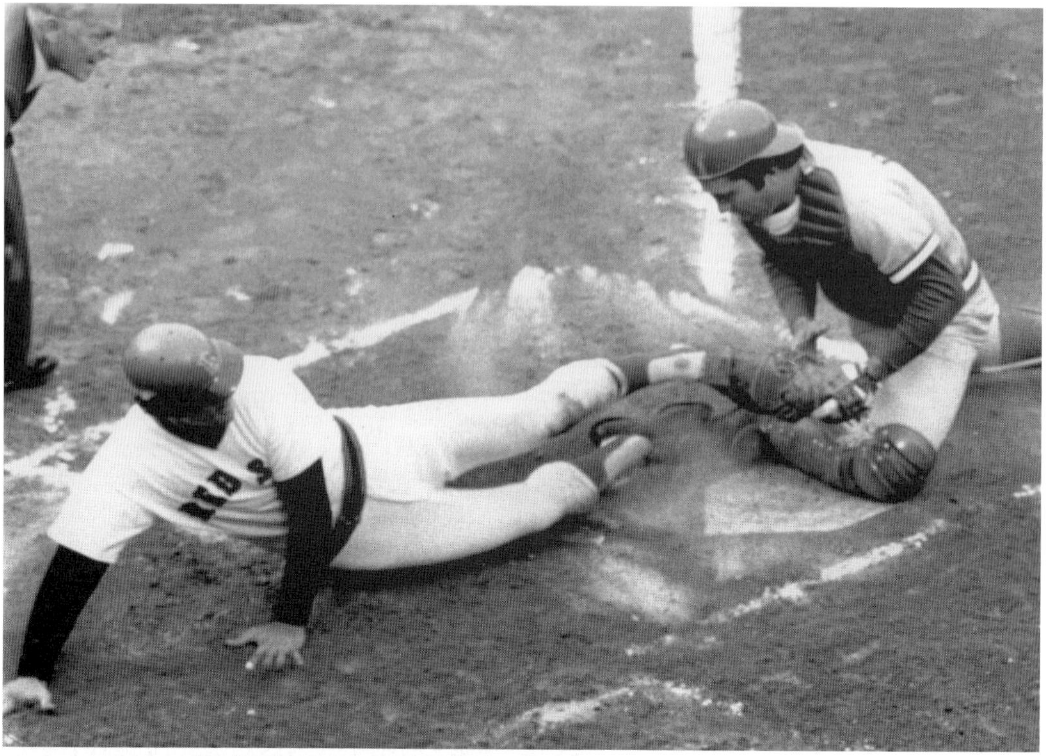

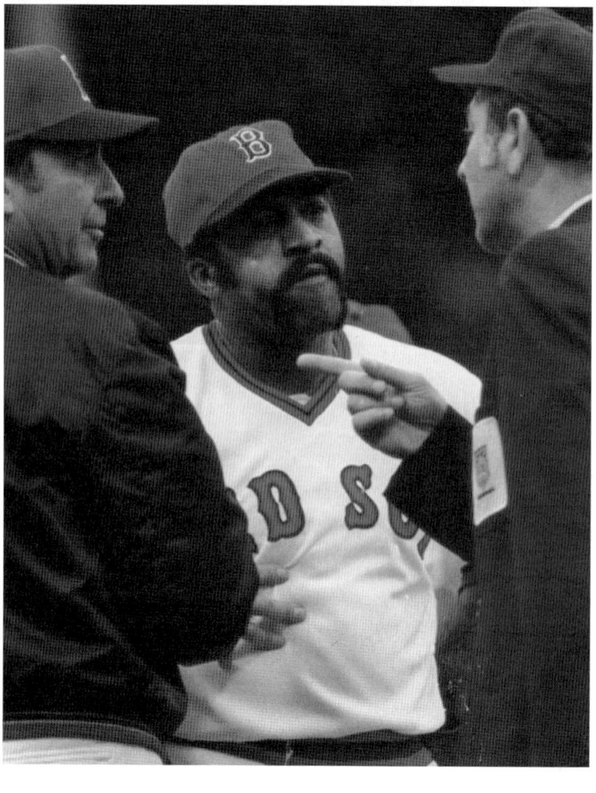

The Red Sox threatened in the first inning, when Dwight Evans led off the game with a single to left. He advanced on a sacrifice by Denny Doyle. When Fred Lynn hit a slow chopper up the middle, Evans, attempting to score, was thrown out by Reds shortstop Dave Concepcion, and tagged by Johnny Bench.

Reds manager Sparky Anderson used a pre-series press conference to put forth the idea that Tiant balked when throwing to first base. After a fourth-inning Joe Morgan single followed by several throws over, umpire Nick Colosi called Tiant for a balk, which brought down a cacophony of boos from the Fenway Faithful, a visit from Darrell Johnson (left), ire from El Tiante, and a futile discussion with Colosi.

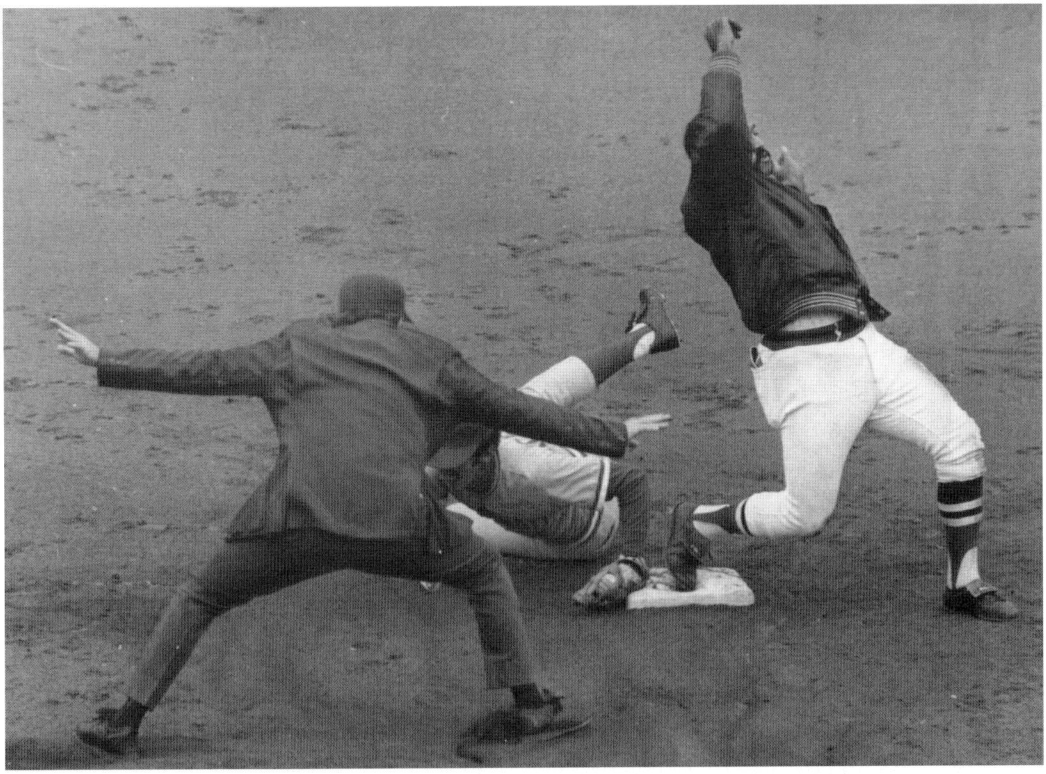

There was never a doubt that Luis Tiant would pitch Game 1 of the World Series, and the Red Sox brass were confident he would meet the challenge on the mound. They got an added unexpected contribution, however, and that came from Tiant's bat. With he and Reds southpaw Don Gullet locked in a scoreless pitcher's duel, Tiant led off the seventh inning with a single. Dwight Evans followed with a bunt, which Gullet fielded and attempted to force Tiant at second. These two shots are different angles of the same play. Luis did not slide and came off the base, and shortstop Dave Concepcion dove attempting, unsuccessfully, to tag him out. He scored the game's first run when Carl Yastrzemski singled to right. It was the only run Tiant would need, as he shut out the Reds 6-0, giving the Red Sox a one-game-to-none advantage in the series.

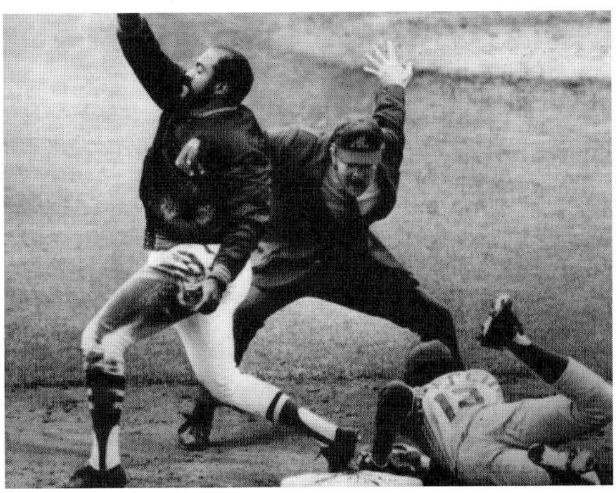

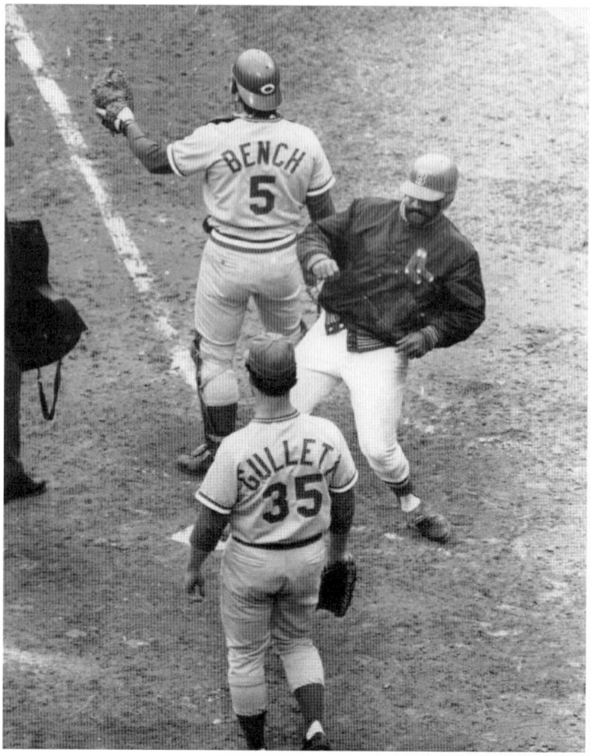

Luis Tiant sneaks back to tag the plate, which he had missed on his first pass, as catcher Johnny Bench (5) directs traffic on the infield and Don Gullet backs up the play. The Red Sox scored five more in the inning; on the very same day that Bill and Hillary Clinton were married and *Saturday Night Live* made its debut, Luis Tiant flipped a shutout in his first World Series start.

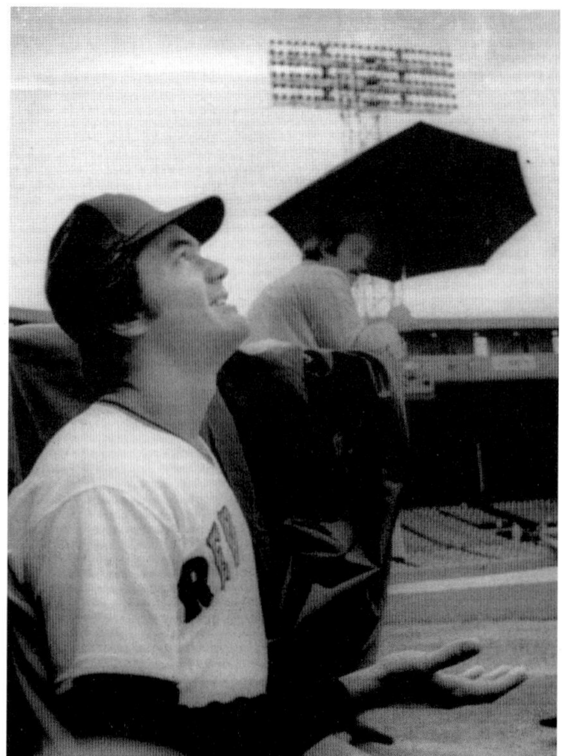

The rains of September returned to Boston and threatened to wash out the second game of the World Series. Here, Red Sox right fielder Dwight Evans checks skyward, pleading for the rain to abate. It did, enough to get the game in, but not before delaying its start.

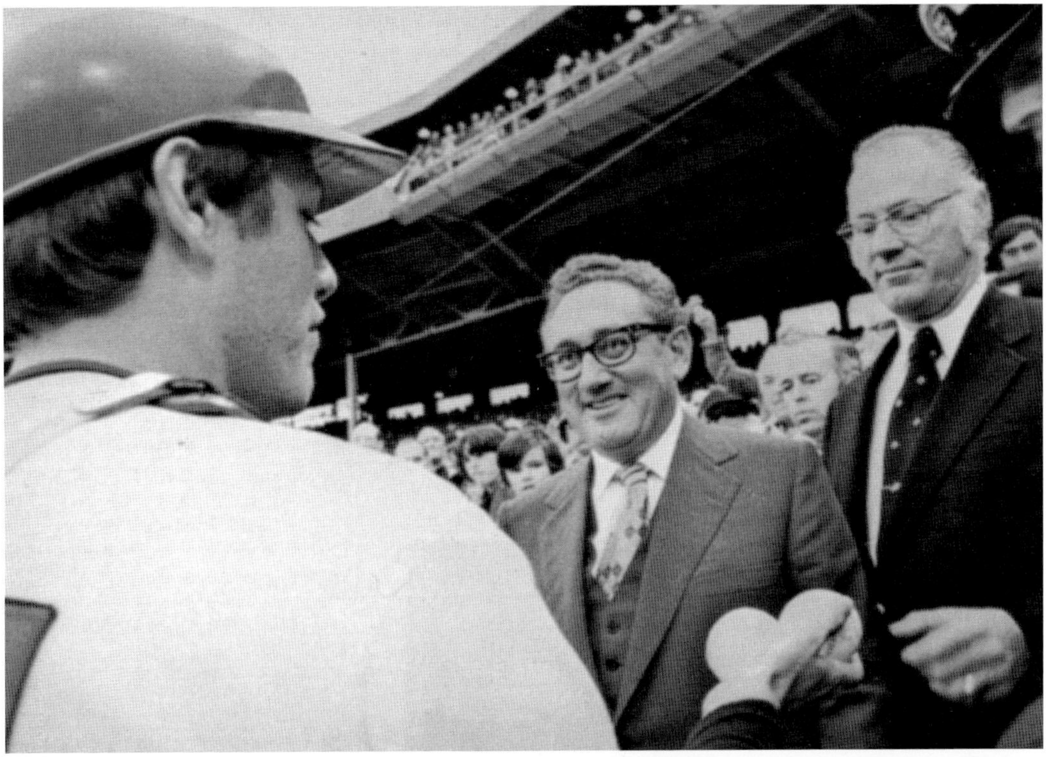

When the rain stopped, the ceremonies intoned the start of the game. In this photograph, Red Sox catcher Carlton Fisk hands baseballs to Secretary of State Henry Kissinger (left) while Major League Baseball commissioner Bowie Kuhn looks on. Kissinger threw out the game's first pitch in pregame ceremonies at Fenway Park.

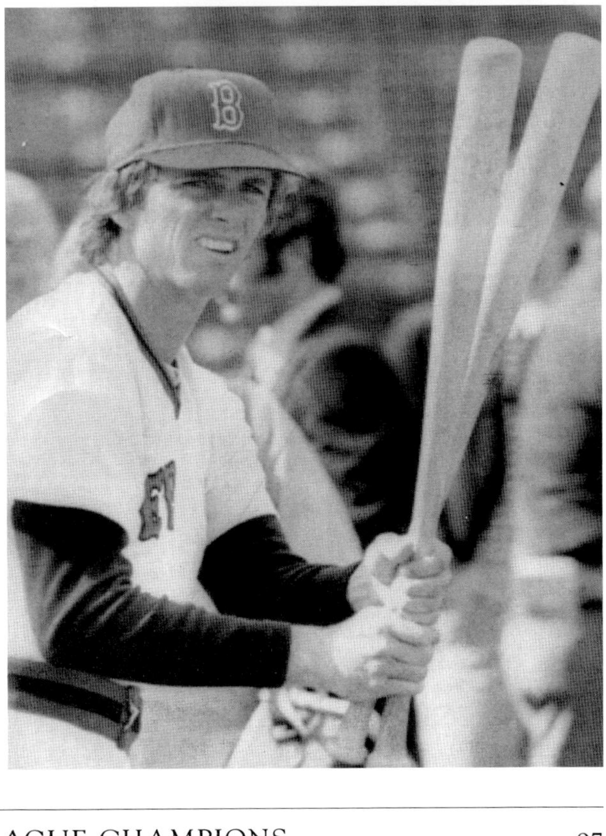

At the urging of third-base coach Don Zimmer, Red Sox manager Darrell Johnson tabbed Bill Lee to start the second game of the series. The zany lefty was not a favorite of either of these old-school former players; however, Zimmer thought Lee's junk-balling style could trouble the Reds. They were correct; Lee gave up only two runs on five hits in eight innings, and he got to hit.

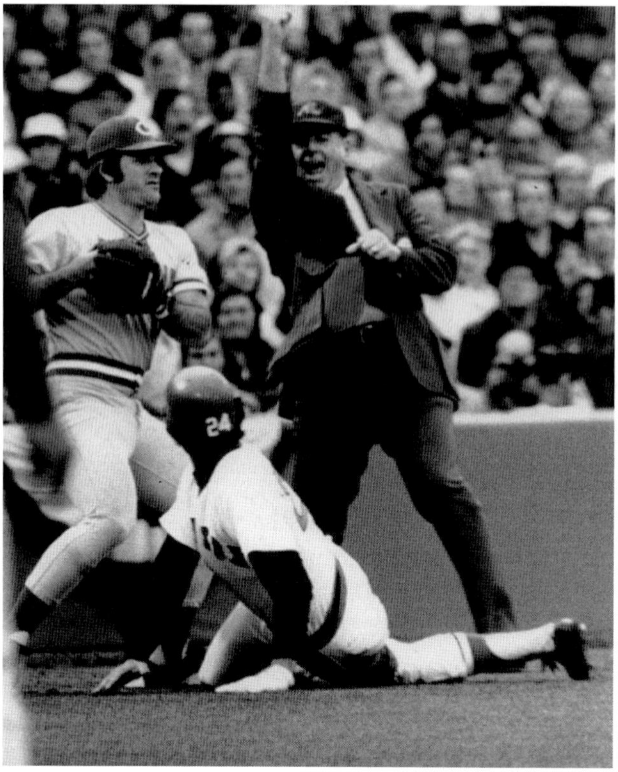

The Red Sox jumped out to 1-0 in the first inning on an RBI single by Carlton Fisk. In the second inning, with one out, Dwight Evans was hit by a pitch, and Rick Burleson singled him to second. Johnny Bench then caught Evans off second with a pickoff throw to Dave Concepcion, who threw to Pete Rose at third, nailing Evans as umpire George Maloney shifts into a good position. Lee struck out to end the inning.

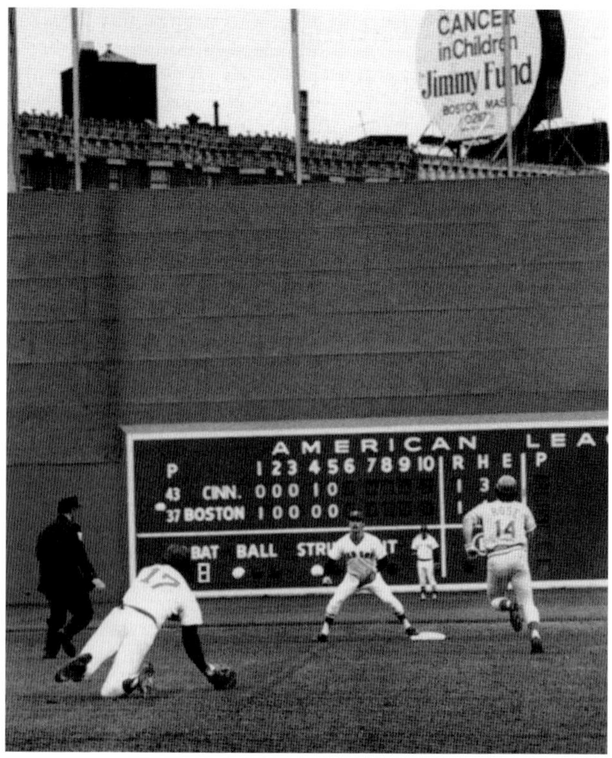

With the score tied 1-1 in the sixth inning, Pete Rose led off with a single. He was then forced out on a nice play by Cecil Cooper (17), who took a hit away from Joe Morgan. Rick Burleson takes the throw at second, and umpire Dick Stello announces the call.

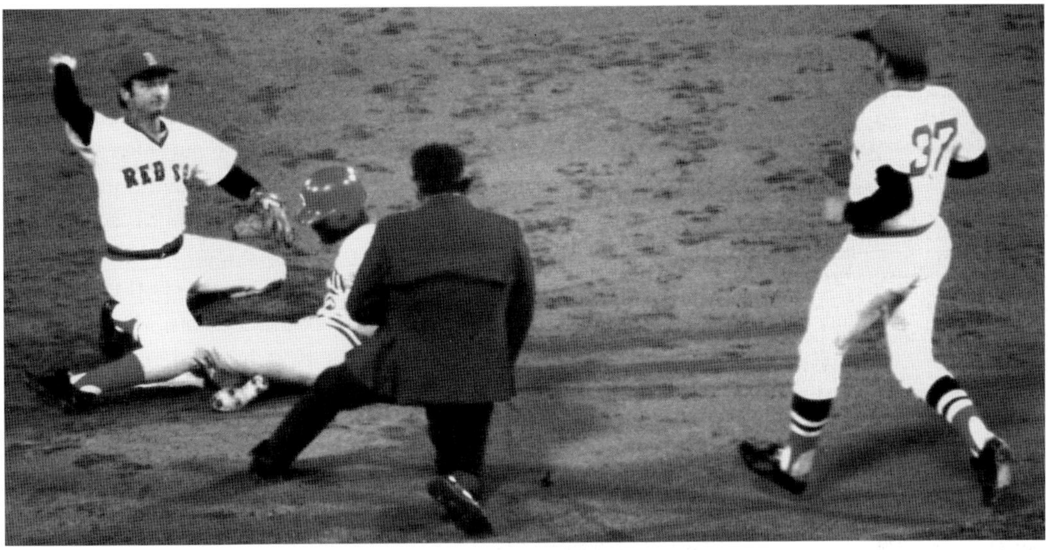

Morgan then attempted to steal second to put himself in scoring position for Johnny Bench to drive him in with a base hit. Carlton Fisk had other ideas and gunned him out on the throw to Denny Doyle. Bill Lee (37) is ready to offer any assistance if needed. Umpire Dick Stello is poised to punch out the sliding Morgan.

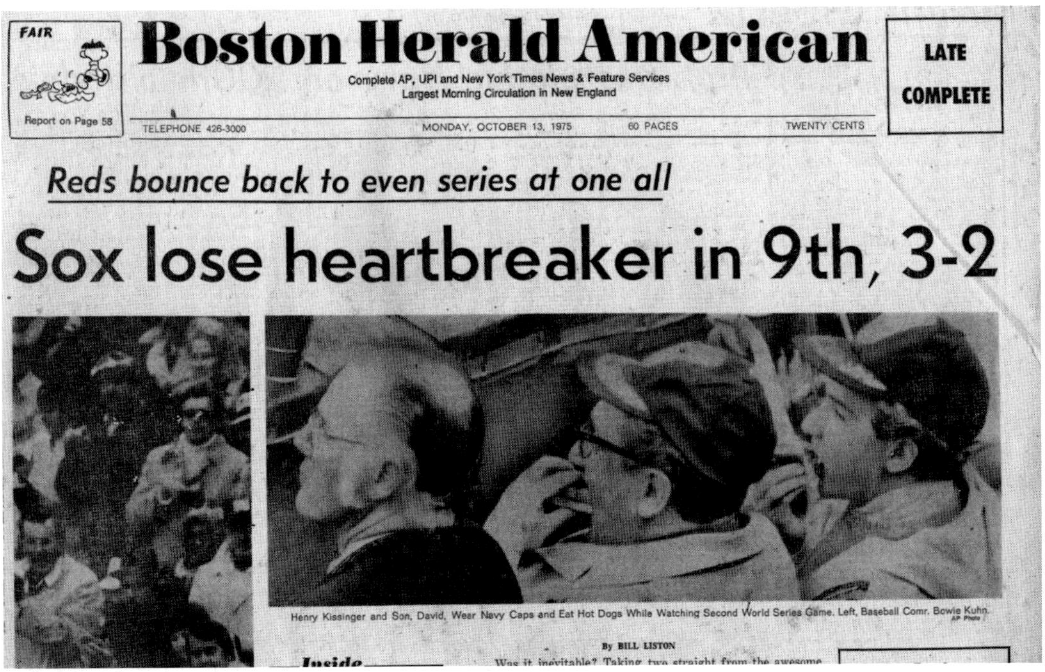

FAIR

Report on Page 58

Boston Herald American

Complete AP, UPI and New York Times News & Feature Services
Largest Morning Circulation in New England

LATE COMPLETE

TELEPHONE 426-3000 MONDAY, OCTOBER 13, 1975 60 PAGES TWENTY CENTS

Reds bounce back to even series at one all

Sox lose heartbreaker in 9th, 3-2

Henry Kissinger and Son, David, Wear Navy Caps and Eat Hot Dogs While Watching Second World Series Game. Left, Baseball Comr. Bowie Kuhn. AP Photo

By BILL LISTON

The Red Sox entered the ninth inning with a 2-1 lead and three outs away from a commanding 2-0 lead in the World Series. However, Johnny Bench led off with double, and with two outs and Bench on third, Dave Concepcion tied the game with an infield single. Concepcion stole second and scored when Ken Griffey doubled him home. The Reds evened the series with the ninth-inning win.

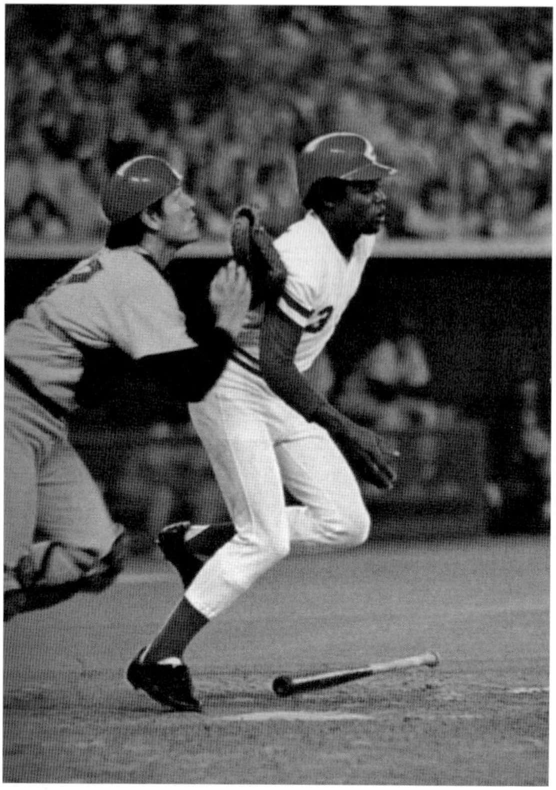

After a two-run, ninth-inning homer by Dwight Evans tying Game 3, Reds center fielder Caesar Geronimo led off the 10th inning with a single, which brought pinch-hitter Ed Armbrister to the plate. He laid down a bunt in front of the plate, and as Carlton Fisk moved toward the ball, he and Armbrister collided, causing Fisk's throw to second base to sail into center field, putting the winning run on third with nobody out. This caused an uproar in the Red Sox dugout as manager Darrell Johnson charged out of the dugout, insisting to home plate umpire Larry Barnett that "the man interfered." Barnett disagreed, and the game ended on a Joe Morgan single, giving the Reds a 2-1 lead in the series. Johnson returned to the dugout, screaming at Barnett, "This is a lousy operation."

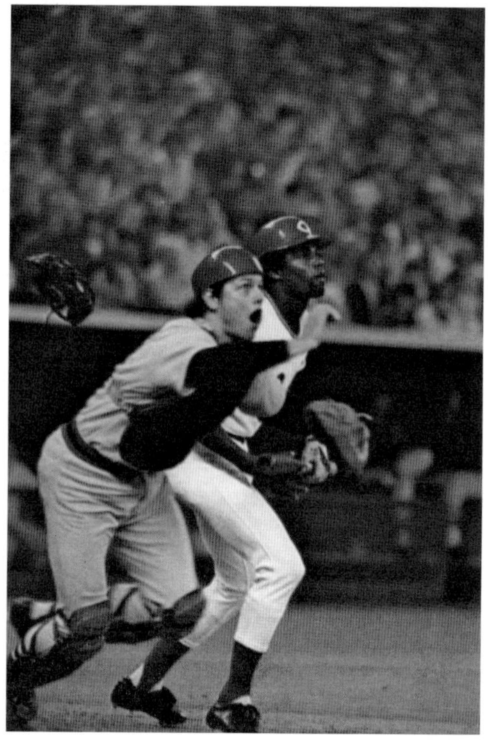

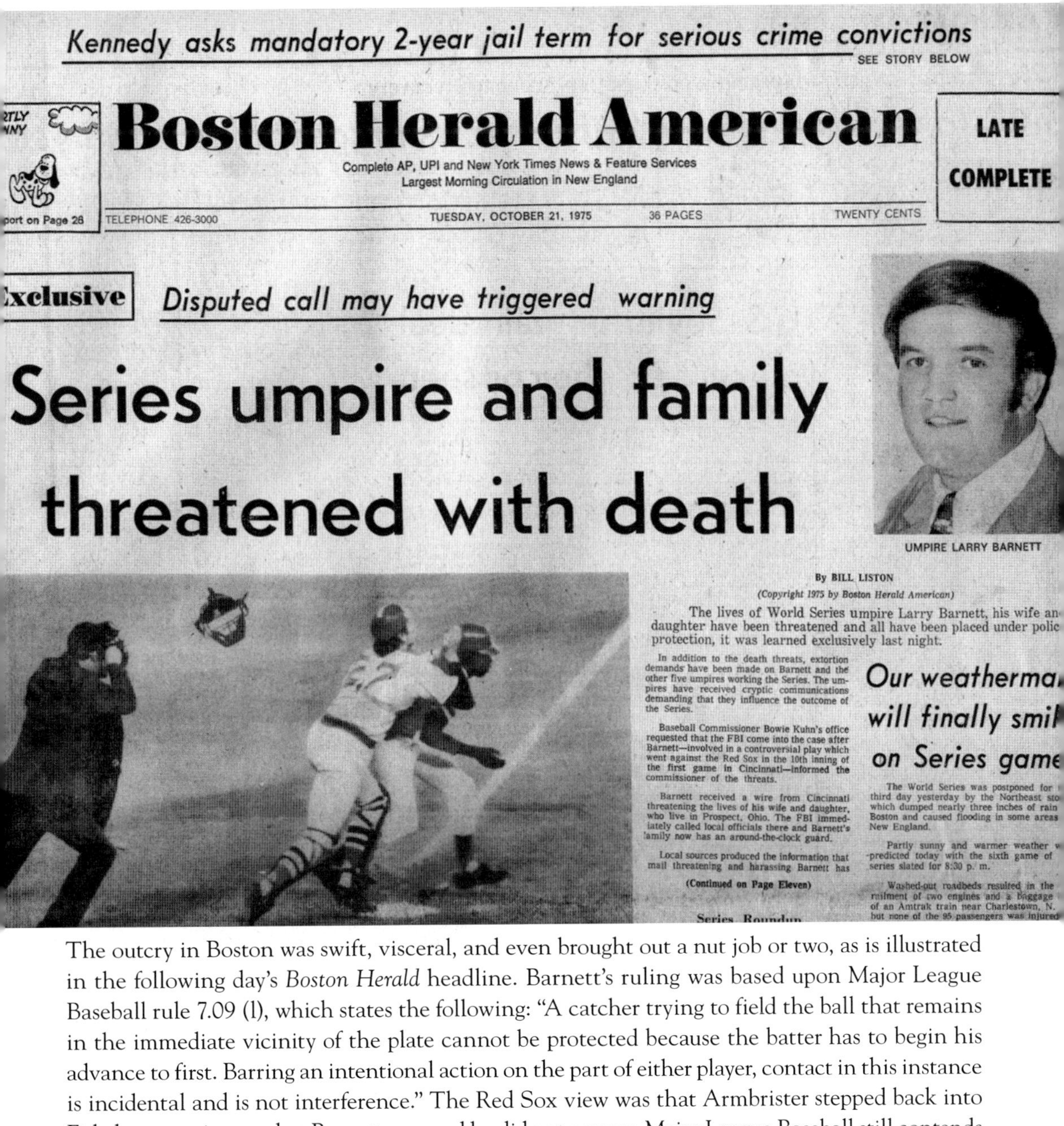

Kennedy asks mandatory 2-year jail term for serious crime convictions

SEE STORY BELOW

Boston Herald American

Complete AP, UPI and New York Times News & Feature Services
Largest Morning Circulation in New England

LATE COMPLETE

port on Page 28 | TELEPHONE 426-3000 | TUESDAY, OCTOBER 21, 1975 | 36 PAGES | TWENTY CENTS

xclusive — Disputed call may have triggered warning

Series umpire and family threatened with death

UMPIRE LARRY BARNETT

By BILL LISTON

(Copyright 1975 by Boston Herald American)

The lives of World Series umpire Larry Barnett, his wife an daughter have been threatened and all have been placed under polic protection, it was learned exclusively last night.

In addition to the death threats, extortion demands have been made on Barnett and the other five umpires working the Series. The umpires have received cryptic communications demanding that they influence the outcome of the Series.

Baseball Commissioner Bowie Kuhn's office requested that the FBI come into the case after Barnett—involved in a controversial play which went against the Red Sox in the 10th inning of the first game in Cincinnati—informed the commissioner of the threats.

Barnett received a wire from Cincinnati threatening the lives of his wife and daughter, who live in Prospect, Ohio. The FBI immediately called local officials there and Barnett's family now has an around-the-clock guard.

Local sources produced the information that mail threatening and harassing Barnett has

(Continued on Page Eleven)

Series Roundup

Our weatherma will finally smil on Series game

The World Series was postponed for third day yesterday by the Northeast sto which dumped nearly three inches of rain Boston and caused flooding in some areas New England.

Partly sunny and warmer weather w predicted today with the sixth game of series slated for 8:30 p. m.

Washed-out roadbeds resulted in the railment of two engines and a baggage of an Amtrak train near Charlestown, N. but none of the 95 passengers was injured

The outcry in Boston was swift, visceral, and even brought out a nut job or two, as is illustrated in the following day's *Boston Herald* headline. Barnett's ruling was based upon Major League Baseball rule 7.09 (l), which states the following: "A catcher trying to field the ball that remains in the immediate vicinity of the plate cannot be protected because the batter has to begin his advance to first. Barring an intentional action on the part of either player, contact in this instance is incidental and is not interference." The Red Sox view was that Armbrister stepped back into Fisk; however, it was what Barnett saw, and he did not concur. Major League Baseball still contends that Barnett got it correct and use this play in teaching today's umpires.

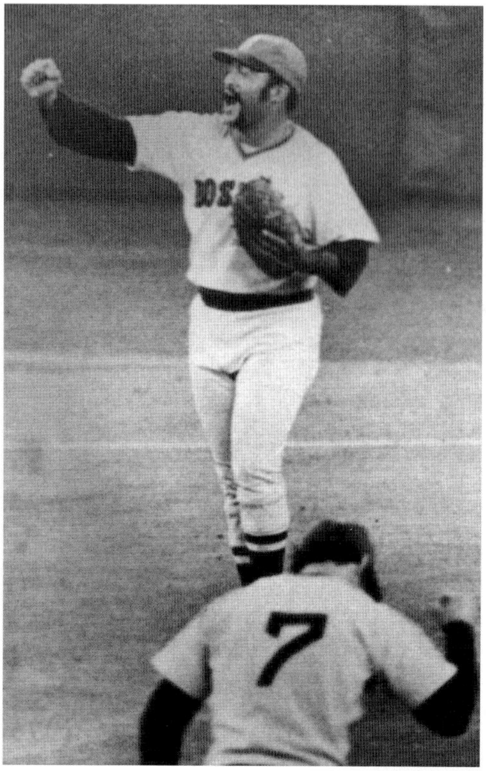

Luis Tiant went back to the mound for Game 4 and surrendered his first postseason runs in the first inning, as the Reds took a 2-0 lead. The Red Sox scored five times in the fourth, and Cincinnati countered in their half of the fourth with two more runs, making the score 5-4. From the fifth inning on, Tiant pitched in and out of trouble as the Reds had the tying run in scoring position four times. Fred Lynn made a spectacular game-saving catch of a line drive from Ken Griffey in the ninth inning, with one out and runners on first and second. Joe Morgan popped out to Yaz to end the game. Tiant and Burleson (7) began the celebration and were quickly joined by Rico Petrocelli (kissing Tiant), Yaz, and Denny Doyle. Tiant surrendered four runs, nine hits, and four walks, throwing 169 pitches.

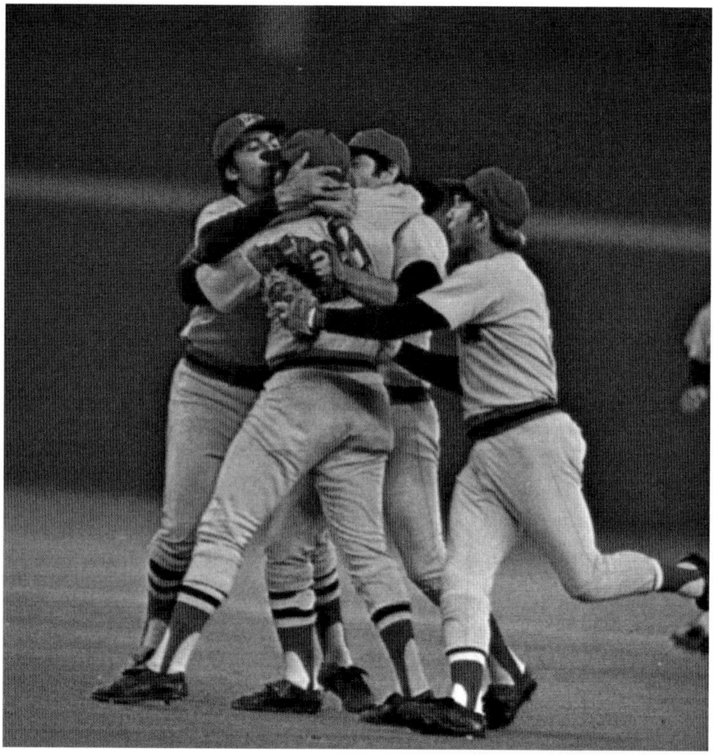

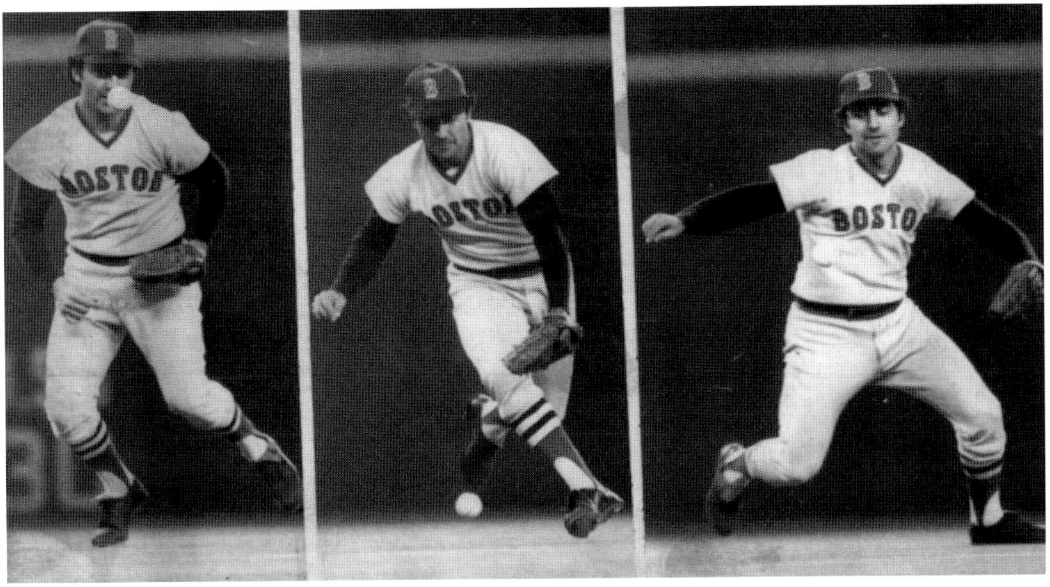

The Reds trounced the Sox in Game 5, behind two home runs by Tony Perez. The Red Sox took a 1-0 lead and held it until the bottom of the fourth as Cincinnati prevailed 6-2. In this photograph, Red Sox third baseman Rico Petrocelli keeps Dave Concepcion's ground ball in front of him before throwing him out leading off the fifth.

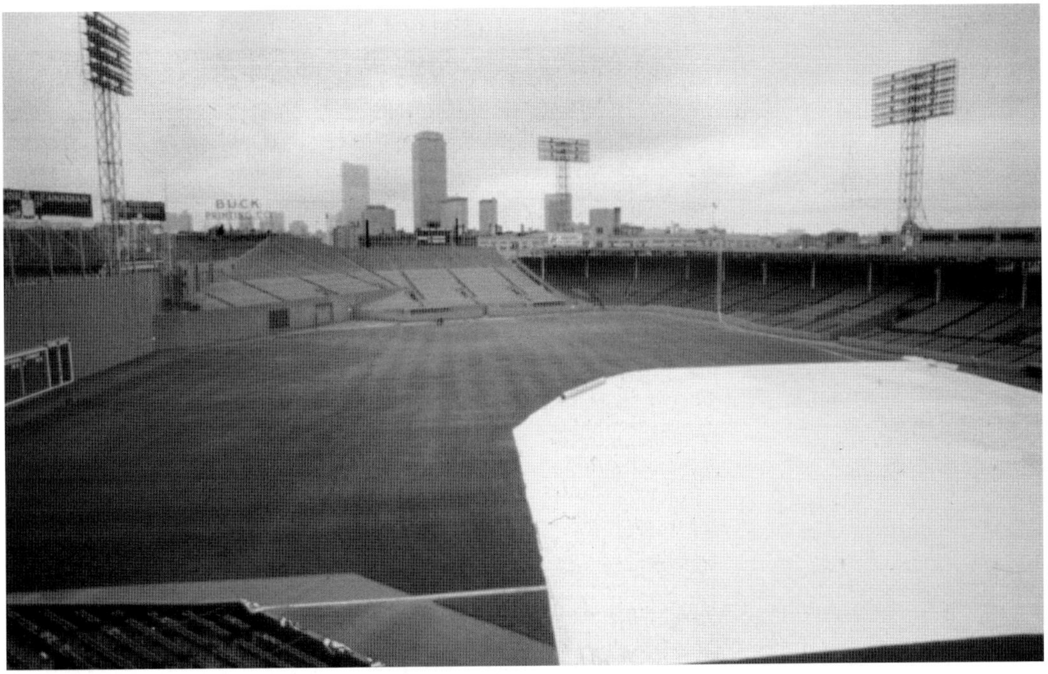

With the Reds needing to win only one of the last two games, it was back to Boston to close out the fall classic. The sixth game was scheduled for Saturday, October 18, but a raw fall rain delayed the game on Saturday, Sunday, and Monday. This was the scene at Fenway for the better part of five days, until the series resumed on Tuesday, October 21. History was waiting.

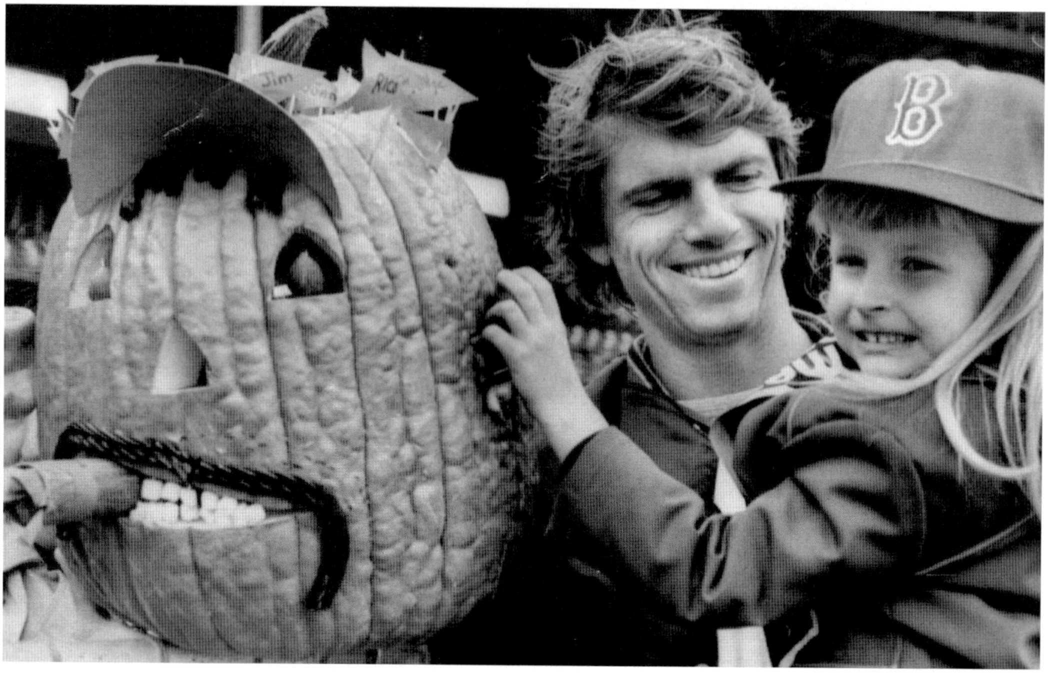

The persisting rains washed out Sunday's game but not before Spaceman Bill Lee had some fun with the 1975 March of Dimes poster child, Tammy Patterson. The six-year-old was a victim of multiple birth defects. Lee was scheduled to start the sixth game.

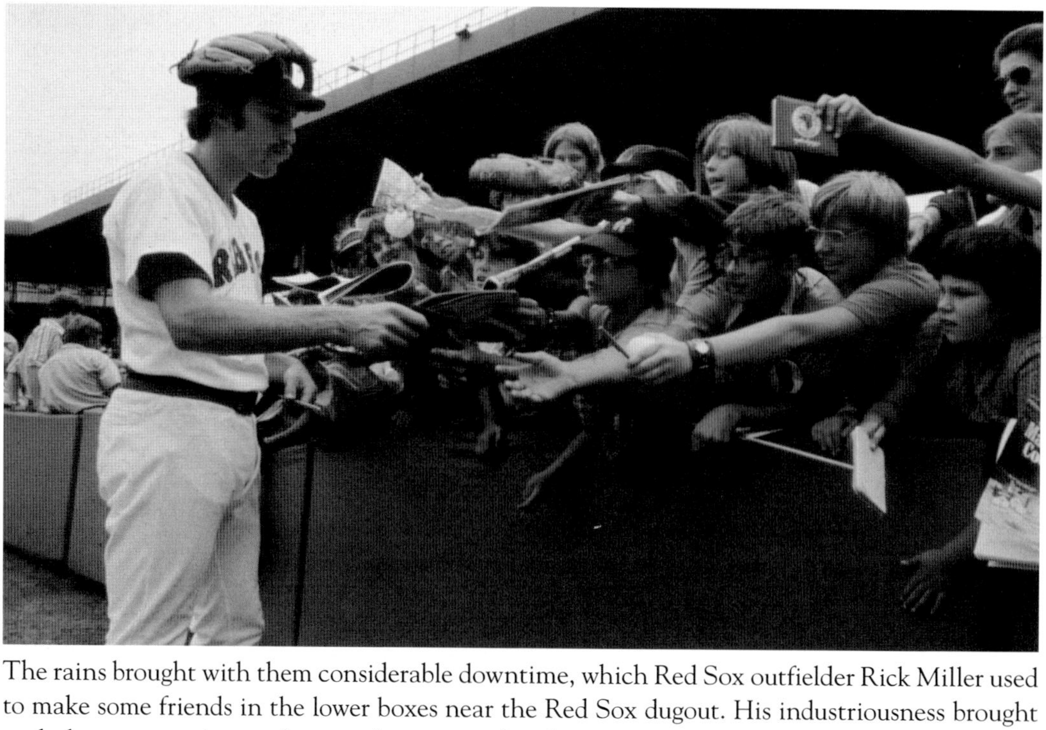

The rains brought with them considerable downtime, which Red Sox outfielder Rick Miller used to make some friends in the lower boxes near the Red Sox dugout. His industriousness brought a whole new meaning to the term "using your head."

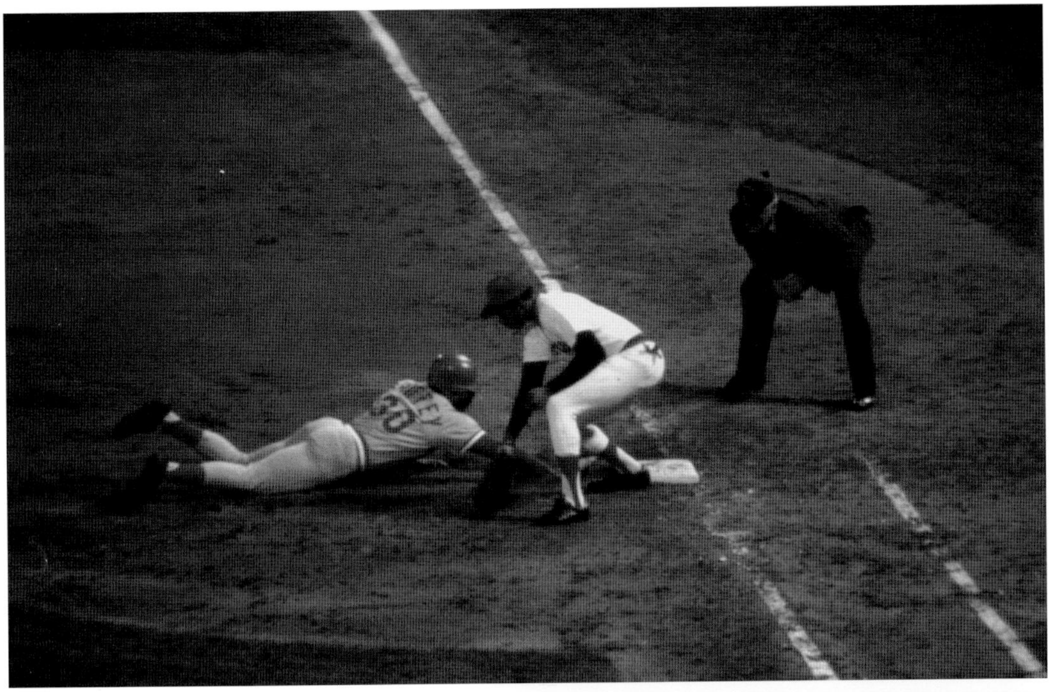

The score was 3-3 when Ken Griffey led off the Cincinnati seventh inning in Game Six of the series. Here, he dives back to first ahead of Cecil Cooper's tag. He, along with Joe Morgan, would score on a two-out double by George Foster, giving the Reds a 5-3 lead, nine outs away from a World Championship.

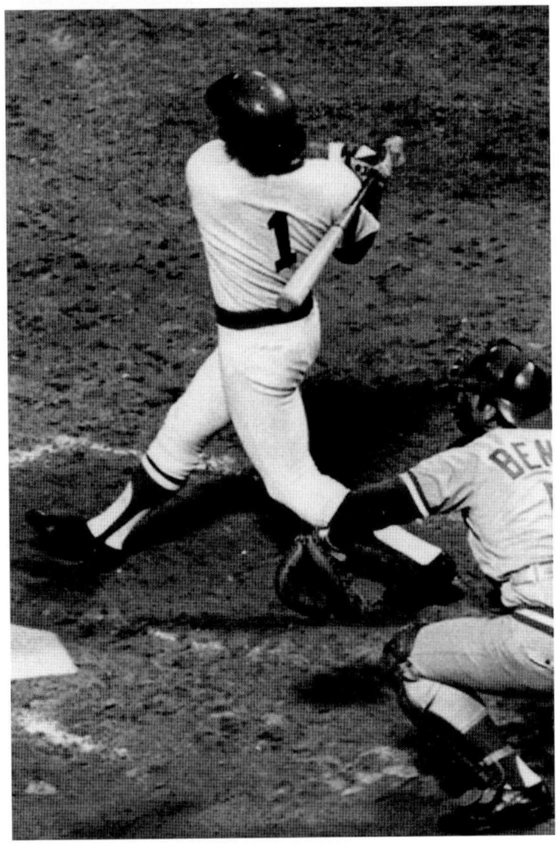

The Reds were ahead 6-3 when the Red Sox came to bat in the eighth. Lynn led off with a single, Petrocelli walked, Evans struck out, and Burleson lined out to left. Bernie Carbo stepped in and with the count two and two, he barely fouled off a pitch to stay alive. The next pitch he deposited 10 rows deep in the center field bleachers, tying the score and unleashing pandemonium in Fenway Park.

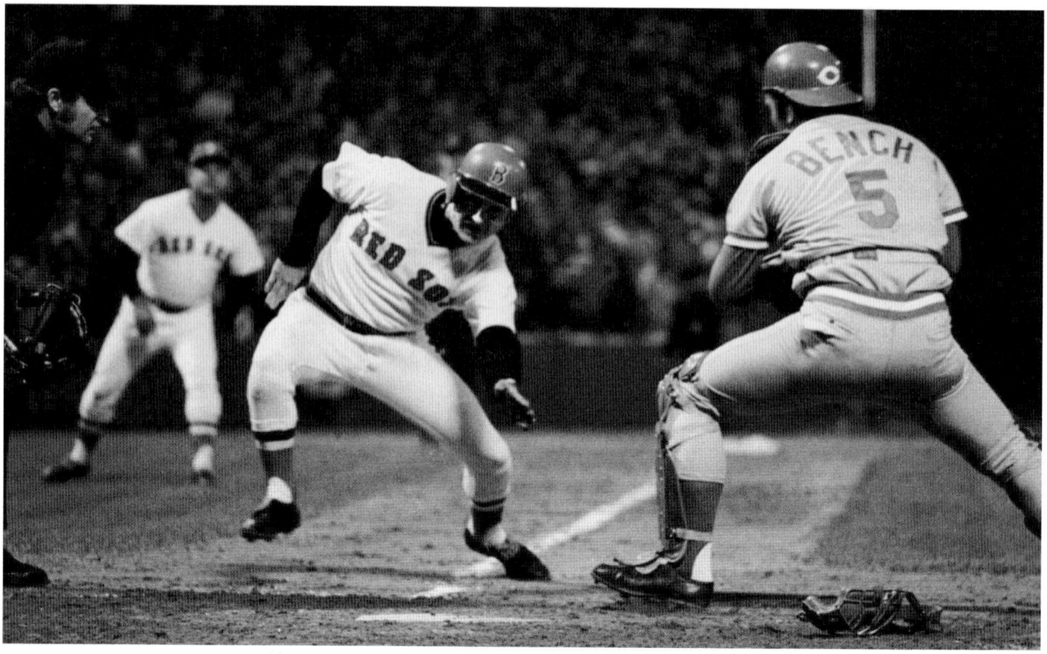

The crowd was still buzzing when the Red Sox came to bat in their half of the ninth. The Reds had gone down one, two, three, and when Denny Doyle walked leading off, the buzz intensified. Yaz followed with a single, sending Doyle to third, and the crowd's energy was now frenetic. Fred Lynn stepped in, and on the first pitch he lofted a fly ball in shallow left field. George Foster tracked it and made the catch right next to the third-base line stands. Doyle tagged up and made a dash for home. The play was close, but the throw was on the money. These two photographs show Doyle attempting to get past and the result of the tag. Fenway Park hushed, and after Rico Petrocelli grounded out to end the inning, it was on to extra innings. (Both, courtesy of the Boston Red Sox.)

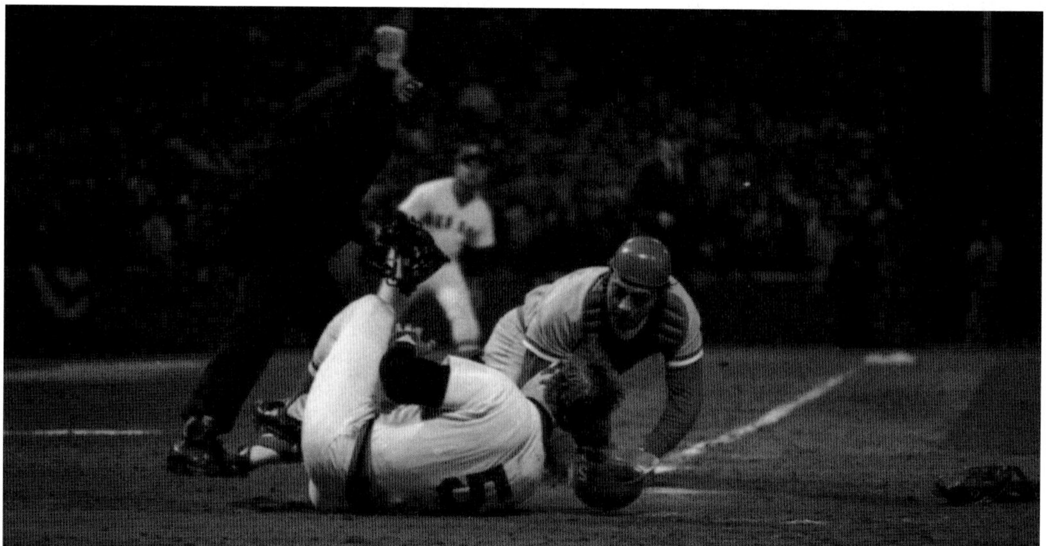

A controversy ensued surrounding this play, centering on whether coach Don Zimmer should have sent him. Zimmer contended that he was saying "No, no, no," while Doyle thought he heard "Go, go, go." Three decades later, the author asked Denny to autograph this photograph with a reference to this play; he wrote, "No is go in some worlds."

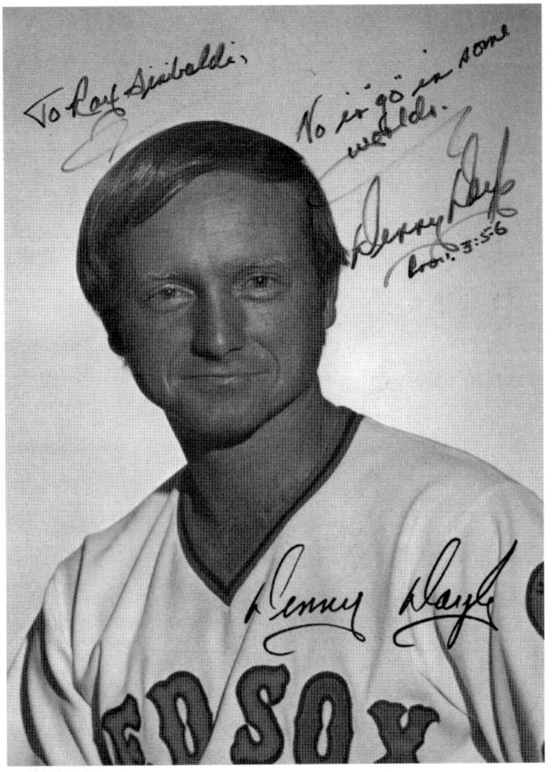

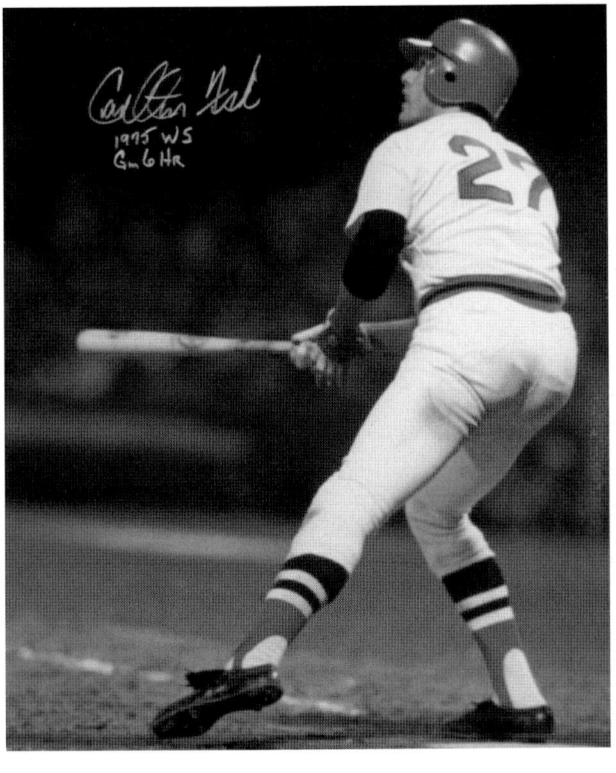

In the 10th, the Reds got the lead run to second base, and in the 12th, they had two men on when Joe Morgan hit a screaming line drive over the head of Dwight Evans. Evans made a spectacular catch and turned it into an inning-ending double play. In the Red Sox 12th, Fisk said to Fred Lynn, "Something good's going to happen, Freddie."

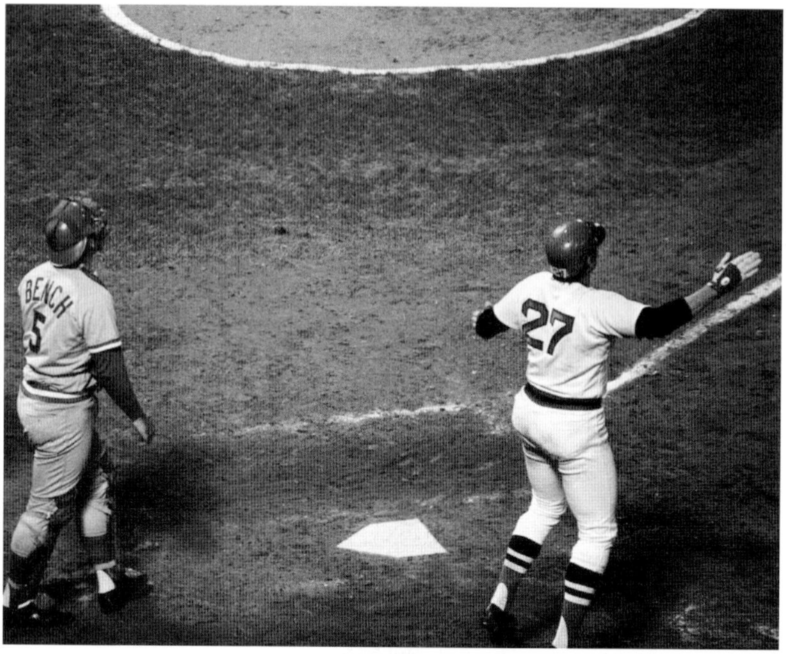

"I'll hit the wall and then you bring me in," Fisk said to Fred Lynn, and on the second pitch, he swung. The ball was heading down the line as Fisk makes his way out of the batter's box with his right arm urging the ball to stay in play. Johnny Bench (5) looks on. (Courtesy of the Boston Red Sox.)

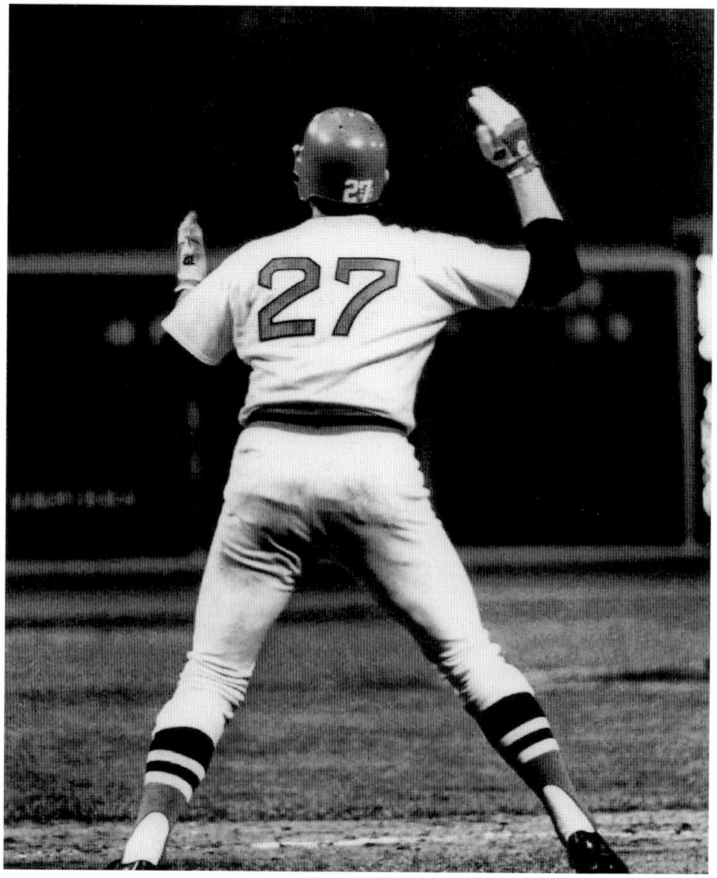

Knowing when he struck the ball that it had home run distance, Fisk is now imploring the ball with both hands to stay fair. As he skipped down the line toward first, he watched the ball clang off the left field foul pole for a home run. This was the shot heard all over New England, as church bells rang throughout the region. The Red Sox had won Game 6, 7-6.

The celebration at Fenway Park went on and on with fans simply not wanting to leave. They cheered, they sang, and they danced, as Fenway was awash in joy and excitement. Carlton Fisk waves to the crowd as he makes his way underneath the left-field grandstands for press interviews. His home run lives in the pantheon of baseball's all-time great home runs.

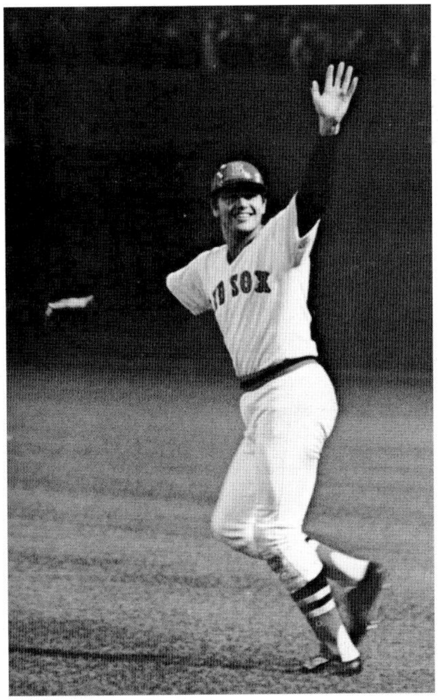

The *Boston Herald* told the story on their front page the following day, with photographs of the three Red Sox home runs. The iconic television shot of Fisk waving the ball fair was taken from inside the left-field wall, and it only exists because when the NBC director told the cameraman to follow the ball, he refused, as he was frozen in fear by the presence of a large rat a mere five feet away.

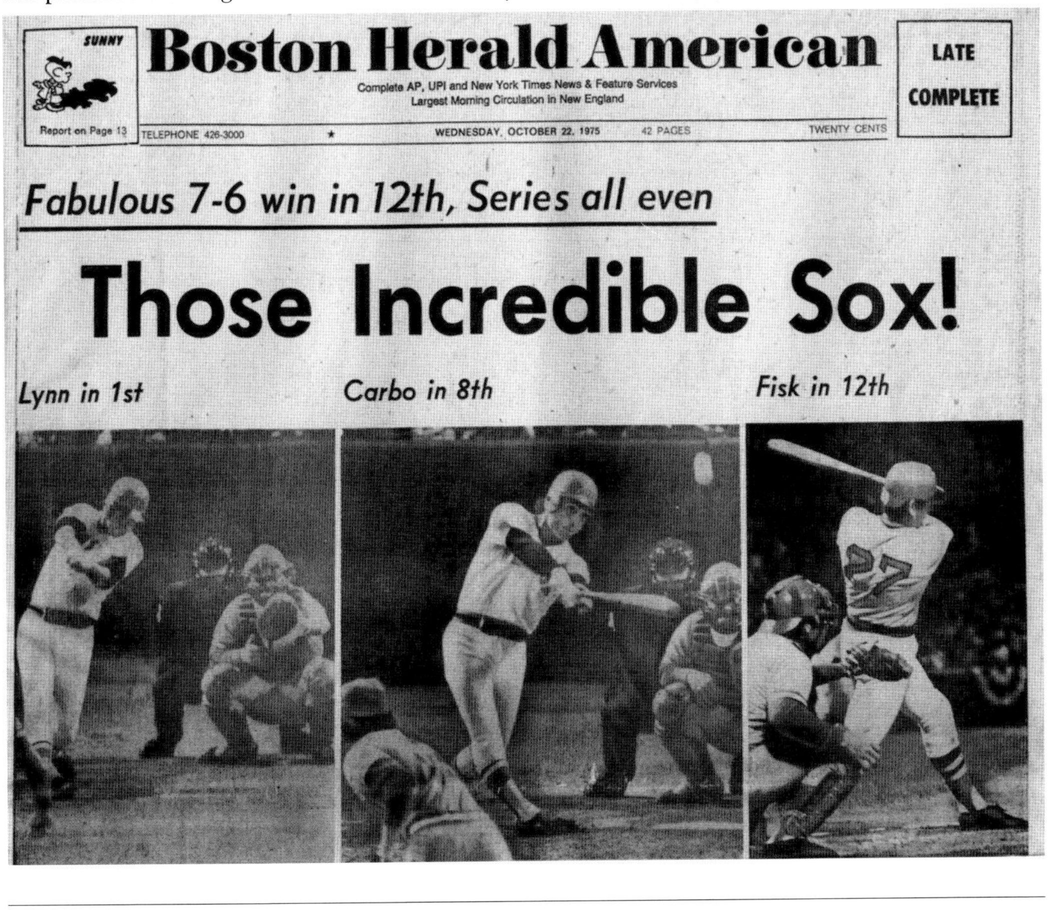

SUNNY
Report on Page 13

Boston Herald American

Complete AP, UPI and New York Times News & Feature Services
Largest Morning Circulation in New England

LATE
COMPLETE

TELEPHONE 426-3000 ★ WEDNESDAY, OCTOBER 22, 1975 42 PAGES TWENTY CENTS

Fabulous 7-6 win in 12th, Series all even

Those Incredible Sox!

Lynn in 1st *Carbo in 8th* *Fisk in 12th*

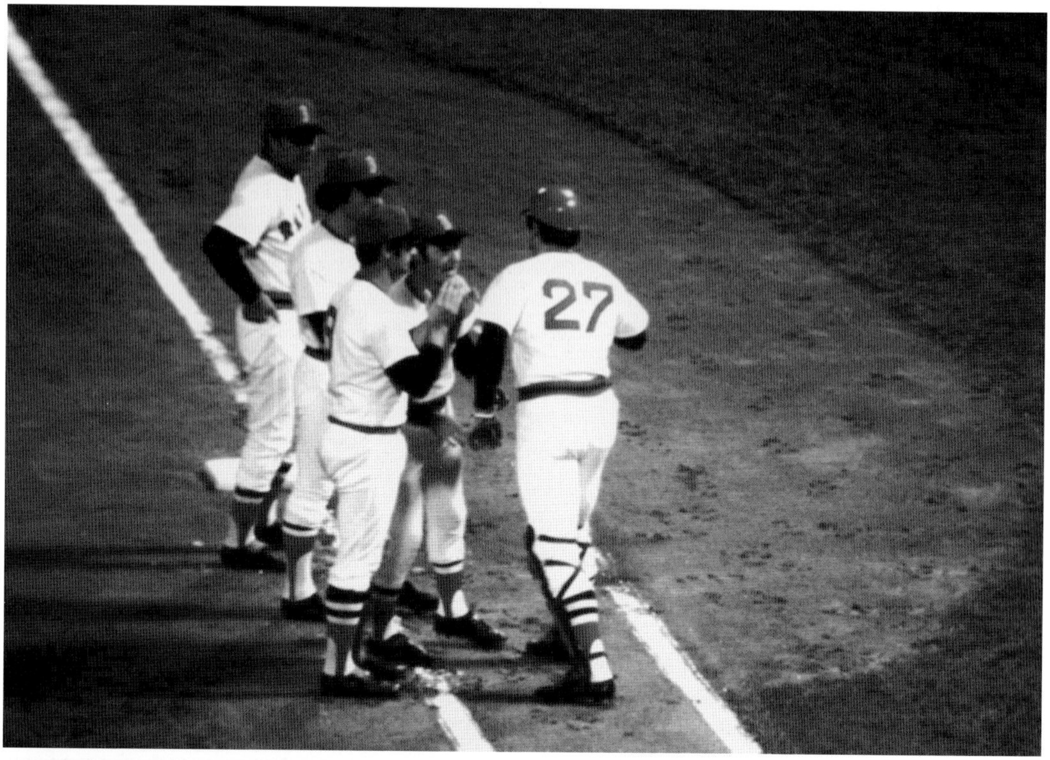

After being introduced by Fenway Park announcer Sherm Feller, Fisk takes his place along the first-base line; joining him are, from left to right, Darrell Johnson, Bernie Carbo, Denny Doyle, and Carl Yastrzemski. Game 7 is about to begin.

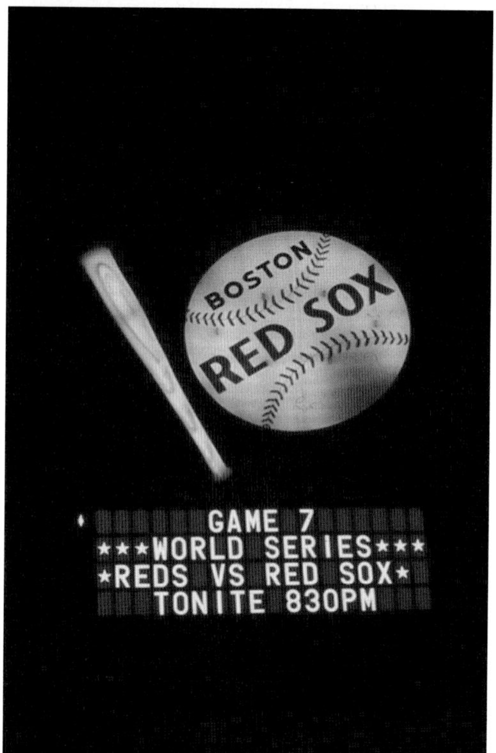

After 171 games and seven months, the championship came down to one game. The sign across from the Red Sox ticket office on Brookline Avenue tells the story. Cincinnati prevailed, coming back from a three-run deficit to win it in the ninth inning. The Reds victory has almost become a footnote, prompting the words of Carlton Fisk, "We won that series, three games to four." (Courtesy of the Boston Red Sox.)

4

The Should Be Hall of Famer "El Tiante"

Luis Tiant arrived in Boston during a tumultuous time in the city. Torn by a federal order to desegregate the schools through the vehicle of forced busing, the city was scarred by the ugliness of racial strife. In its midst emerged a pitcher who came to be known as "El Tiante," a moniker he proudly bore, as it was the same name they bestowed on his father.

The original El Tiante was a southpaw pitcher from Cuba who Luis still says was better than he, but the color barrier of bygone days kept him from claiming his stake in American baseball history. His exploits, to this day, are as legendary in Cuban baseball as Babe Ruth's in America. His son picked up his father's mantle, and while paying a deep personal price, rose to the pinnacle in Major League Baseball, where he became one of the game's most dominant pitchers.

He spun, he twisted, he twirled, and he pirouetted his way into the minds of opposing hitters and the hearts of Bostonians. Given up on and discarded, he battled back from oblivion to stake his claim as one of the game's best. And 30 or so times a year, he unified the city.

In Game 4 of the 1975 World Series, Tiant pitched a complete game 5-4 win. He did not have his best stuff. He was in trouble all night. He fell behind, his team battled back, and his opponent surged and was nipping at his heels. Throwing 169 pitches, he prevailed. It was a gallant effort, and he prevailed with his heart, an unquenchable competitive drive, and an indomitable will. That one game in Riverfront Stadium was a microcosm of his career.

There is a heated debate in baseball circles concerning his worthiness for enshrinement in the National Baseball Hall of Fame. Some say he is borderline. The old-fashioned numbers of wins, losses, ERA, strikeouts, and shutouts put him on par with contemporary Hall of Famers Jim Bunning, Don Drysdale, and Catfish Hunter. The new Sabermetric evaluation mechanism known as WAR places him above all three, as well as guys named Feller, Ford, Marichal, Eckersley, and even one named Koufax.

As for the immeasurable aspects of a winner, he is second to none. As Jim Palmer put it, "You can talk about everybody else over there, but Luis Tiant is the man." He is the greatest pitcher not in the National Baseball Hall of Fame. Hopefully someday and soon.

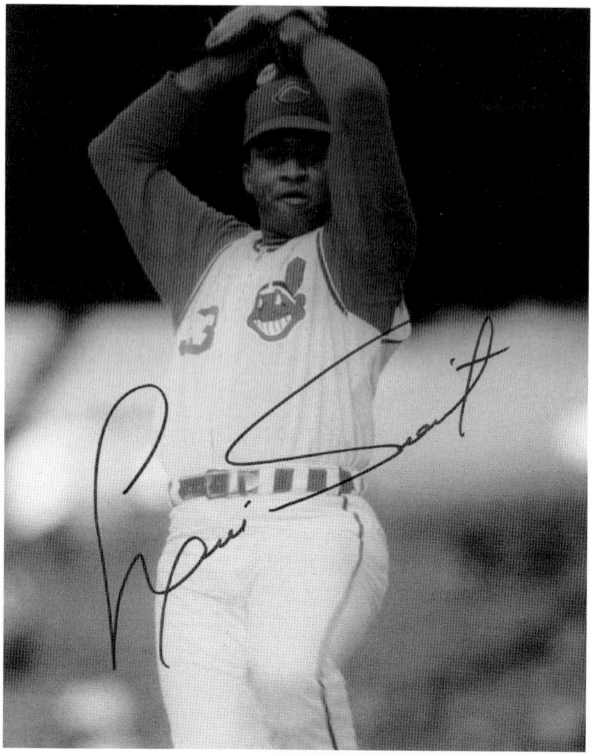

Luis Tiant played two years with the Mexico City Tigers, and it was from them in 1961 that the Cleveland Indians purchased his contract. It was a joyous time for Tiant, as he was beginning his dream to play in the major leagues; however, his joy would be tempered when his father told him not to return to Castro's Cuba. It would be 15 years before he would see his father again.

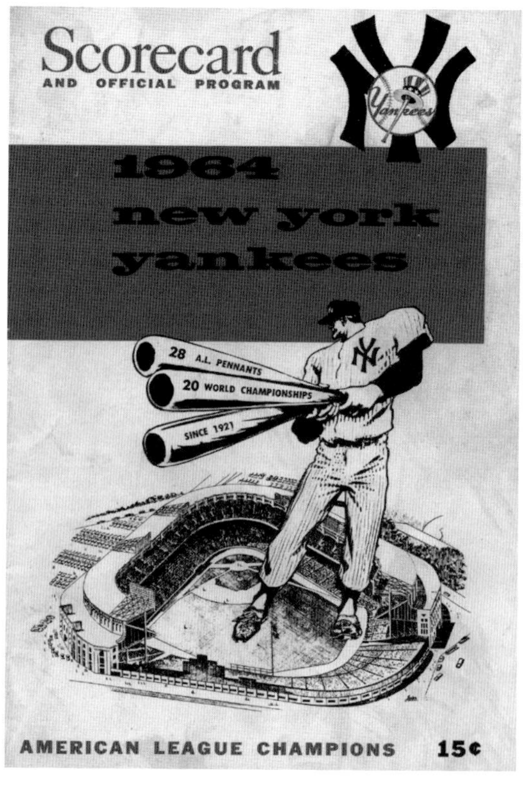

In July 1964, Tiant's Portland Beavers were battling for first in the Pacific Coast League with the Cincinnati-affiliate San Diego Padres led by Tony Perez. The city and the league were abuzz in anticipation of the matchup between the Cuban expatriates. It was not to be however, as Tiant got a call that he was bound for Yankee Stadium. The scorecard is from his debut game, and Perez and Tiant would not square off until the 1975 World Series. He threw a four-hit shutout, struck out 11, and beat Whitey Ford; Luis Tiant had arrived!

Struggling with shoulder difficulties, Tiant slipped to 9-20 in 1969, following his outstanding year in 1968. A falling-out with Indians manager Al Dark led to a trade with Minnesota. However, his continued arm miseries led them to believe his career was at its end, and following a year in which he threw 92 innings, he went 7-3 with a 3.40 ERA. He was released on the last day of spring training in 1971.

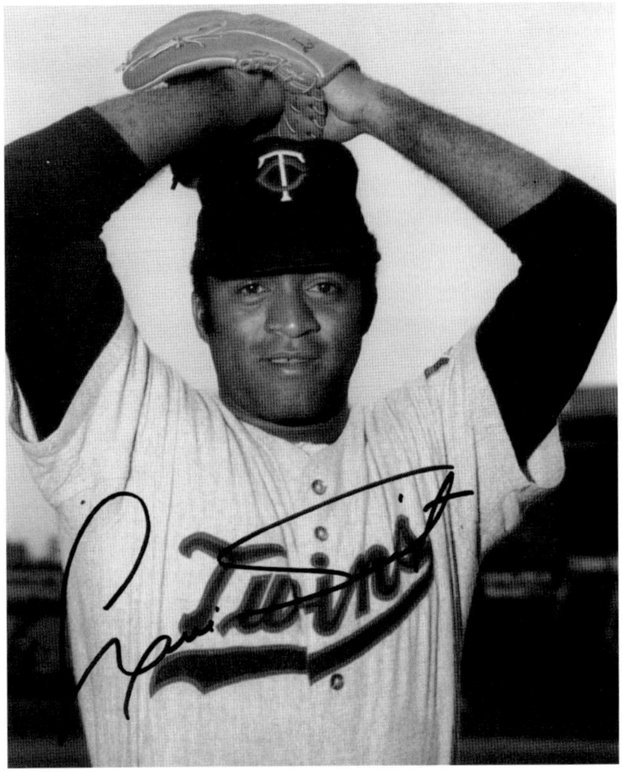

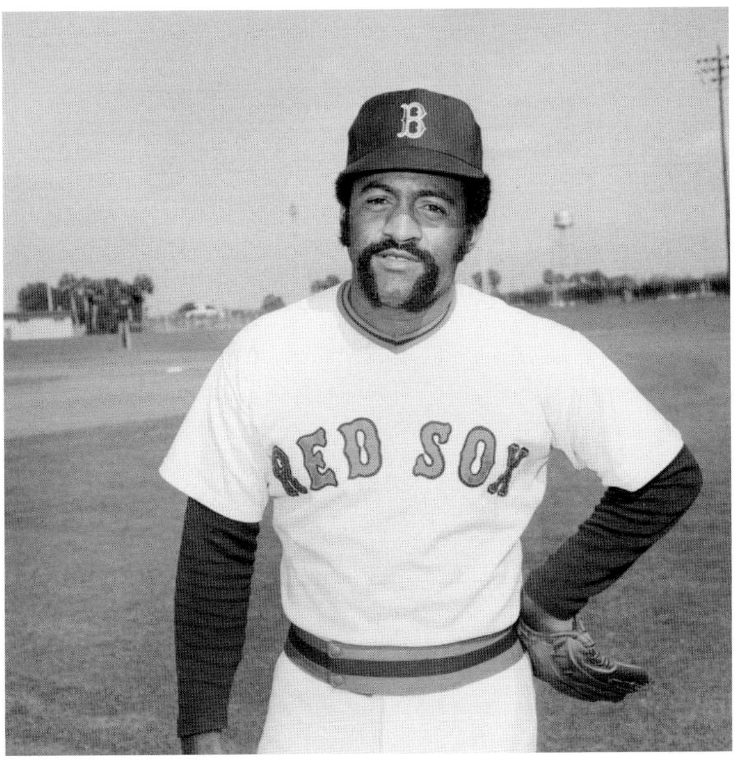

The Braves were his next stop, where he pitched for their Richmond AAA team for only a month. They too believed Luis Tiant was finished and granted him his release. Two days later, he was signed by the Red Sox and joined their AAA team in Louisville, Kentucky, managed by Darrell Johnson. Tiant was in Boston by mid-summer, and although he struggled a bit, all were excited about 1972.

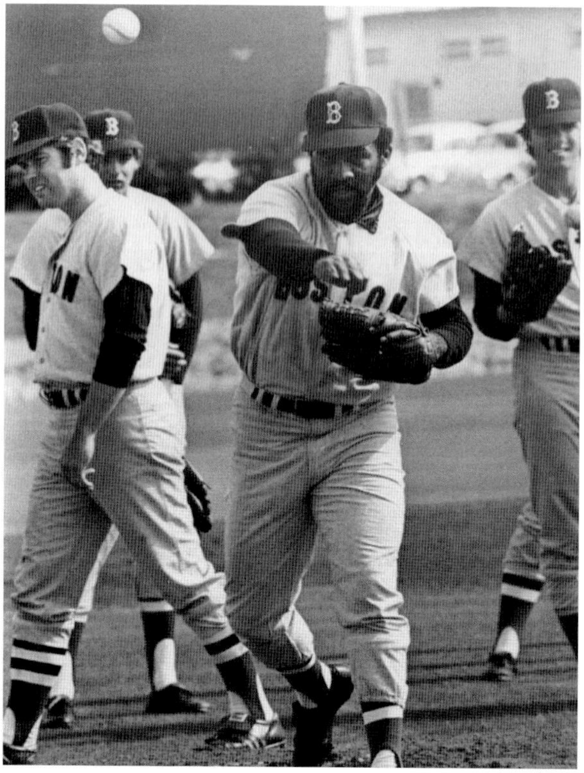

In 1972, Tiant arrived at spring training in Winter Haven, Florida, convinced that his arm woes were finally behind him. By the year's end, he would convince the rest of the American League as well. Here, he tosses a ball toward the camera while Bill Lee (right) looks on and smiles. Of Tiant's 43 appearances in 1972, twenty-four were out of the bullpen, but on August 23, he went into the rotation to stay, with a 3-0 shutout of the White Sox at Comiskey Park. He then won nine of his next 11 starts. Six of his nine wins were shutouts, with four of them coming in a row. His fashion sense was rubbing off, as both Carl Yastrzemski (left) and Rico Petrocelli (center), pictured here before a September game, began sporting mustaches. For the second time in his career, Tiant led the league with an ERA under two—1.91.

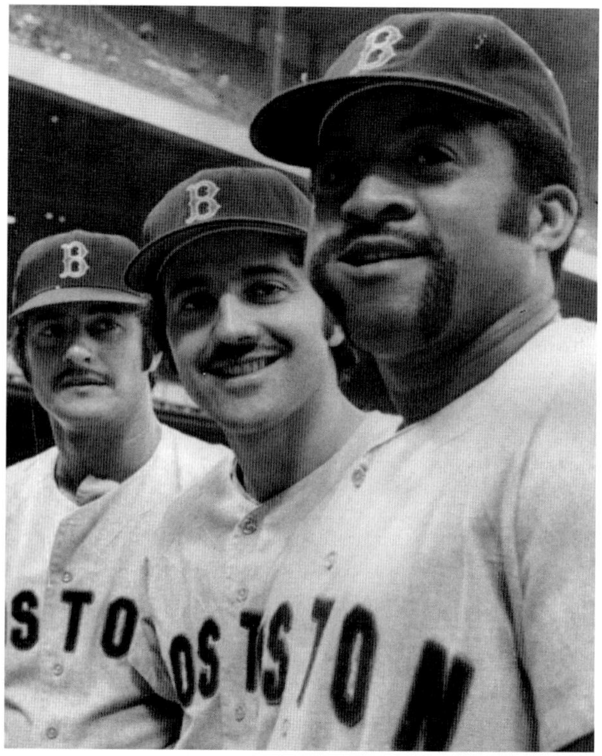

Luis Tiant's arrival on the Red Sox changed the culture of the team. An unmatched competitive drive, an unyielding desire to win, and a passion to never give in endeared him to teammates, opponents, and of course the Fenway Faithful. The master of the practical joke, Tiant always kept the team loose. His omnipresent cigar became the trademark of El Tiante; wherever he is, cigars are there as well. His propensity to smoke a cigar anywhere and everywhere was always good for a photo opportunity, as these two photographs illustrate. Today, Luis's son Daniel is the CEO of the Tiant Cigar Group, purveyors of El Tiante Cigars.

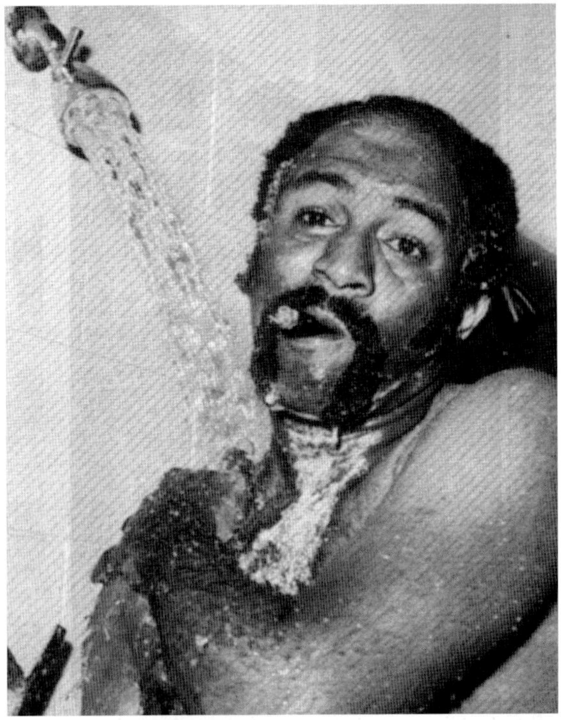

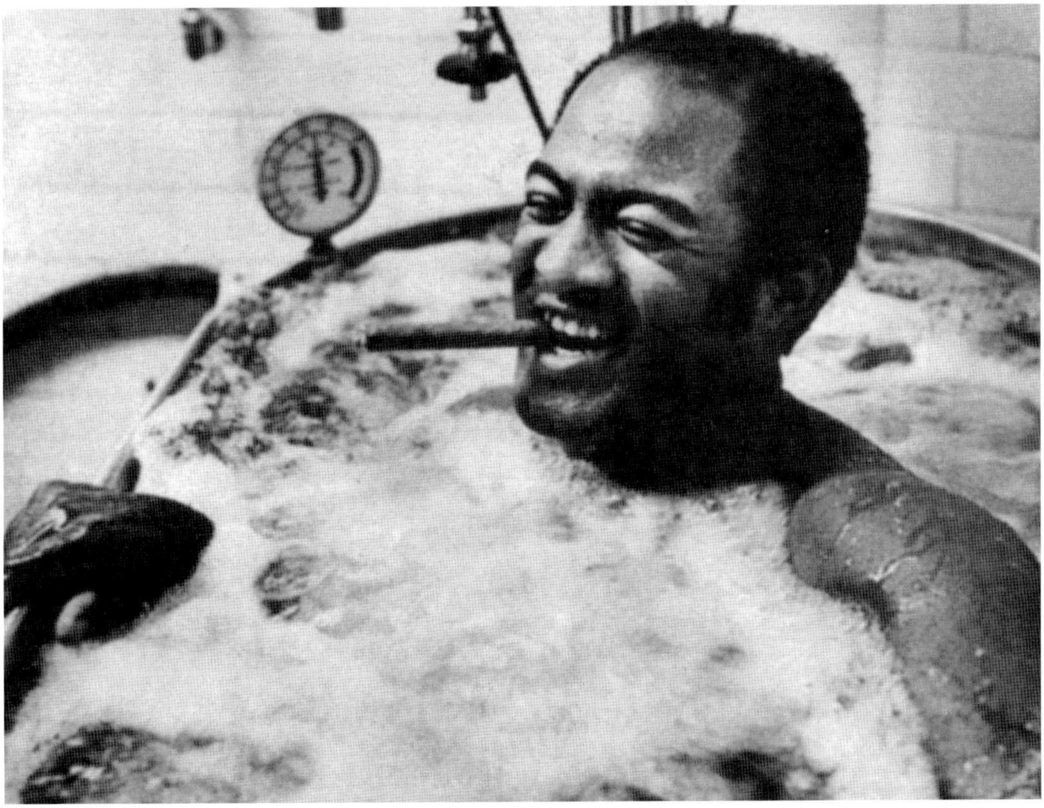

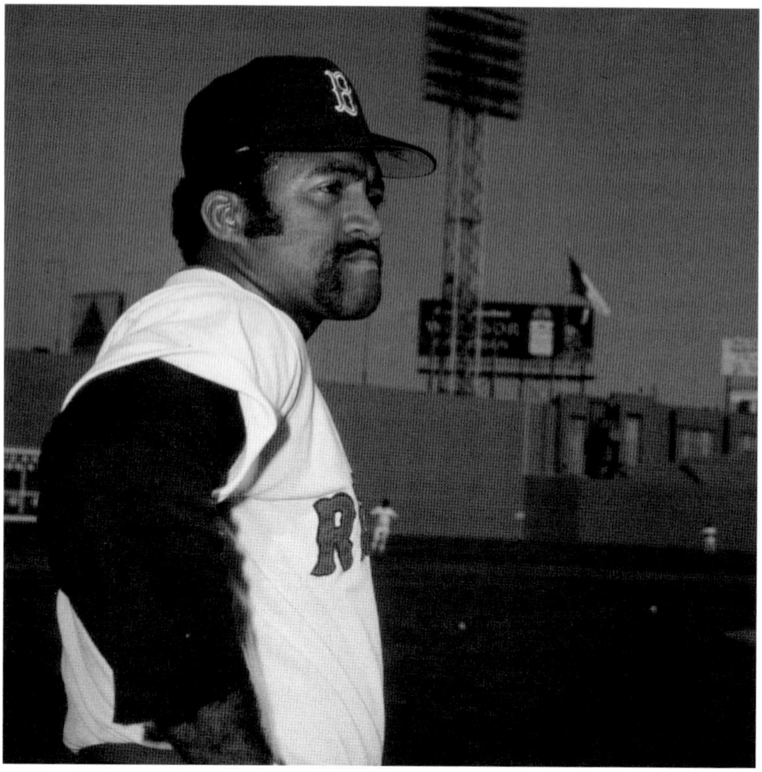

During the 1973 season, Tiant's relationship with the Fenway Faithful deepened. He became a 20-game winner for the second time in his career, going 20-13 pitching 272 innings. There was no doubt the physical maladies that had derailed him were a thing of the past. His 20th win came on the last day of the season, an 11-2 win over Milwaukee with nine strikeouts.

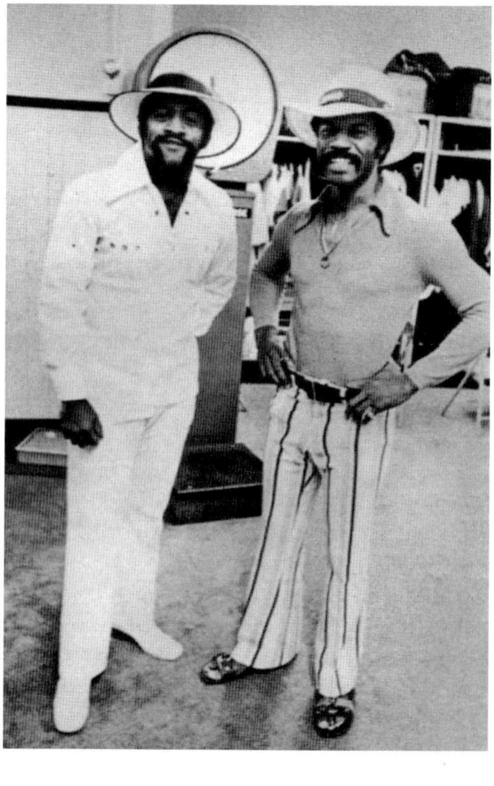

Tiant and his best friend Tommy Harper rock civilian threads in 1974. Harper played with the Sox from 1972 to 1974, setting a stolen-base record with 54 in 1973. Tiant, bedecked in white, chose 1974 as a year in which he wore all white and did not drink or gamble to thank God for all his blessings. The only exception was his Red Sox uniform.

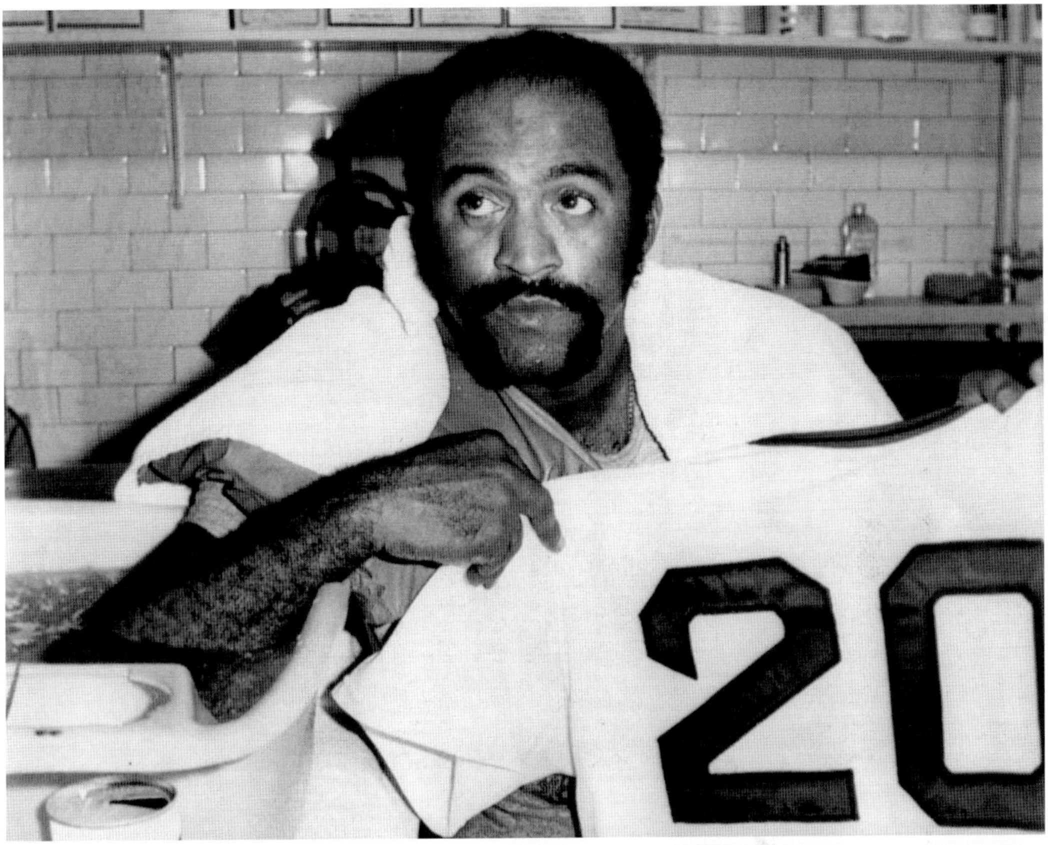

Tiant's year of gratitude also proved to be a year of tremendous frustration as well. On August 23, he shut out the Oakland A's 3-0 at Fenway Park for his 20th win of the year. It was his 12th win in his last 14 decisions and ran his record to 20-8. The Red Sox were seven games ahead in the American League East. However, his next three starts were losses in which the Red Sox did not score a single run. In a stretch of four games, he surrendered six runs and was 0-3. By September 19, Tiant lost his fifth straight decision, was 20-13, and the Red Sox were in third place, three games back. They finished seven out, and Luis finished 22-13. At right, he disputes home plate umpire Ron Luciano's strike zone during a 3-1 loss to the Tigers.

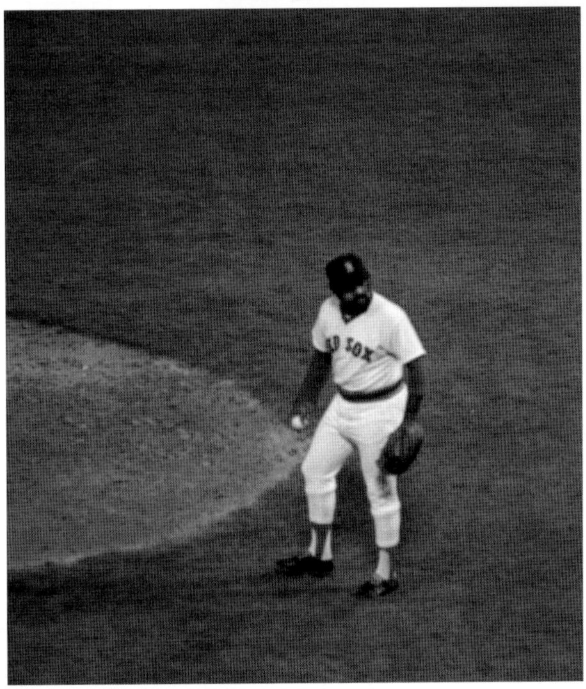

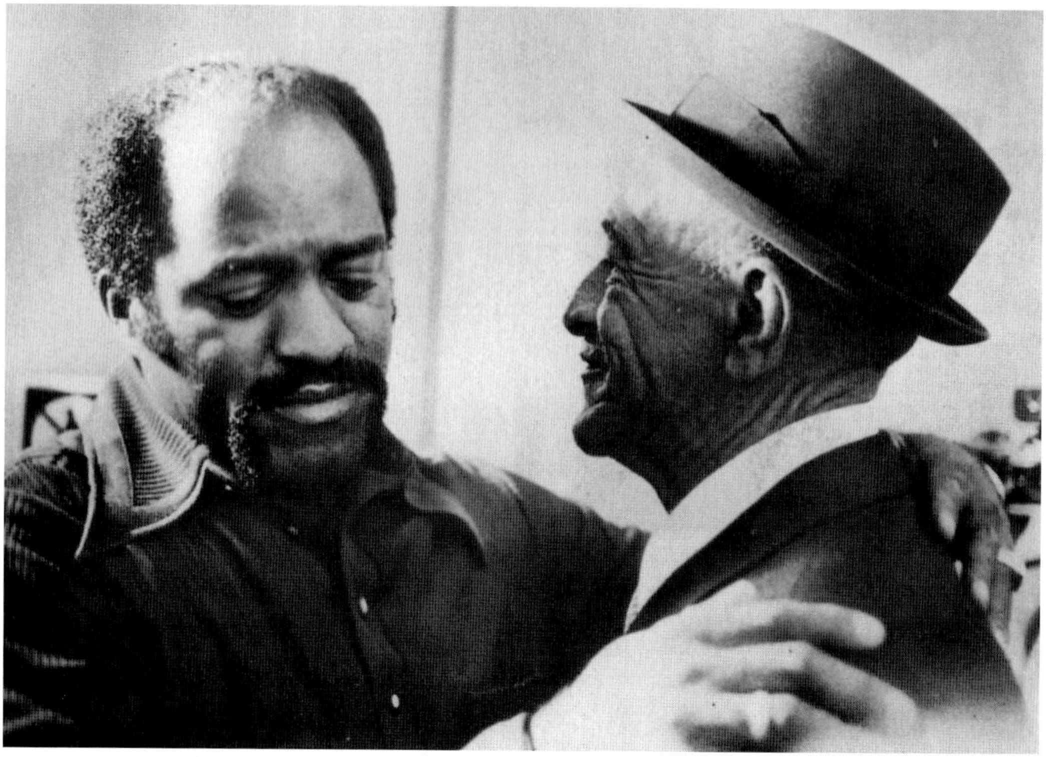

In August 1975, a 15-year wait came to an end at Logan Airport in Boston. Through the efforts of Sen. Ed Brooke of Massachusetts and Sen. George McGovern of South Dakota, Tiant's parents were allowed to leave Castro's Cuba. It had been 1960 when Tiant had last seen his father and seven years since his mother visited him in Mexico City. In the above photograph, father and son embrace. In an emotional moment, Luis Tiant Sr. said to his boy, "Don't cry, the cameras will see you," to which his son replied, "I don't care . . . It's the way I feel." A few days later, they were in the younger Tiant's workplace, Fenway Park. Tiant, clutching his omnipresent cigars, watches the action.

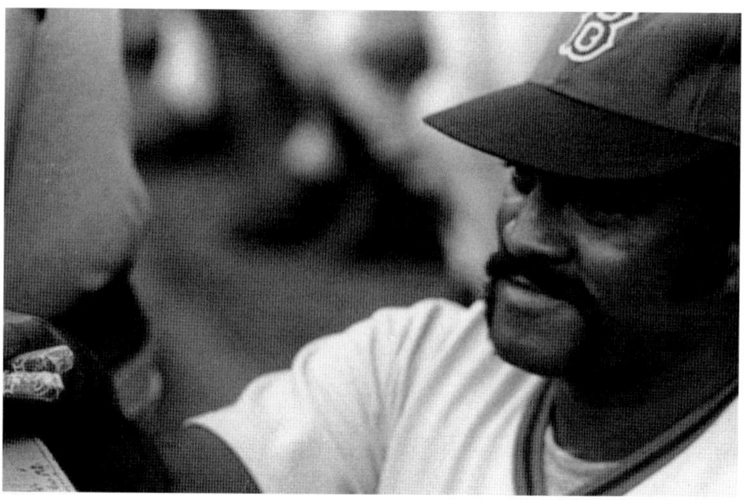

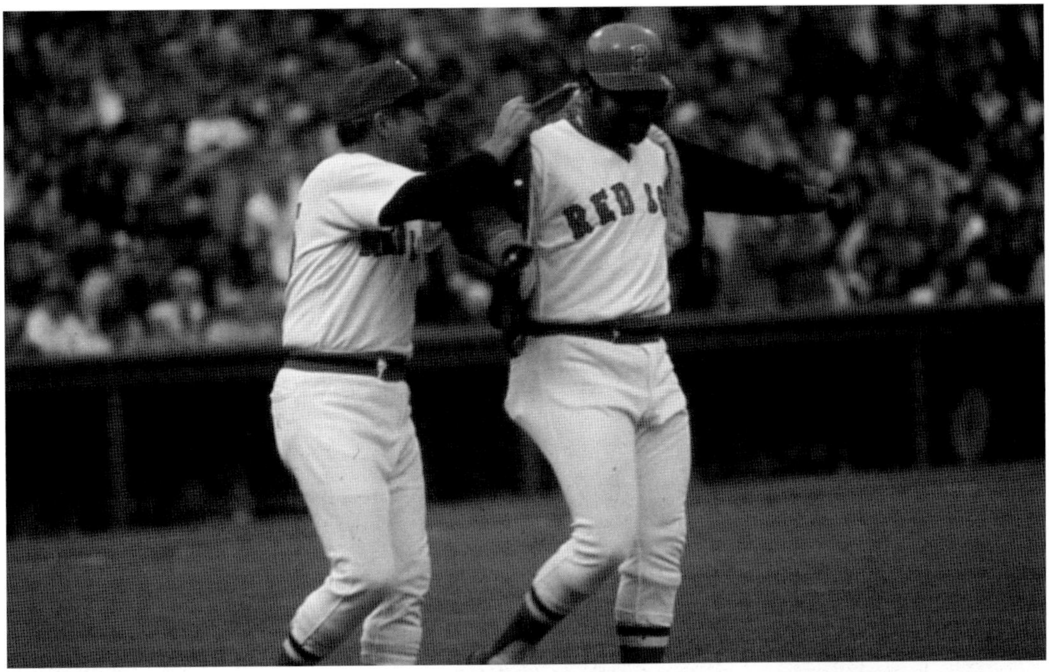

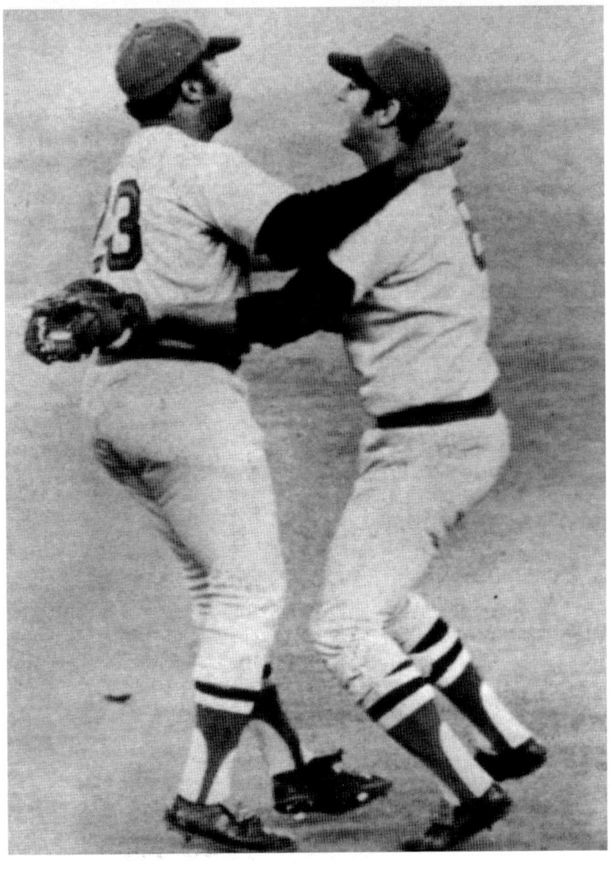

The culmination of Luis Tiant's professional career came in 1975, when the Red Sox won the American League pennant, and Tiant rose to the occasion. On the mound he was 3-0, with a win over the A's in the opening game of the playoffs and two wins in the World Series against the Reds. His 3-0 postseason record with a 2.86 ERA adds to his Hall of Fame–worthy credentials. He also gave a significant contribution with his bat as well, going 2-8 with two walks and an OBP of .400. In the above photograph, Johnny Pesky helps with his warm-up jacket after his single leading off the seventh inning of Game 1 of the World Series. In the photograph at right, Tiant and Yaz rejoice after his 169-pitch complete game win in Game 4 of the World Series in Cincinnati. (Above, courtesy of the Boston Red Sox.)

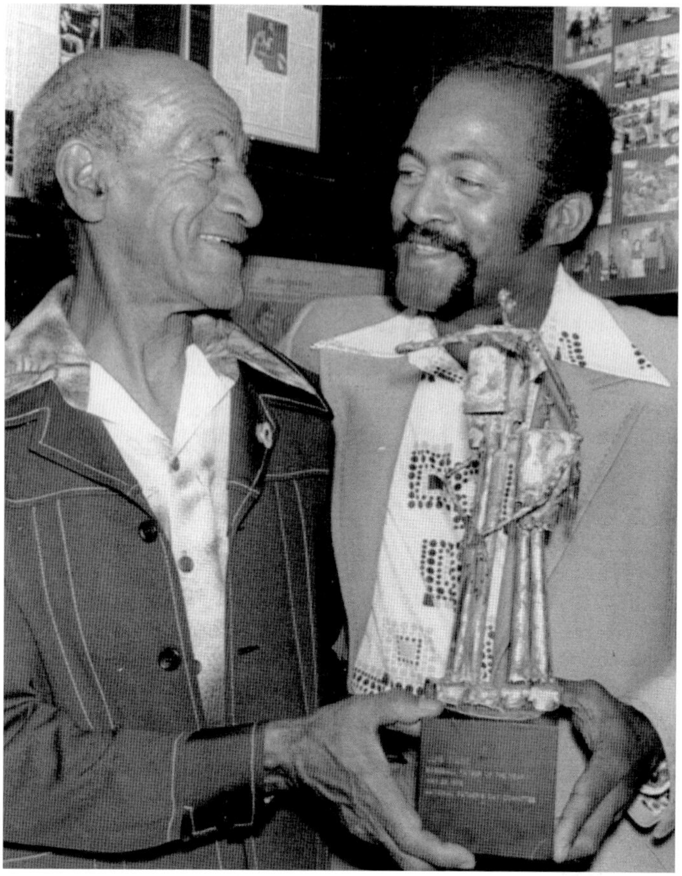

The joys of 1975, reunification and victory, were short-lived for Luis Tiant and his family. Father and son share a moment in June 1976 when Tiant was named Baseball Father of the Year by the National Father's Day Committee. The senior Tiant passed away just six months later on December 10. Three days later, while attending services for her husband, his mother, seen below flanked by her grandchildren, suffered a heart attack and passed away. Both of them were 71 years old. Luis Tiant shared the last 16 months of his parents' lives while riding the apex of his career. He laid them to rest together in Milton, Massachusetts, where he and his wife, Maria, had made their home.

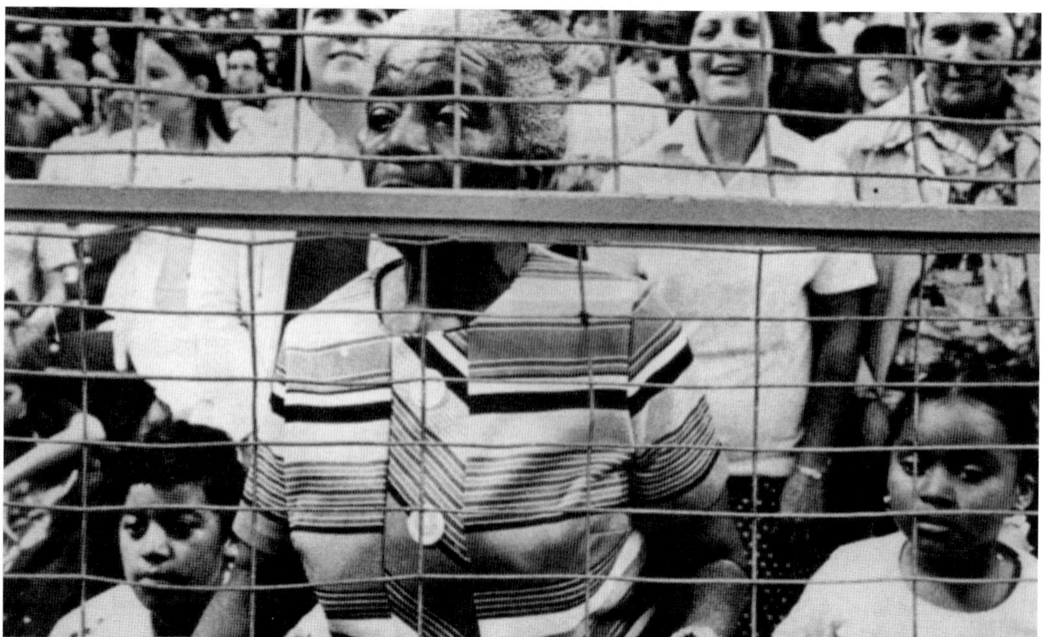

In November 1978, El Tiante switched uniforms when he signed a two-year contract with the New York Yankees. After a 13-8 season with the Red Sox in 1978, Red Sox ownership refused to offer their 38-year-old ace more than a one-year deal. This despite the fact that Tiant threw a three-hit shutout on the last day of the season to get the Red Sox to the 1978 playoff game with New York, his last game in a Red Sox uniform. Seizing the opportunity, Yankee owner George Steinbrenner swooped in and offered Tiant a two-year deal. The sight of Tiant in pinstripes was for many of the Fenway Faithful too much to bear. In the photograph below, catcher Terry Kennedy flipped Tiant the ball after he was called out on strikes in a spring game at Al Lang Stadium in St. Petersburg, Florida.

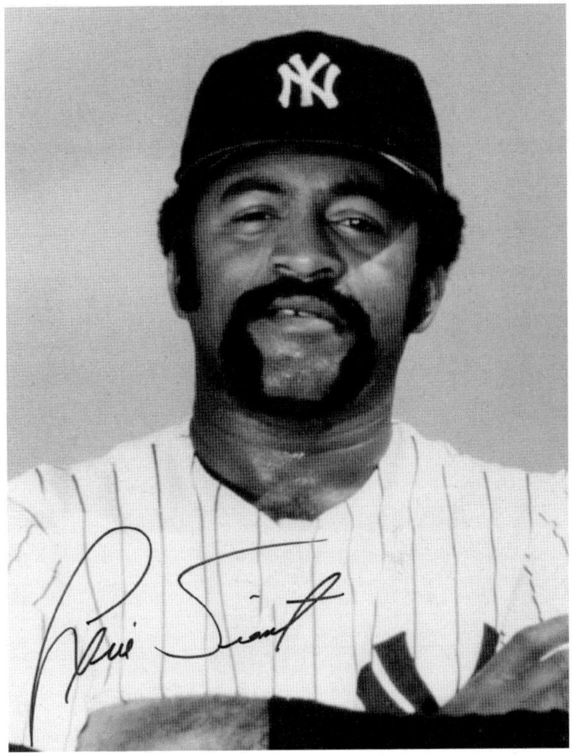

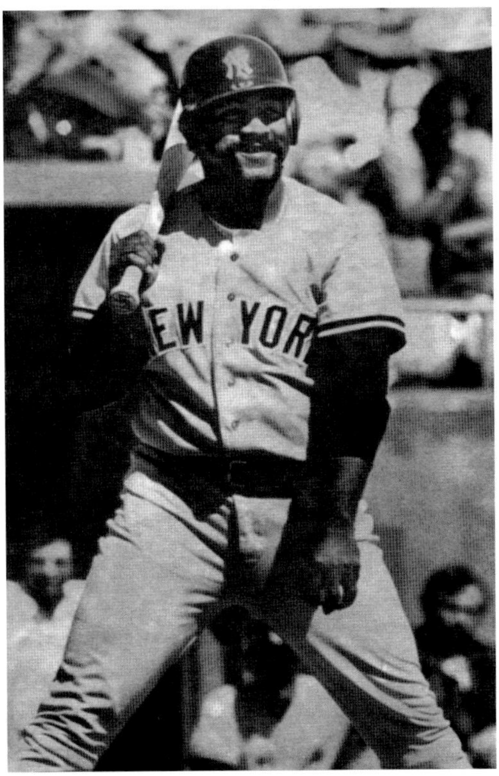

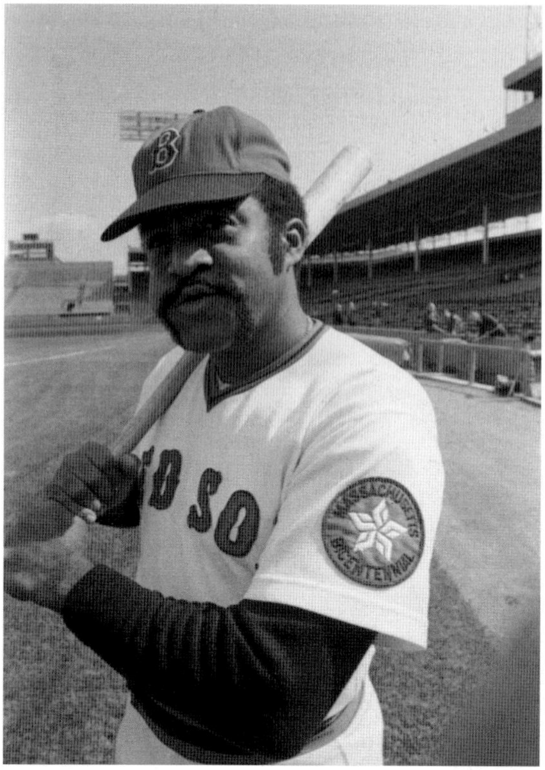

Luis Tiant played nine seasons when pitchers hit. A pretty good hitting pitcher, he actually hit .406 with the Twins in 1970 in 32 at-bats. His best year at the plate came in 1967, when in 71 at-bats he hit .254 with a home run and 10 RBI. With Boston he hit .117 with five RBI before the designated hitter, but he stood out with his bat during the 1975 World Series.

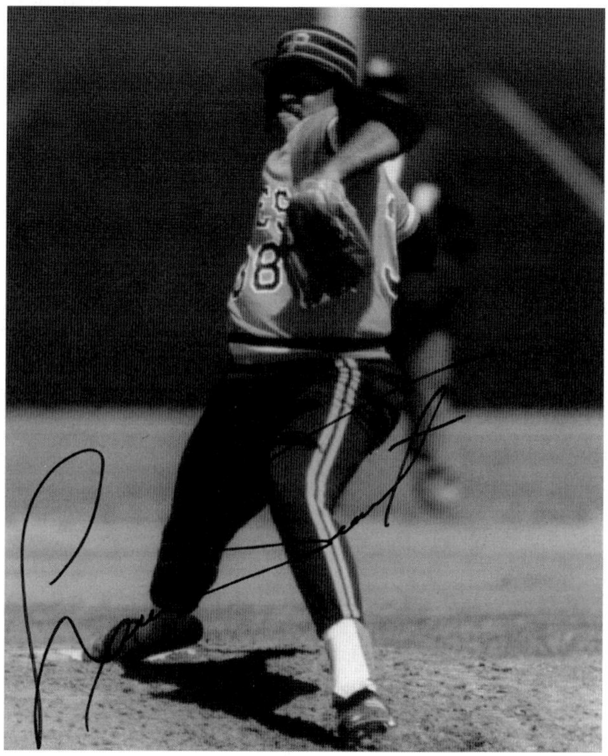

The Yankees released Tiant in October 1980, and he signed with the Pittsburgh Pirates. He threw 57 innings for them in 1981 in his only stint in the National League. After they released him, he went back to where it all began, the Mexican League, where the California Angels purchased his contract in August 1982. He pitched 29 innings for California in 1982, closing out his career.

These two scenes were repeated 122 times while Luis Tiant wore a Red Sox uniform. For it was in the uniform of the Boston Red Sox he recorded 122 of his 229 career wins. In the photograph at right, he is congratulated by catcher Carlton Fisk. In a phone interview with the author on the *Scott and Jake* radio show in Sarasota, Florida, Fisk was asked if he had to win one game who would he want on the mound, and his answer was immediate: "Luis Tiant." Carl Yastrzemski (below, shaking Tiant's hand) has repeatedly stated throughout the years that Tiant would be his choice in a must-win situation. Fellow pitcher Bill Lee said of Tiant, "He has the most tenacious killer instincts in the game."

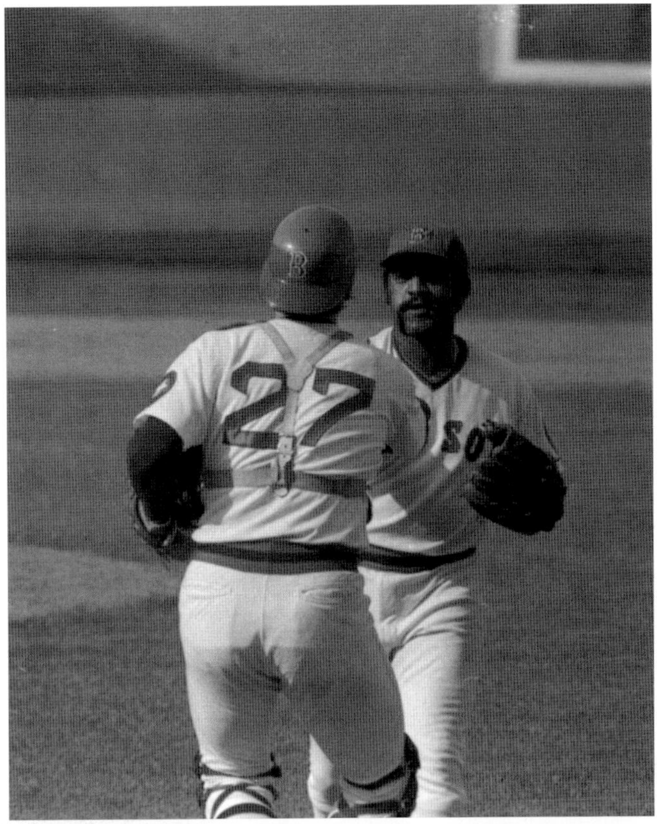

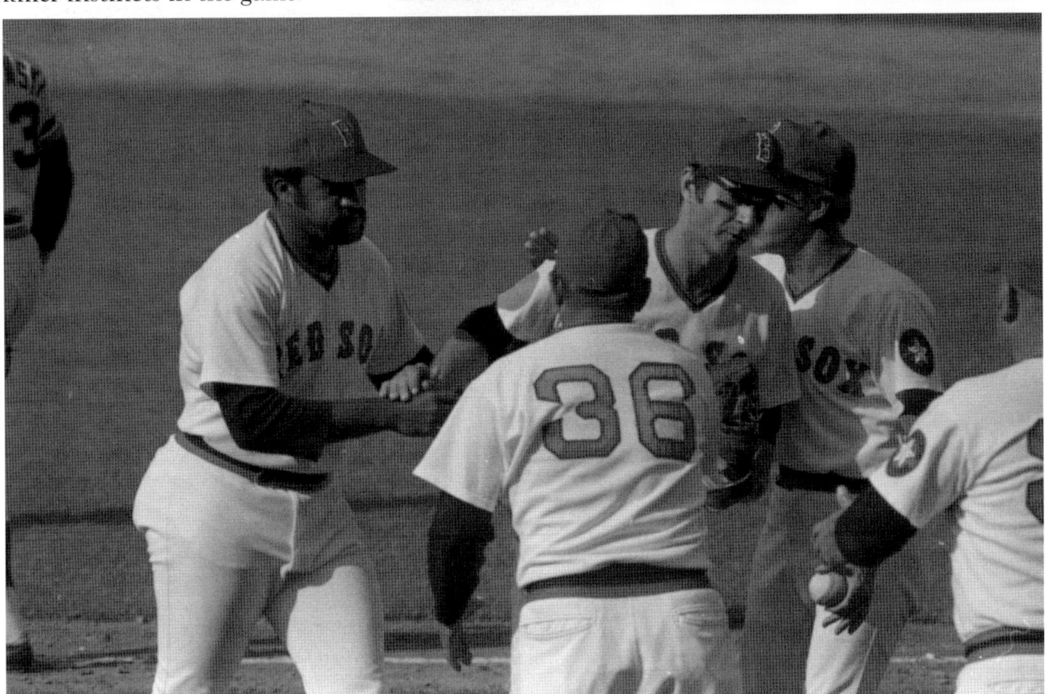

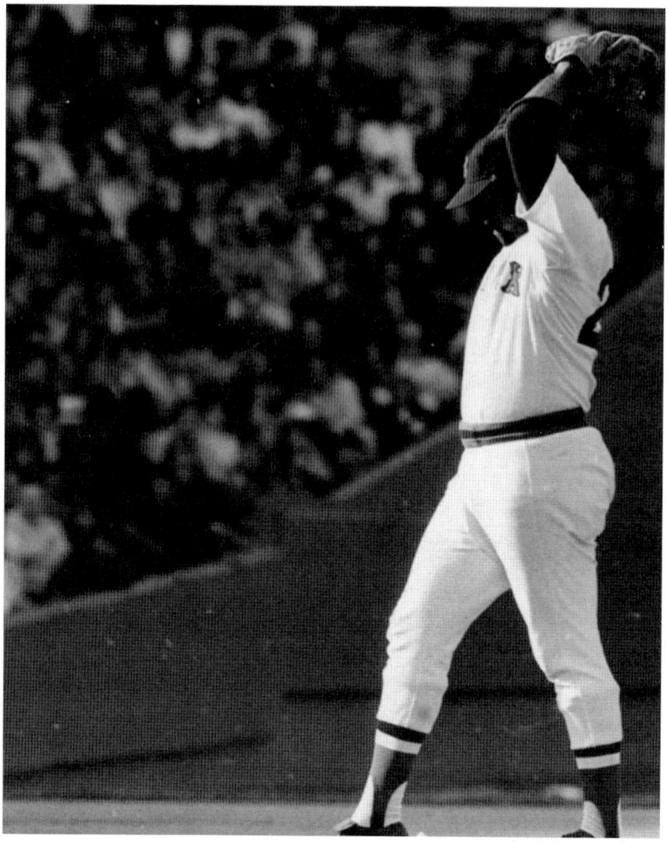

Luis Tiant played 19 years in the majors with six different teams, and although his best season was in 1968 with the Indians, there is no doubt his best years were with the Red Sox. He was 122-81 with Boston, and he threw 26 of his 49 shutouts in a Boston uniform. He had three 20-win seasons, and he dazzled the fans like nobody before him. Carl Yastrzemski once said of the fans' relationship with Tiant, "He owns this place and he should." So it was natural for him to stay in the Boston area, where he remains today. In the photograph below, Luis greets baseball historian, noted SABR member, and author Kerry Keene at a Fenway Fest at Curtis Liquors in Weymouth, Massachusetts.

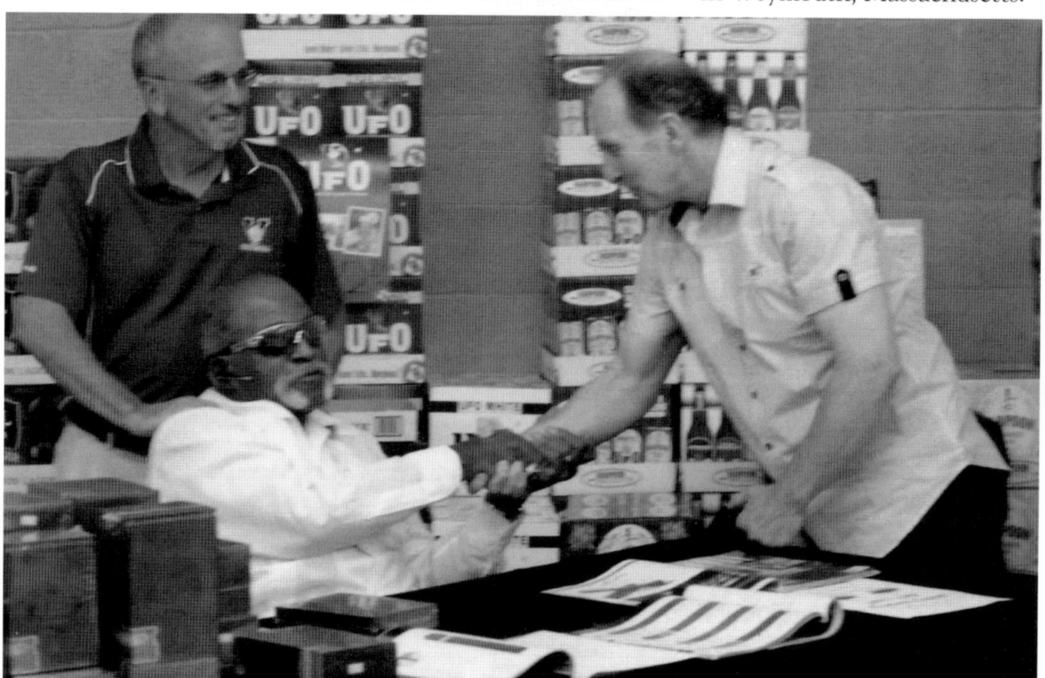

Today, Tiant is a special instructor for the Boston Red Sox, working with young pitchers in Fort Myers, Florida. He also is the proprietor of El Tiante's, a restaurant on Yawkey Way outside of Fenway Park. He can often be found there greeting generations of the Fenway Faithful. Here, he is with Alice Desaulniers of Weymouth, Massachusetts, and her grandson Jake Kinsherf of Ann Arbor, Michigan. (Courtesy of Lynda Fitzgerald.)

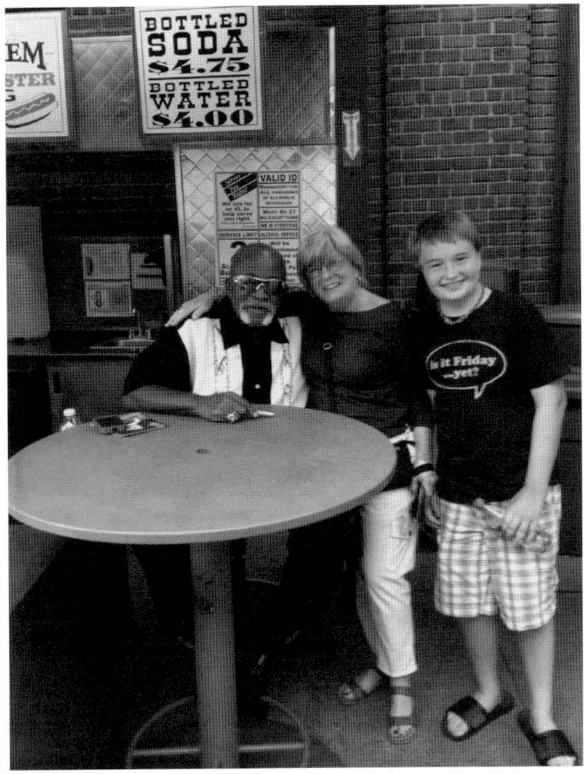

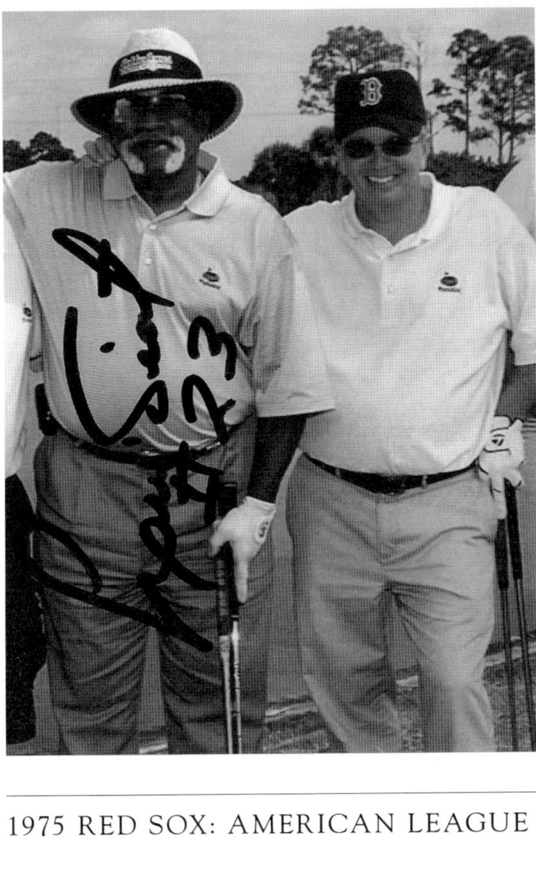

A passionate golfer, Tiant plays in many charity events. Here, he is with the author at the event for the Plantation Foundation of Venice, Florida. Still a fierce competitor at 74 years young, Tiant told the author that golf is the closest thing he has found to pitching. (Courtesy of the Plantation Foundation Venice, Florida.)

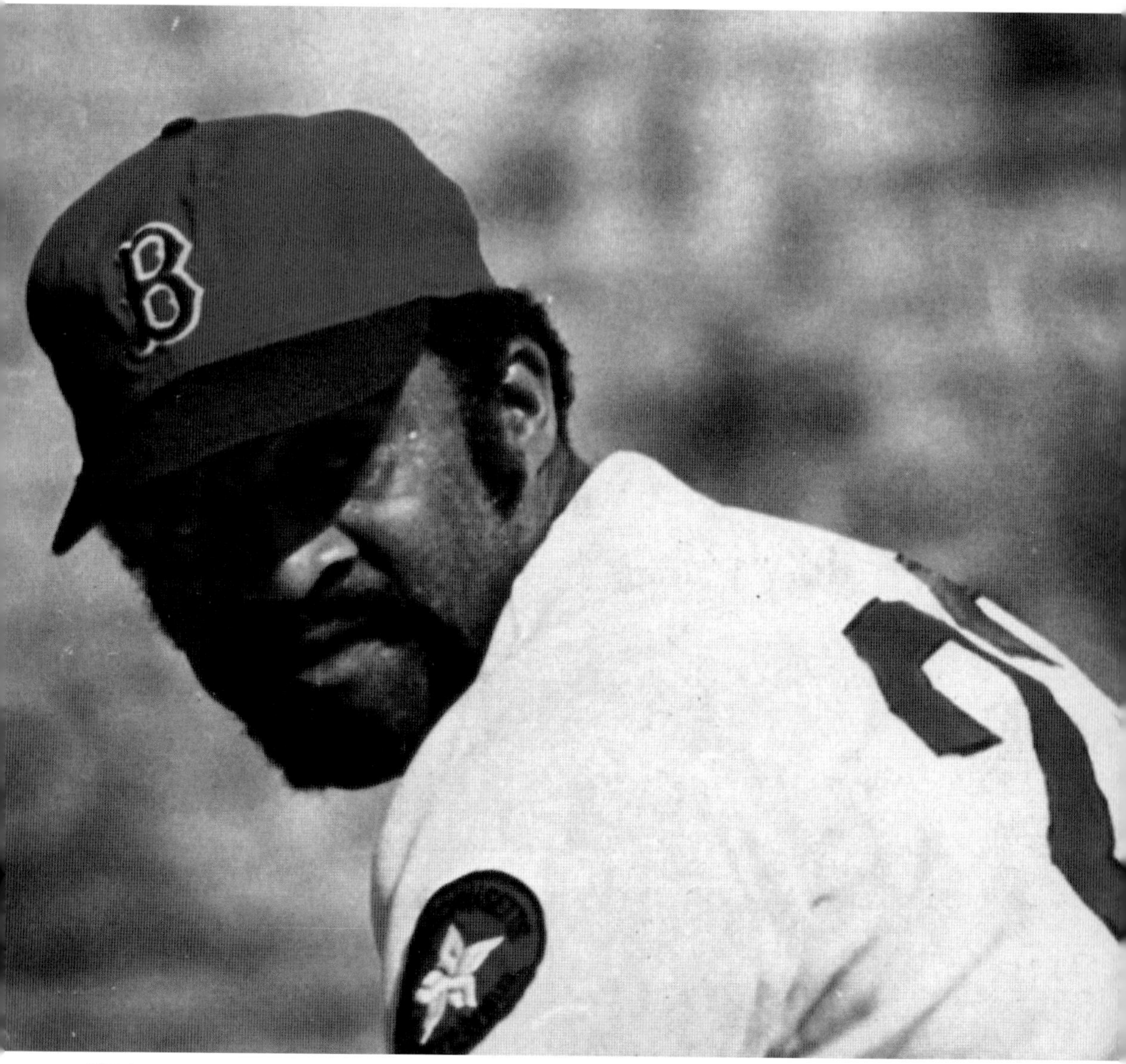

El Tiante was one of the most indomitable pitchers of the 1970s. Contemporaries Don Drysdale, Catfish Hunter, and Jim Bunning are in the National Baseball Hall of Fame. By every measurable statistic that has afforded these players induction, Luis Tiant belongs. By the immeasurable intangibles of those special athletes, Luis Tiant has always belonged. Among the all-time greats of the game, the author adds his name to the list of players and fans who in a game one's team must win, wants the ball in the hands of El Tiante. In December 2014, his name appeared on the Golden Age ballot. He did not make it, and he cannot come up for reconsideration again until 2017. Here is hoping that the day will come when he will join Carl Yastrzemski, Carlton Fisk, and Jim Rice, his teammates on that 1975 Red Sox team that helped restore the game of baseball to its rightful place as America's pastime, in the hallowed halls of Cooperstown where he belongs. (Courtesy of Dick Raphael.)

BIBLIOGRAPHY

Adelman, Tom. *The Long Ball: The Summer of 75–Spaceman, Catfish, Charlie Hustle and The Greatest World Series Ever Played.* Boston, New York, London: Little Brown, 2003.

Carbo, Bernie and Dr. Peter Hantziz. *Saving Bernie Carbo.* Fort Pierce, FL: Diamond Club Publishing, 2013.

Frost, Mark. *Game Six: Cincinnati, Boston, and the 1975 World Series: The Triumph of America's Pastime.* New York: Hyperion, 2009.

Sinibaldi, Raymond. *1967 Red Sox: The Impossible Dream Season.* Charleston, SC: Arcadia Publishing, 2014.

Tiant, Luis and Fitzgerald Joe. *El Tiante: The Luis Tiant Story.* Garden City, NY: Doubleday and Company, 1976.

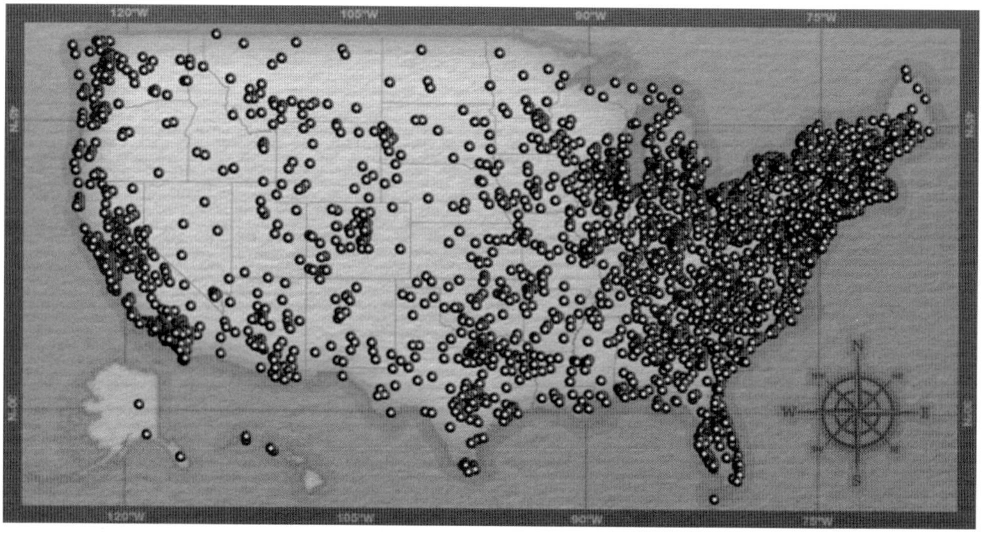

Consistent with our mission to preserve history on a local level, this book was printed in South Carolina on American-made paper and manufactured entirely in the United States. Products carrying the accredited Forest Stewardship Council (FSC) label are printed on 100 percent FSC-certified paper.

MADE IN THE USA